FOR THE LOVE OF BOOKS

Arthur Machen—an unpublished sketch
by Sarah Bixby-Smith

FOR THE LOVE
of BOOKS

*The Adventures of an Impecunious
Collector*

by

PAUL JORDAN-SMITH

Essay Index Reprint Series

 BOOKS FOR LIBRARIES PRESS
FREEPORT, NEW YORK

STANDARD BOOK NUMBER:

8369-1065-6

LIBRARY OF CONGRESS CATALOG CARD NUMBER:

79-80397

PRINTED IN THE UNITED STATES OF AMERICA

To

GORDON RAY YOUNG

ACKNOWLEDGEMENT

Some of the chapters in this volume first appeared in *The Overland Monthly*, *Tomorrow*, *Racket*, and *The Los Angeles Times*. To the editors of these publications I am indebted for their courteous permission to reprint.

P. J. S.

"These books of mine are become magic mirrors. For whenas I look upon their pages, they give back to me a vision of a self more free, whereof I like to make believe. Here my leane virtues are made to seem robust, and my immoderate vices are thinned to amiable shadows of themselves ; my slight achievements are filled out to assume august proportions, and my feeble courage hath been transformed into Puissance itself. Sure, 'tis mine own self I see, but 'tis a self now grown vast and noble . . . I. O. V."

— *John Collingsworth's Diary*

"In a very real sense, our own bad taste is worth more to us than other people's good taste. The wholesale swallowing of opinions can lead too often to a kind of snobbery : culture becomes mere intellectual etiquette. . . Now it cannot be too often repeated that the basis of all real criticism is enjoyment. Criticism starts from three simple words : 'I like that.' "

— *L. A. G. Strong*

CONTENTS

ILLUSTRATIONS

AN UNEXPLANATORY INTRODUCTION

AN UNEXPLANATORY INTRODUCTION

IT IS at times when the more obvious values begin to totter, when land and house, bank and government are threatened that we realize the truth of the old Greek saw, πλοῦτος ὁ τῆς ψυχῆς πλοῦτος μόνος ἐοτιν ἀληθής — the wealth of the mind is the only true wealth. And while it is a fact that the scholar is no less uncomfortable than the barbarian when his belly gnaws for food, it is likewise a fact that, given a crust of bread, he has a greater capacity for happiness than the unfortunate whose standard of values depends upon a foundation of gold. Both the scholar and his less systematic brother, the mere lover of books, have a refuge — and means of escape from the bitterness of so-called reality. Did not M. Jerome Coignard find the *Consolations* of Boethius a very fortress against adversity? Though a fugitive, did he not enjoy reading his beloved book while resting in a fountain? Did not the *citoyen* Brotteaux, through the pages of his Lucretius, escape the raging terrors of the French Revolution?

Though I have addressed myself hereinafter to the book collector, and write with the unction and swagger and fanaticism of the bibliomaniac, I am in the first place concerned with the collector as a bibliophile — a lover of books. I take little pleasure and less interest in those who gather books as small boys accumulate their marbles or fat dowagers their diamonds. And I note without surprise that the simon

3

pure collector — the man who has collected for speculation, for show, and without love, is as miserable in these uncertain days as his banker.

Therefore I write but little of dollar values. I, too, have had my bargains, and found the "sleepers" on neglected shelves. My days have been gladdened therefor, and, dog that I am, I have boasted of besting the dealer. But the deal has never been my object in these matters ; hence as prices crash I shed no tears over the books I have bought. I am unmoved when my friend bewails the fact that a Boswell which last year fetched a thousand dollars, today goes begging at a paltry hundred. A first Boswell remains a rare thing, though its market price fall to a dime — and I should still be proud of owning one. It has long seemed to me that the writing collector has made too much over his bargains, and written at forbidding length concerning books that only museums and millionaires could afford. When men begin to talk of having paid a thousand for this and ten thousand for that I am frightened, and, given to reckon in pennies, lose all interest in what they are pleased to call "the game." It is too big a game for me. To buy books because they are cheap or because they are dear is to proclaim oneself a fool.

Nor do I write for the collector of fads and fashions. To the Devil with novels that are "now being eagerly collected" ! I see them being carted off by empty-faced younglings and rich, ignorant widows, all inflamed by some smart young cataloguer from New York's East Side. I shall stick to my own tastes, and lick my own platter. To be sure, if I see this current trash in a junk-pile, I shall stoop to pick it up, convey it to the clever salesman and exchange it for an honest copy of *The Ship of Fools*.

We love books for their wisdom, their beauty, the pleasures they afford, and the comfort they give : they open doors to the only freedom we may know. Let us collect them for those reasons and no other. Then, when the golden bowl is broken and the grasshopper has become a burden, we shall not look upon our shelves with reproach, but welcome their time-tested tenants as companions in adversity.

But if I have not permitted myself to be swayed by the fashions that booksellers have created, I have no quarrel with the bibliopoles themselves. I like them. I consort with them daily : I rejoice in their shops, smart or shabby. With that most charming and amiable of modern bibliophiles, Mr. A. Edward Newton, writer of our own most joyful of books on collecting, I heartily commend the trade. By and large they are the most honest fellows in the world.

And if I feel myself more at home at the shabby little places on the back streets, it is not because I have been cheated or snubbed by the more prosperous. The shops of Maggs and Quaritch in London, and Edouard Champion in Paris have received me with hospitality and displayed before my envious eyes volumes fit for kings, and they continue to enrich my shelves with their sumptuous catalogues, though I am but a poor and unprofitable customer. Yet, even in these vast treasure houses I have found books, usually uncatalogued, that a poor man might easily afford. And, as has often been pointed out, at these notable shops, they know their books and are scrupulously honest with their clients. When you get a book of Maggs you will not afterward be saddened by finding a leaf wanting or a title in facsimile. Nor may I ever forget the courtesies bestowed me in certain notable American shops lifted well above traffic's noise in New York and Chicago, where booklover and scholar are always welcome to examine treasures reserved for Masters of the Market; nor the hospitable rooms of a cloistered place in Pasadena where no imperfect book may cross the threshold; nor a dozen places in Los Angeles and San Francisco, where books I could never afford have been held from sale merely to satisfy my insatiable curiosity. I name no names, but I recall a most lovable bookman who specializes in Whitman at the "Sign of the Sparrow" on a certain avenue in New York. He has spent many hours explaining his rarities, when he knew there could be no profit from the guest collecting an author whose books were then dear at two bits the volume. And it has been thus over all America. The book-folk seem to have the faculty of forgetting business and losing themselves in the clouds. Is it possible that some of the devil-may-care, art-for-art's-sake spirit of the garret-writers oozes out of old leather and saturates the air of these places where books are kept? Be that as it may, the book business — with notably slight exceptions — is characterized by honesty, courtesy, amiability and (though I despise the word) service. If I want a friend I go to the book shop. If I want information, I have learned that the folk who work in these shops will spend days of time in doing research when all they can reasonably expect in return is the exultant grin of gratitude. With the next bottle of Dow's 1904 Port I propose a toast to the most generous, genial and dependable of all business folk I have ever known — the booksellers: and if I have laid stress on the Americans it is because, for more than a score of years, they have been busily engaged in bestowing favors upon a comparatively impecunious customer.

But for all their guidance and friendship, the poor devil of a collector must turn ferret, and go seeking about in unlikely places if he would hope to possess himself of books that are rare. A dust-gathering, time-killing search it will be ; but not being rich I can afford to prowl about amongst the litter of a dusty, second-hand furniture store : in such places, for no more than a silver dime, I have picked up some of the choicest books in my library. Resting on Mr. Blurp's protected shelves at this moment is a volume that on the morning of a day was lying uncomfortable in the bin of that same unsightly furniture emporium ; at noon it was bought for ten cents ; in the afternoon it was traded, at a smart shop, for a first edition of Erasmus ; a few minutes later Blurp was called by phone and was delighted to add it to his collection for thirty-five dollars — a third less than the catalogued price ! But Mr. Blurp could not be expected to prowl, not he. These joys are reserved for the impecunious who, after all, may have pretty nearly as much pleasure, and much less worry, than the rich.

What I have really tried to do, in this little book of mine, is not so much to indicate my methods of collecting — though I have not always refrained from boasting gossip — as to reveal my reasons for loving and collecting the books I have about me.

For the book is the thing : not the "item," nor its speculative value. I back my taste against that of the world, — when it suits me. It may not be your taste, it may not be good taste, but it is mine. I shall eat no parsnips, however well they may be held among the gourmets, or however they be praised on the price-less pages of Louys Elzevir's *Le Pastissier François*. 'Twould be mere affectation for me to collect Dante ; but I am honest about loving Aldine Homer : for Homer I enjoy ; Dante puts me to sleep.

Thus I have for years collected the books of Eden Phillpotts and John Trevena with but little compe-tition. When I began collecting Arthur Machen, James Branch Cabell and Stephen Crane their first editions could still be had in mint state at fifty cents the volume. Few of Jerome Cardan's interesting works are sought by those who collect in his century ; and Norman Davey is almost foreign to the catalogues. No man requires advice about what to collect. Tell the man who next asks that silly question to collect cigar coupons.

I am not presuming to suggest that these worthies should be collected. I but explain my own reasons for *reading* them, and hope that some other may thereby discover a pleasure as keen as my own. Let the collecting be secondary ; otherwise it will be silly.

Again, I have dwelt at some length upon the books I have "discovered" in footnotes. Centuries before my time these were known and admired, but some of them have been all but forgotten. Apart from my own enthusiasm in rediscovering them for myself, my principal interest has been to indicate a connection between the pleasures and the uses of collecting. The collector, to derive the greatest amount of satis-faction from his sport, should be somewhat of a re-search student, digging out the secrets of his rare editions, unfathoming their mysteries, tracing down their origins. His collecting will then lead him into new fields, the growth of his library will be organic, natural ; it will be original ; it will possess unity (for him), and will prove a source of both joy and benefit, to himself and to his fellows.

Writing thus, with the reading collector uppermost in my mind, I am conscious of having neglected the supreme matter of "points"— those peculiar blunders made by writer or printer which enable us to distinguish a first edition from all other claimants. I acknowledge the importance of these signs and am slave to them, along with other members of my tribe. Though it seems to me that it is high time for the collector to exercise a healthy scepticism in this regard.

I ignore, for example, those who make a point of dust jackets — detachable, detestable things that may be slipped off and on at will, and are better tossed into the waste basket. They form no part of the book, and prove nothing.

The publishers' catalogues (dated or not), seem likewise questionable. Publishers of large editions have a habit of putting unbound volumes aside, awaiting trade demand. As the books are bound up for shipment current catalogues are tipped or sewed in. Some copies escape lacking the catalogue. Only from the most methodical house is it possible to learn anything definite about the order of binding. Perhaps the first book off the press was placed at the bottom of the stack and was last to the bindery. The book with the September catalogue may have preceded the copy containing the July list. I have two copies of the 1840 Burton's *Anatomy*, published by Thomas Tegg. The copies are identical (plates and type impression no guiding sign), yet in one of these volumes is a Tegg catalogue for 1843 ! They are of the same edition :

9

the so-called "point" is pointless, and a hundred years hence, when the books are rebound, it will have completely disappeared. Moreover it is worth noting that when publishers' new catalogues run short the binders are apt to sew in the old ones, or none at all. I see no reason, then, for believing that Arthur Machen's *Hill of Dreams* with the catalogue at the end antedates an otherwise correct copy without these pages : still less reason for questioning a sound copy of Maugham's *Of Human Bondage* for its lack of the Heinemann book list. Without definite and authoritative statements from printer and binder on such points, arguments are worthless — and definite knowledge is usually lacking.

A more serious problem is that of broken letters — such as the split "i" on the last page of Mark Twain's *Jumping Frog* (my copy has the sound letter and is said to be "right," so this is no case of sour grapes). Dr. Le Roy Crummer, as astute a collector as I know, maintains that with books printed prior to the introduction of linotype machines it is impossible to accept the broken or dropped letter as a test of priority. Printers' assistants in the old days were careless. A bolt slipped ; type was loosened, a letter stuck to the ink ball and was dropped. Adjustments were presently made and the dropped letter would go unnoticed until many sheets were struck from the press, then, perhaps, the error would be discovered and corrected. As a result the early and late sheets of a given signature might have been correct ; the ones run off while the printer was nodding were wrong. Unless then the proprietor came upon the scene — a scrupulous proprietor — the faulty sheets were bound into some copies, corrected ones in others. If such things

occurred — and old printers testify that they frequently happened — what does a broken letter in a
Longfellow item signify ? We know that during the
17th century these accidents were repeated. In those
days the author was wont to do his proof revisions at the
printer's shop. He would correct and perhaps revise
a few sheets and then be called away. The printer
would print enough of the corrected sheets and then,
if the author did not return, would begin work on a
new sheet. When the author returned he would
resume his corrections, after many sheets had been
done. The remaining sheets of that signature might
then differ considerably from the ones first struck.
He might or might not succeed in removing the faulty
ones. When it came to binding, one volume would
be made happy by the presence of a corrected signature "A," defaced by an incorrect "B" and "J" ; in
the next copy bound the reverse might hold. I refer
the reader to the testimonies of Mr. Ronald B.
McKerrow and the late Dr. Aldis Wright concerning
these puzzles. If no two of ten copies of the 1625
Bacon's *Essays* examined by Dr. Wright, are exactly
alike, what "points" will determine a first issue of the
first edition ? And were the printers of America
during the early days of the 19th century much more
accurate than their English forerunners ?

I have no wish to seem an utter heretic concerning
these delicate matters, but when I see two volumes
of X's verses, both dated 1828, both alike in binding
and all other particulars save that one has an "h" at
such and such a line of such and such a page and is
therefore held to be worth seven dollars, while the
other has dropped its aspirate and is priced at three
hundred, I wonder if it would not be wise to enquire

more closely into the history of printing and the habits of the craftsmen?

But I have digressed far afield and perceive that this introduction has lost its character — if indeed it ever had one. All I had meant to say at this point is that the collector should preserve both common sense and a sense of humor. Let him respect bibliographers and catalogues, and follow their guidance within reason, and no further.

A library reflects one's prejudices, one's limitations, one's personality. As Mr. Birrell remarks in one of his suggestive essays, the wise collector may look at his books and say, "These are mine, and I am theirs." A library that fails to mirror its owner's personality has neither life nor meaning. It is a mere affectation.

True, the collector — though he be blessed with fortune — is never completely expressed by his books. He grows. Some of his wants remain forever unsatisfied — and his wants multiply. He is always in need : a more perfect binding for his *Horace,* a better copy of *Tom Sawyer,* an item missing from his Gissing. The impecunious collector is always planning, always seeking, but is never hopeless, for tomorrow his alert instincts may lead him to a cave of treasures. And so long as he is tormented by these sweet desires life is rich in romance.

And during these precarious days when men are putting patches on last year's trousers, and counting themselves happy if they have the patch, one is indeed fortunate if one is able to find refuge in dreams — a fool's paradise if you will —, or lose oneself in a pursuit that is by no means as extravagant as it has sometimes been described.

AN UNEXPLANATORY INTRODUCTION

This is no time for the collector to quit his books. He may have to quit his house, abandon his trip to Europe and give away his car ; but his books are patiently waiting to yield their comfort and provoke him to mirth. They will tell him that banks and civilizations have smashed before ; governments have been on the rocks, and men have been fools in all ages. But it is all very funny. The gods laugh to see such sport, and why should we not join them ?

Come then, let us read about the laughter of the gods ; let us read of the permanent and abiding : of man's loves and hopes, of pity and of tears. Let us forget patches and mortgages, and the criminal stupidity of politicians. Read Aristophanes and Rabelais ; economize on the daily paper.

This is the collector's hour of opportunity. Prices are at bottom. Or, if the collector's own favorites have not yet tumbled, he may conveniently adapt himself to the times and go in for items less dear than those he was used to buy in times less lean. I can think of a dozen interesting fields waiting for the impecunious. Books of curiosities and wonders, for example : Aubrey's *Miscellanies ;* Jones on *Credulities, Past and Present ;* Mackay's *Memoirs of Extraordinary Popular Delusions ;* Wanley's *Wonders of the Little World ;* Nathaniel Crouch's numerous collections of oddities. I could enumerate an hundred titles of books that have chronicled marvels, even as Mr. Charles Fort did lately in his *Book of the Damned,* and all of them much more amusing than those of this popular writer. These that I have mentioned (and more hereinafter), are despised by the Blurps, and may be picked up for a trifle. But the collector is a man of individual taste : let him name his own pizen.

The personal pronoun has been vulgarly conspicuous throughout these essays. But I have been voicing mine own enthusiasms, explaining my prejudices, and making a tour through a section of my own library ; therefore I make no apology. Let other collectors discount my dogmatisms and damn my taste as they will. I applaud them, and wish them Godspeed on their own secret errands.

I

COLLECTING AMERICANS

"We make the market for English books in this country ;
let us turn our attention to our own too-long-neglected
authors."

—From *This Book-Collecting Game*,
by A. Edward Newton

I

COLLECTING AMERICANS

THERE are two kinds of private libraries that depress me : one is that made by agents at the order of some Croesus who has to be told by experts what books to collect; the other is that formed by the man who copies his list of books, without having read them, from some collector's manual. Of these the first kind is apt to be far the better. It may have no personality, show no sign of love, but, assembled by experts, it will contain fine examples of the best books. Moreover, it will probably reveal intelligent purpose and be a useful addition to the country where it is housed. There is something to be said for the collection of the great millionaire, even if it leave one cold and spiritless : it covers some field of human thought, represents some cultural age, and is probably destined for the use of scholars.

But the second collection is apt to be a sorry mess : a sad assemblage of step-children. It is not infrequently an imitation of something very bad. Thus, Bibliopolus writes an essay about what he considers to be the best books of Tierra del Fuego, therein printing a list of "Hot Points of Fuegana." The wealthy innocent has heard that book collecting is *being done,* and that even a man who has founded his fortune bootlegging may, by virtue of the possession of a fine library, be admitted to the circles of the cultured.

Knowing bottles better than books, he seeks advice, and is told that Bib's book will tell him what to get. Following this cue he buys the entire list of "hot points." If Bib's list has been well considered the collection may present a good appearance, and the knowing may approve. The chances are, however, that the list will be made up of the author's favorites, a mixture of good and bad. In Bib's own cases even the bad books may rest happily, for Bib is there to love and defend his purchases. This he may do on the following grounds : pure sentiment, association, typography, political history, etc., etc. He has a copy, say, of "Ten Nights in a Bar Room" : he would never think of defending its literary merit, but for a unit in a collection dealing with prohibition, or ethical theories of nineteenth-century America, apology is not required.

My prejudice in these concerns no doubt arises from the circumstance that I have about me none but the books that I love ; that I feel a warm glow in my heart when I sit in the libraries that express their owners' personalities, even though I may despise the books. If these fools that collect for name and fame would only turn to cans or cog wheels, I'd like 'em better : they'd make better collections and be happier men. Had I lived in Turkey during the early days and been possessed of wealth, I dare say, being by nature a wicked, venturesome fellow, I might, seeing that it was the custom of the country, have collected pretty girls for my harem. But would I have ordered them by large lots ? Would I have sent out expert agents to collect these damsels ? Would I have read collectors' manuals, recommending blondes or high cheek bones ? Not I ! Fancy reading : "Brunettes have fallen off sadly at this year's auction, and the wise collector will turn to blondes, especially the rare and dumpy little creatures from the Khorbo Mountain district. In unpressed condition the values of these dainty ones are likely to remain very high for some years." No, I should have collected my own in my own manner, and so would you.

Now that was a rather nasty illustration, but it conveys my feeling perfectly. To collect books for love, for information, for some past or present sentiment, for the satisfaction of intellectual curiosity, is a rational and amusing occupation. To gratify that passion by assembling the first editions of these darlings is something admirable. To join collectors' ranks for any other motive is a waste of time, money, life : the silliest of pretences, and, to say it roundly, damned rot.

Of late a number of collector-writers have essayed to establish just what American books are worthy of the collector's shelves. An interesting speculation, this, but not one that should influence another man against his own judgment. For it is but speculation. I "roll my own." Few American books are old enough to have met the tests that only time can bring to bear, and even as ancient literary prejudices are now apt to but provoke an indulgent smile, so may the pronouncements of such as I tickle the risibles of later generations. Timely books are read by the thousand, and are easy of appreciation. We think them great as we read, but they seldom survive our laughter or our tears. If the book that lays hold on its own generation have not some word too big for its decade, it will prove too little for even its own century. 'Tis clothes that deceive us : the lady who was so meticulously clad in the mode of 1890 cannot now be seen for her sleeves ; she fascinated her contemporaries. How many novels escape the sure destiny of the fashion-plate ? I regret that Trollope's brave company are forever hidden from my eyes by their beards and tea-tables. But Don Quixote's angular form cannot be hid under the fantastic trappings of the 17th century. He lives : his tragic figure was too vast for even his creator's satire.

What American books have survived the few years since that first press was set up in Cambridge ? I speak not of text-book immortality, wherein all that made a stir in their own day are called to remembrance in a foot-note. Nor do I refer to those whose only value is to the research scholar. Living books remain translatable to the present, yielding minted joys and wisdom, without regard to years.

We begin with the 17th century. Captain John Smith's *True Relations* (1608), Bradford's *History of Plymouth* (1607-46), and a handful of other journals are important to the collector of historical items, but they have little other merit. Wigglesworth's *Day of Doom* may amuse us as it horrified our forebears. It has jingle, and that is all. However, this book, and Anne Bradstreet's *Tenth Muse* are necessary to a complete collection of American verse. Neither can be called good reading. Aside from George Sandys' translation of Ovid (1626), perhaps Cotton Mather's *Wonders of the Invisible World* (1693), is the only book of that day with literary merit.

Coming to the 18th century we find that the collector of historical items (as such), still has the field to himself — a dozen or more journals, volumes of letters and the like are there for him. *John Woolman's Journal* (1774) may be considered an exception ; there's good reading there, as Lamb has testified. Thomas Paine's *Age of Reason, Rights of Man,* and *Common Sense* are important ; Paine was a great man and patriot but his books offer no temptation to a modern reader. John Trumbull is an exception to the desert dryness of the period, and we may still laugh with those revolutionary soldiers over the rollicking lines of his *McFingal,* with its frankly Butleresque satire. But Joel Barlow's famous *Columbiad,* full as it is of uncannily accurate prophecy, is as dull as Timothy Dwight's *Conquest of Canaan ;* Barlow, however, did redeem himself in *Hasty Pudding,* whereas Dwight now defies reading. And the same might be said of the novels. Our first novel was Sarah Morton's *The Power of Sympathy* (1789), an exceedingly rare volume, suppressed by her family, but reprinted many years later. In 1790 came Susanna Rowson's widely-read *Charlotte Temple,* followed by Hannah Foster's *The Coquette* (1797). These pioneer women fashioned their tales of sin and sentiment after the worst eighteenth-century English models. Charles Brockden Brown holds his own a little better. Mystery, horror and romance are the stuff of his fiction, and it is still possible, with some dogged persistence and a few yawns, to get through such books as *Wieland, Arthur Mervyn* and *Edgar Huntley.*

It would be amusing to make a collection embracing, say, the first fifty American novels, an equal number of our earliest verse writers — God forbid that they should be called poets ! — and dramatists, beginning with Hugh Brackenridge's *The Battle of Bunker Hill* (1776), Royall Tyler's *The Contrast* (1787), and William Dunlap's *The Father* (1789). These last are a little better than the novels of the same period. It would be a patriotic thing to do, would be useful to students of American letters, and, this to speculators, would ultimately be worth a fortune. Blessings upon such a collection : but may I be spared the boredom of reading it !

But the man who wishes to collect books worth reading, books of some literary value, will not pay too much heed to their historical significance. He will trust his own instincts.

I should be inclined to say that Benjamin Franklin's *Autobiography* is the first American book to show any symptoms of livingness. Franklin was our first all-round man, and his vitality still runs over in the pages of that queer, stodgy little record of his foresight and thrift.

Of Poe and Hawthorne we may speak with some degree of certainty. Poe's *Tales of the Grotesque and Arabesque,* his *Poems,* and Hawthorne's *Scarlet Letter* are not mere collectors' items, though they will probably remain near the top in any assemblage of Americana. Irving may still be read with vast pleasure : a civilized man of genial humor. Holmes retains his urbanity, though the edge of his wit has been a bit dulled by time : his *Autocrat* is a tasty thing and ought to be treasured as long as Irving's *Sketch Book.* Lowell has not done so well as he deserves— the best critic we have produced up to this day of Livingston Lowes. His essays have not lost their power to inform and amuse. And Emerson, for all the young intelligentsia of this smart age, is yet a true prophet and a man of fire. He took some rather poor stuff from German philosophy, has some pulpit airs, and has produced a flock of nitwit religious cults, but his *Essays* remain tonic and stimulating.

Thoreau's *Walden*, a book for odd hours, is more talked about than read ; but Americans, of whom but few remain, would do well to ponder upon the outspoken individualism of this forthright mystic in a day of butter-fingered cowardice wherein we cry "surrender !" to the God Machine.

There is no need for me to mention old Walt Whitman's *Leaves of Grass*. "The barbaric yawp" is still heard around the whole world, and while his faith in democracy may amuse us now, he stands alone as our most original poet and anarch.

For the rest I should choose Melville's *Moby Dick*, Mark Twain's *Tom Sawyer* and *Huckleberry Finn*, Harris's *Uncle Remus*, Miss Alcott's *Little Women*, and Lanier's *Poems*,— all with considerable assurance.

These I have just named possess the magic, of one sort or another, that makes for what we call literature. And with the naming these my own assurance (take it for what it is worth), ends.

If, however, I were invited to choose first editions from this rather abbreviated list of Americana ; first editions of the books I would like to have fitted into my own shelves, and which I, quite privately, believe to be the ones most deserving of immortality, they would be :

Franklin's *Autobiography ; The Scarlet Letter ;* Poe's *Tales*, and his *Raven and other Poems,* both of 1845 ; *The Sketch-Book ; The Autocrat of the Breakfast-Table ;* Emerson's *Essays ; Tom Sawyer, Huckleberry Finn ;* and *Uncle Remus.* To these I

would add two great American translations : Bayard
Taylor's *Faust*, and Longfellow's *Divine Comedy*.
Then, from the historian's shelf I would filch the
three very exciting volumes of Prescott's *Conquest of
Mexico*, and I might be tempted to add Richard
Henry Dana's *Two Years Before the Mast*. Croesus
may have the *Tamerlanes* and *Leaves of Grass* to do
with as he will.

Then, before plunging into mad speculation concerning our contemporaries, there is an intermediate
period to be considered, though I am not much concerned here with keeping a strict order or a rigid classi-
fication, God knows. But there were some worthy
books written during the Eighties and Nineties in which
are the strong seeds of survival. Edward Bellamy's
Looking Backward, for all its stiff lack of literary
merit, was the product of a creative imagination of
no low order, and takes a respectable place in utopian
fictions. Stephen Crane's *Red Badge of Courage* and
Frank Norris's *McTeague* stand near the top of realistic fiction : they stand in no need of praise from me.
And if one is minded to collect regional novels, Miss
Murfree's novels and stories of the Tennessee moun-
tains, and Mary E. Wilkins Freeman's chronicles of
lonely souls in shivering New England are too much
neglected. There is a real tip for the collector who
demands quality and is not too entirely given over to
the fad of dust-jackets, and such nonsense. Finally,
we must not forget that it was during those derided
eighteen nineties that the work of perhaps our finest
poet, Emily Dickinson, was first printed.

What I have just set down, as you are quite well
aware, is by no means revolutionary — not even
original. It boils down the platitudes of the text-

books, and lists, I believe, the outstanding American books, without too much enthusiasm. For, as Mr. A. Edward Newton has well observed, "they are not absolutely of first rank." But from now on to an inglorious end I shall depart occasionally from this beaten path ; I shall give offense, both by omission and by commission. For what I am about to say, I take blame upon mine own shoulders.

Do not collect the books I am about to praise because of any words of mine : collect rather the things I condemn, if you love them. Follow no man's advice, unless you are, indeed, a mere speculator.

At this moment I am disgusted to learn that people of intelligence and taste have come to the collecting of trash, merely because an overstocked second-hand dealer has quoted it at an extravagant price : *Josiah Allen's Wife, Samantha at Saratoga, Tempest and Sunshine, Peck's Bad Boy, Ten Nights in a Bar Room, When Knighthood Was in Flower,* now find place in the catalogues : "These popular American books are rising in value daily." Let them rise ! The patent medicines displayed this day in my druggist's window at thirty-nine cents a bottle may rise to a dollar tomorrow, but why should I fill my medicine chest or my belly with the abominations ? Nor shall I clutter my shelves with stuff written with an eye on the butler's pantry and back stairs. Let people read what they will, so be they are amused : but to preserve these toys of the intellectual underworld is nothing short of depravity. Of old, the collector may have been quite mad, but he was at least a man of taste.

The knowing tell us that this sad state of affairs has been brought about by the advent of the post-war millionaire who, piloted by his agents and handy-guides, has determined to seem a gentleman, and who, by the application of business methods, has quickened the market. Whatever the cause, the prices of the good old books have risen with almost incredible rapidity since 1918. Seventeenth and eighteenth-century masterpieces, which in 1914 could have been bought from, say twenty-five to fifty dollars, are now marked by three and sometimes four figures.

The average impecunious collector, therefore, who used to browse comfortably in the stalls on the lookout for a *Tristram Shandy* or a North's *Plutarch*, finds that these treasures have gone beyond his reach ; they have been promoted. Very well, what is he going to do about it ? Obviously, he will either be quit of the collecting mania, and content himself with late editions of the first rate, or turn to what he deems best among those moderns who have not taken to large paper.

Not unless he has gone quite mad will he be tempted to litter his library with the world's worst. I, too, have eaten sour grapes, but I shan't bite off my nose to spite my face.

I return to my former illustration. Were I in Turkey, deprived of the ten prettiest wenches in the land, should I, therefore, revenge myself by taking the ugliest trollops of the Orient ? If the collector cannot have what he wants at first he will take the best he can get, and watch his chances.

Thus, now that *Tom Sawyer* has swaggered into libraries of affluence, and the *Autocrat* has become the creature of the plutocrat, it would seem fitting that the impecunious collector (known hereafter as the Imp) might well and wisely turn his attention to more recent writers and play a new game with himself.

It will be a game of chance in which the Imp will

match wits against Time and the hypothetical tastes of the future. One must not swagger overmuch. The more recent the book the greater the risk. But just here lies the pleasure of the game : one is to choose, from out a multitude, one's own particular favorites, regardless of jacket "blurbs" and critics, and collect for the sheer fun of it.

I propose, then, that the American Imp declare his independence of the manuals intended to shape his prejudices (including this poor thing), that he free himself from those limited, large-paper editions intended to mislead his judgment, betray his purse, and do his own selecting among the moderns where a few dollars will go a long way. The man who protests that he is helpless before such a maze of books and asks assistance in making his decisions, should leave collecting and seek simpler amusements. For this collector must be made of stern stuff, and fortified with a stout belief in his own judgments. He will make his selections according to some plan, most like, wherein he will have such latitude as his tastes may dictate. But in selecting his authors he must be far more circumspect and cautious than when he was privileged to play among the classics.

Yet even here there are some rules it might be wise to follow.

The popular is suspect. Popularity is the whim of the multitude. The popular novel is apt to be merely a gauge of ephemeral fashion. The wise collector will study his author carefully, looking for the eternal values. Does his author have brains ? originality ? insight ? Does he take pains in his writing ? Or does he pound out words with the zeal of a columnist for the daily press ?

The collector looks, in the main, for the writer who thinks ahead of his age, or has studied it with unwonted sagacity ; for the writer who seeks out the very heart of human nature, and has the wit and wisdom to interpret it ; for the writer whose desk has been, quite plainly, something of an altar, and whose work is somewhat more than secular. Let me not here fall into cant, for I refer not to those affected humbugs who proclaim a holy mission, or who write as though they were intoning psalms. A Rabelais will shout his imprecations and announce his satisfactions quite lustily : a Sterne will be sly with his barbed wit : a Pater will chant of lonely but lovely themes : a Samuel Butler, without adornments, will explain the merits of common sense. These are all collectors' men : they share as little in content as in manner, yet their desks were to them as altars, whereon they offered up their highest and best to their several gods.

On the other hand, the collector may seek for the writer whose work is distinguished by originality of style, whose literary manners set him far apart from his fellows. Whatever his taste may be, the collector seeks the writer who is apt, for these very reasons, to be overlooked by his contemporaries. Style seems but snobbery to the masses ; an original thought is deemed an impertinence.

In the back of the collector's mind is the hope that he is saving some of the immortals from oblivion, and no small part of his joy lies in the pleasant conceit that he is treasuring a storehouse of delights for the future.

The man who sets out to collect his contemporaries will meet disappointment and suffer chagrin. The author whose first book was so promising, may, in all likelihood, descend to banality. But even so, Imp may retain the one and cast away the rest with but little loss of time or money. All collecting is a gamble, and for that the odds are so great, the zest should be the greater.

So, after this long preamble, I shall turn to a few of those now collected Americans (born, say, between 1840 and 1910), and, as others have done, make out my own list of books (including some who have no other merit than having for a little time given me pleasure), of the "high spots"— of the American books that in my opinion are destined to live, not omitting scornful words concerning books I most heartily despise.

I take up a handful of American catalogues issued during this present year and see that James Lane Allen's novels show an increasing demand. I read and wept over these daintily written bits of sentimentality during my adolescence, and still confess to a sneaking fondness for them, though I cannot bring myself to read them. I have them tucked away where they will not readily be seen, all of them, beginning with *Flute and Violin*. Allen was a gentleman of taste, but one must own that, like many another gentleman of taste, he had but little originality. He was a fond — too fond — observer of the gentler aspects of pastoral life, but his thought forms never escaped the platitudinous. The charm that characterized his slight novels is as patently made-to-order as the pointless pathology manufactured by Mr. William Faulkner. I keep these books because of the pleasure they gave to a lonely youngster ; they are utterly lacking in vitality or power, and I shall not be deceived by my own sentimentality.

The catalogues likewise record an increase in demand for the first editions of Ellen Glasgow, whose first novel, *The Descendant*, appeared during the year in which Allen's *The Choir Invisible* grew into a best seller (1897). But in the case of Miss Glasgow the American collector has reason to be well satisfied. Miss Glasgow's fiction, from the outset, has been distinguished by able craftsmanship. She has drawn her backgrounds with meticulous care, and that in a region where the details are apt to be generously overdone in an almost uniformly antique fashion. Her men and women are neither types nor puppets, and she has never succumbed to the myth of southern chivalry, knowing full well that, at its best, it was no more than an airy gesture. And I wonder if Miss Glasgow's *Barren Ground* be not the most candid novel of gentility the South has produced. Certainly, if one is to collect modern Americans, there is more satisfaction to be had from these thoughtful chronicles of Virginia than from those of her more popular contemporaries : and, I dare say, the speculator will find them less of a "risk." But whether prices rise or fall, I shall lay hold on every good Glasgow first edition that chances to come my way.

Falling book prices and the thought of Ellen Glasgow must inevitably turn one's eyes toward the books of another Virginian, James Branch Cabell, whose prices have lately taken a most disgraceful tumble. Even *Jurgen* is down, as they say. And the book-sellers nod wisely and mutter I-told-you-sos. There is one very excellent reason for this state of things, and one having nothing to do with the quality of Mr. Cabell's work. Too many expensive, limited editions killed the Imp's enthusiasm. Arthur Machen's sales suffered for the same reason. When an author prints or permits the issuance of signed pamphlets — and those of no great merit — intended to fetch handsome profits from the gullible, the sensible collector calls a halt.

But as I write I have before me an inscribed first edition of that *Jurgen* concerning which there was such an indecent pother a few short years ago : I would not exchange it for a car-load of the "high-spots" that have been so successfully thrust upon unsuspecting Americans during the past decade. *Jurgen* is a wise and beautiful book, setting forth the tragi-comedy of sex, and, quite incidentally, detailing to us the story of the betrayal of what we were wont to call our American liberties. I sometimes believe that it is the greatest of American novels : certainly it is by all odds the cleverest.

Another American first that stands high on my own shelves is Stephen French Whitman's *Predestined*, which appeared in 1910. Well-conceived, polished, powerful, it proved to be strong meat for the sugared tastes of its decade. Had it been published ten years later a whole symphony of critics would have applauded. For besides his keen powers of observation and broad human sympathy Mr. Whitman possesses a superior artistry, a sense of both phrase and form that few of our time have equalled. He chooses his words with fine precision, and keeps his themes well in hand, refusing to tristram-shandy up those friendly little blind alleys where so many novelists lose both themselves and their readers.

But it was not the realism of Whitman that was to thrive in America. He was too civilized for 1910. Perhaps, too, there is something mordant about his wit.

His appreciation of the ironic is too keen. When we finally went in for realism we wanted it vulgar and heavy. *Predestined* should have waited until 1925.

Mr. Whitman has, during a score of years, done remarkable short stories, clever, carefully-executed things, read with envy by writers who would give their right hands could they but master his secret : but he has not ventured a second time to speak out what he knows of the worm that burrows at the core of life.

Few of our modern American story tellers seem to have been seriously inhibited by what was once upon a time called "style." Even sound English seems offensive to many of them. Mass education seems to have begotten a contempt for the language of distinction. Journalism is the academy of the trade nowadays, and were it not for the author's name on the title-page, one might attribute almost any smart novel of the times to pretty nearly any prolific reporter of the land. If low writing went hand-in-hand with high thinking, one might count it a distinct gain, but it is not so. These chaotic blunderbusses are as loose in their thinking as in their construction, and the facile journalist is superficial. The stylist whom they deride took pains with his sentences that he might the more clearly express his thought.

It is more than a relief, therefore, to come upon such a book as *The Time of Man,* by Elizabeth Maddox Roberts. Here is the South of the poor white, the transient laborer. But Mrs. Roberts has not felt it necessary to resort to dull trivialities to emphasize poverty. Through Ellen Chesser's eyes the world outside seems an invitation to romance, and even when her picture is framed by the hoops of a dilapidated farm wagon, it never loses its magic quality.

32

The Time of Man provides a true picture of the itinerant farm laborer, his simple pleasures, his sloth, his incapacities and his tragedies. But it is much more than that : it is the story of the dreamer who, fully aware that his delectable visions are far other than reality, yet mutters to himself, "But this last, surely now, *this* is not a dream ? "

Mrs. Roberts has an intimate knowledge of her Kentucky background, and has used that knowledge to good purpose. Her men and women are never suffocated in a honeysuckled loveliness. The word idyllic, so often misused with reference to her work, suggests better the weaknesses of her predecessors. Her pen is indeed the poet's, she sees with a poet's sympathetic vision, but she looks through to reality. Some realism is a lie, and the romantic may, at odd times, perceive truth.

Concerning *The Great Meadow*, I shall not permit myself more than a word. It is an interesting tale, delicately told, but the pilgrims of that adventurous chronicle are made to pass through my own land of enchantment, and I am thereby deprived of the power of judgment. Mrs. Roberts' later books (up to and including *Buried Treasure*), I read with but little pleasure ; but that is no matter, *The Time of Man* is a rare thing, and that is enough.

I recall another Kentucky novel not yet listed by those who catalogue scarce first editions. In 1923 was published a novel called *Weeds*, the only book yet recorded under the name of Edith Summers Kelley. Here we have realism, powerful realism. This story of the poor tobacco farmers of the southern hills has never received the attention it deserves, but I am convinced that it is one of the finest things America has yet produced, deserving a place close beside *Mc-Teague* and *The Red Badge of Courage*.

In this book, as in *The Time of Man*, we get a picture of poverty, hardship, defeat. I would hazard a guess that before doing this book Mrs. Kelley had studied the Kentucky tobacco growers with a care and thoroughness comparable to that bestowed upon *Middletown* by Robert and Helen Lynd. Such books are not born of a summer's vacation.

The final surrender of Judith Pippinger to life's futile treadmill is a real tragedy. Death and defeat, the inevitable outcome of the so-called realistic novel, are not always tragic. The end, for example, of Dreiser's hero in *The American Tragedy*, affords comic relief ; there is no contrast between noble aims and a terrible downfall. In the case of Judith we know of her buoyant hopes, her unavailing prayers, her fine, free spirit, her appreciation of beauty. For all her pitiful limitations of knowledge, this girl of the tobacco patches is heroic, splendid ; and the contrast between her deserts and life's rewards is sharp. In a word, Edith Kelley has written excellently of noteworthy matters, of profound emotions, of stirring dreams, of bitter realities, and, for that she has not toyed with the sentimental, she has succeeded in catching hold of the reader's heartstrings. I dwell on this for the reason that realism has come latterly to be flat, stale and all too profitable. Smart young men, empty of the more desirable human qualities, lacking urbanity, wit, insight, and the selective genius, snatch tales of crime from the daily press, and, with a smattering of Krafft-Ebing and Freud, convert them into novels which are at once described, by their log rollers, as "profound, stark realism." Thus Mr. William

34

Faulkner tells a story of how a half-witted bootlegger assaults an inconsequential college girl with a corn-cob, and how, from that simple beginning, she proceeds to prostitution. I am unmoved. Let the nitwits die. What of it ?

Miss Kelley has found the significant in the commonplace, and has dramatized it with great power. *Weeds* is a book to keep, to re-read, to preserve for the future.

Elinor Wylie's *Jennifer Lorn* is an exquisite bit of fiction, utterly unlike the novels just named : whimsical, slight, ironic, subtle, sophisticated, cruel, but civilized. I marvel at the catholicity of culture back of this extraordinary book. And it is a book that requires more than one reading. What seemed ice turns out fire. Elinor Wylie was a great artist, hiding from a reality with which she had once been on intimate terms. The wise bibliophile will treasure her first editions — there are only eight of them, and, alas, there will be no more — in chests of rosewood.

Among Americans now writing my own favorite novelist is Robert Nathan. I especially commend him to the Imp. Not seeking to please the general, he wastes no time on banalities, and his editions are not, I fancy, too unlimited.

Mr. Nathan adds charm to simplicity, tolerance to wit. He is urbane, wise, humorous and honest. In his delicate hands allegory takes on the colors of romance, and fantasy acquires an authentic verihood. He has uses for satire, but none for a bludgeon. He chuckles over tricks played by the imps of Satan, and is soberly aware of injustice ; but, seeing clearly these imperfections, he does not hastily conclude that life is an unsupportable evil. He has balance. In brief,

35

Mr. Nathan is a sane, intelligent man, and one of the finest craftsmen of this generation : I do not know his equal in America.

Here again are collectors' wares. At present it is no difficult task to assemble the eleven slim volumes : even *Peter Kindred* (1919), Mr. Nathan's first book (and the last one for any admirer of his to read), is not impossible to come by, dust-jacket and all : but, for the reasons I have set forth, one may be sure that they will rank high among the rarities.

I especially commend — to those who may, quite reasonably, be sceptical — *The Fiddler in Barly, The Woodcutter's House*, and *Autumn*. Of these the first two are intimately related : stories of Ezra Adams, who didn't amount to much but felt mighty friendly ; of Metabel, his daughter, who danced and dreamed ; and of Musket, the incomparable dog who danced and moralized — there is no wiser nor more amusing canine in fiction,— no, not even M. Bergeret's Riquet. Musket's advice on matters of courtship and marriage is as profound as it is diverting, and the lovelorn mouse, to whom, on application, he offers his suggestions, is not without a measure of sagacity. Prior to the mouse's marriage, Musket had insisted upon the superiority of the experienced woman — "who has learned that vigor without wit is of no use." And, after Mouse had followed this sophisticated suggestion and had lived with his wife for a time, he returned to Musket with the droll testimony : "I am very happy . . . my wife's experience is a constant source of gratification to me. All I have to do is to forget where she got it."

Of our other contemporary novelists but few, I believe, merit the attention of the collector. Thorn-

36

ton Wilder ought to remain near the top of any carefully considered list of American prose writers : *The
Cabala* quite definitely places him among the best, both
as observer of life and master of medium. *The
Bridge of San Luis Rey* is lacking in the clear, crys-
talline qualities that distinguish his first book, and even
if that were not so, its rather too heavy vein of popular
mysticism provokes a doubt. *The Woman of Andros*
is charmingly reminiscent of Walter Pater, slight in
conception but profoundly sympathetic in treatment.
My own confidence in the future of this remarkable
young writer is based upon the solid authenticity of
his timeless themes, his discriminating selectivity, and
his almost reverent use of words. His first editions
are already so relentlessly hunted down by collectors
that there is no need for further emphasis.

Nor can the collector overlook the fine work of
Louis Bromfield, who just now occupies a conspicuous
position among our civilized writers. Discount some
of his things as you will, his *The Strange Case of
Miss Annie Spragg* has back of it a clear understanding òf the psychology of religion and a very definite
knowledge of certain curious phases of American cultural history : the story is more than clever ; it is
powerful, and, for all its bizarre details, convincing.
When he chooses, Mr. Bromfield can write as well
as Norman Douglas, and, indeed, there are pages in
The Strange Case that the author of *South Wind*
might well wish he had written.

The works of Willa Cather are listed, at steadily
increasing prices, in practically all the catalogues that
offer modern first editions ; I wish I might share the
enthusiasm of her collectors. But I confess that most
of her stories seem to be dull and stodgy. I make,

37

however, one exception — *A Lost Lady*. There, now, is a chronicle that is solidly American, convincing, thoughtful, honest, and ably written. There is a keenness and zest here that seems lacking in Miss Cather's other work, an ecstasy that lifts this tale of a Nebraska village up to the level of an epic. I shall not crowd my shelves with such things as *The Professor's House* or *My Antonia*, but the shelf of moderns would be sadly lacking without this one outstanding novel.

Nor shall I collect the novels of Joseph Hergesheimer, whose *The Lay Anthony*, *Java Head*, and *The Three Black Pennys* once led me to make false prophecies. His later books smother in a junk shop of detail, or descend to triviality. For all that, however, the name linked to the three books just listed will not soon be forgotten. Hergesheimer had the artist's power of observation and utilized it in the study of really important aspects of life ; he had a sound historical sense, and was prompt to lay hold on essentials ; nor was he lacking in narrative skill. I regret that these abilities are not revealed in his later work.

Is Glenway Wescott, hailed as a rising star back in 1924-25, already forgotten ? The catalogues would seem to indicate a waning interest, but I cannot credit their transient testimony.

The Apple of the Eye is a book of emotional power and depth, boldly conceived and finely executed : *The Grandmothers* is one of the tenderest and truest of American novels. Mr. Wescott's stories are compact and unpadded ; his prose supple enough for every changing mood. In manner he is easily the foremost of the middle-western novelists. To these

virtues he adds another and greater — one that gives
assurance of his future place in our world of letters —,
his singular ability to portray character. Bad Han
and Jule Bier are as alive as Marty South or Clym
Yeobright. Bad Han's life-story is told in the first
eighty-five pages of *The Apple of the Eye,* wherein
she is the leading character. Her death, ending the
first episode, seems quite enough to destroy the reader's
interest in the book, but Mr. Wescott has the suggestive skill and subtlety, the thaumaturgic power to
evoke the spirit of this noble "bad" woman, so that,
throughout the full-length novel, it dominates the
whole : a notable performance for any novelist.

Here again the wise collector will discount fashion.

I note with satisfaction that James Boyd's work is
beginning to attract collectors. There, I believe, is
a man to watch. Born in 1888, Mr. Boyd has done
but three novels : *Drums* (1925); *Marching On*
(1927); *Long Hunt* (1930). Quite obviously he is
not in a flutter to fill the shelf-space of his admirers,
nor anxious to keep his name before a blurb-harried
public (Wise man that he is, let him bid prodding
agents go hang themselves !). He takes his time,
studies his ground and his period, brings to them a rich
creative imagination, and tells his story with grace
and ease.

Drums is a story of North Carolina life from the
days when Americans first began to grumble about
taxation, down to the close of the Revolution, and
John Frazer, who grows to manhood during those
troubled times, is permitted to see the best and the
worst of Americans and Englishmen. Thoughtful,
he is slow to take a stand. He dislikes equally the
bumptious, dull-witted English official and the hot-

headed, unscrupulous American revolutionary. Democracy he views with distaste; snobbery he loathes. Convinced at last, however, that there is but one course open to him he elects, though not without regrets and proper reservations, to throw himself into the fray.

I believe there is no finer novel dealing with this dramatic period of our history, and I am quite sure that none has shown so keen an understanding of its more intimate problems.

In *Marching On* the descendants of John Frazer are tried by the fires of the Civil War. This novel is an excellent companion to its forerunner, and while objectively it may not be so exciting, it displays, if possible, a greater mastery of the inner life and struggles of its hero.

Mr. Boyd is primarily concerned with the human soul, and the trappings of the period about which he happens to write never obscure his vision. Thus, in his last novel, we first come to know Murfree Rinnard as hunter, frontiersman, Indian fighter, moving faultlessly against an authentic background of forts, forests, huts, trapping, shooting and trading. Then, bit by bit, we are made aware that Rinnard's subjective life is far more interesting than his exploits. Rinnard is Everyman, torn between the love of woman-home and a life of carefree adventure.

Here, then, are books filled with soldiers and the sound of drums; old stuff that has been mishandled to the delight of the childish for generations : but Mr. Boyd, unlike most of his predecessors, subjects his marching men to very subtle processes of analysis, discovers the motivations that lie back of heroic action, the spiritual conflicts that beget adventure. And he does all this without for one moment dulling his reader's interest in the drama of vivid action. It is superfluous to add that he has quite ably mastered the art of writing.

I forbear to speak of futures ; I offer no recommendations, but after reading these three excellent tales I have promised myself to lay hold upon a first edition of everything Mr. James Boyd chooses to write.

Another southern novelist whose work will bear watching is Mr. T. S. Stribling. Since the appearance of his first novel, *Birthright*, in 1921, he has given evidence of a steadily increasing mastery of his medium. One felt his power from the outset, but his early work lacked the incisiveness, the clarity of vision, and the broad humanity that have gone into the making of such excellent novels as *Teeftallow* and *The Store*. I think, too, that Mr. Stribling has gained in courage since his first venture in fiction. He lives in the most sensitive part of America (Tennessee), and yet he dares expose its most cherished vices, its secret sins, and to drag forth its closeted skeletons. He has gained courage in telling of the negro and his achievements, and has not hesitated to make evident his superiority to shiftless whites.*

It must not be inferred that Mr. Stribling is a propagandist. In *Birthright* one feared that he might turn pamphleteer and preacher, but the artist in him

---

* Had I been writing in 1933, I should have included in this speculative list of immortals the names of Vardis Fisher, Erskine Caldwell, John Steinbeck and Hervey Allen. For Fisher's *In Tragic Life*, Caldwell's wicked *God's Little Acre*, Steinbeck's *To a God Unknown*, and Allen's *Anthony Adverse* are more than "promises of notable performance."

41

is triumphant, and his creation of such clearly etched characters as Abner Teeftallow or Colonel Miltiades Vaiden reveals to us a man whose feelings of outraged justice are more than balanced by a sympathetic imagination and a growing sense of tolerance and humor.

Henry L. Mencken has been collected for several years, and the catalogues indicate that he will continue to be in demand, barring certain fluctuations of the market. I confess to having been enthusiastic about Mencken's work back in 1912-16. But he grew monotonous — stereotyped. I like the man's gusto and admire him for his common sense, though he does cut a sorry figure at literary criticism and would do well to keep clear of comparative religion. But as a commentator upon the current events in what he is pleased to call "the American scene," we have no more useful writer in this republic. He is saving salt for high meat exposed at the near-by city of Washington. He is condemned for the wrong things. His opinions are sound enough. His diatribes against our political stupidities deserve respectful hearing. His remarks about American manners and the national vulgarity are applauded by all thoughtful citizens. Unfortunately, he displays nearly all the vulgarities he sets himself to castigate. He is salesman turned critic ; a pulpit-pounding evangelist shaking his fist at his own tribe.

He is not a man of letters, but he is a man of sense, and for this single reason his books should do home-missionary service. Apart from that, his *American Language* is a monumental thing that will survive everything else that he has done.

Of dramatists there is little need to speak. We never had one until the appearance of Mr. Eugene

O'Neill, and perhaps he has been well enough advertised.   Certainly he will continue to be collected : the wise collector began quite early.   Mr. O'Neill's concepts have widened and deepened with time, he has gathered power and acquired a greater mastery of his medium.   *Desire Under the Elms, Strange Interlude,* and *Mourning Becomes Electra* have definitely placed him on a level with his European contemporaries.   In my own mind there is no question concerning his place in the future : let him write what drivel he may, the work that he has already done makes him the only American dramatist whose plays are worthy of preservation : he is the first American playwright.

The poet's corner is not crowded.   In the past we had Poe, Whitman, Lanier and Emily Dickinson. Of living poets there are eight who, for one reason or another, challenge attention : Conrad Aiken, Joseph Auslander, Stephen Vincent Benét, Robinson Jeffers, William Ellery Leonard, Edgar Lee Masters, Edna St. Vincent Millay and Genevieve Taggard (I wish that I might name also Elinor Wylie, who but a little while ago stood at the head of the list).   I confess that I do not wish to speak above a whisper concerning the poets, and I dare say some of these that I name may be forgotten before the end of the century.   I but name those who, in my opinion, are the most original and vital of our time.   Jeffers appalls me, but I am gripped by his majesty and power ; Masters is given to awkwardness and curious mannerisms, but who has etched finer portraits of Americans in verse ?   Aiken sums up the melancholy and madness of our age better than any other modern, and it seems quite impossible that the elfin music of Edna Millay will ever lose its power to charm.   With some deference I leave the matter of the poets to the whim of the collector.

For the last I have reserved two men, non-fiction writers (though one of them did once write a novel, concerning which the less said the better): Henry Adams and John Livingston Lowes.

It may be objected that Adams is not a modern, but the tremendous sale of his *Education* is certainly among the modern incredibles, and it was to moderns of this century that his books were sold.

One hundred copies of *The Education of Henry Adams* were privately printed in 1906, but the book was not published until 1918. It is a document both subtle and profound. It is pessimistic, anti-democratic, and bristling with scepticisms. It is the warning cry of a civilized man, conscious of approaching social catastrophe, addressed to a thoughtful minority. And the book became a leading best-seller!

But I, for one, doubt if it was read, really read, by but few of those who seem, for one reason or another, to have purchased it from the shops. One wishes it might be read by every politician in America. It would quicken sluggish consciences (if politicians possess these organs of discomfort), clarify foggy minds and arouse a kind of patriotism that is compatible with intellectual self-respect. For *The Education of Henry Adams* is, frankly, a noble piece of propaganda. It is written under the spell of melancholy, and is not inspired by great hope, but for all that if it were carefully read and understood by any considerable number of Americans in positions of power it might yet save a nation from chaos and anarchy.

The Road to Xanadu is no statesman's manual. It

is an encyclopedia of literary criticism. That last has an appalling sound, so let me hasten to say that it is one of the most thrilling and *the* most learned work of criticism I have ever touched. *The Road to Xanadu!* The title is magic, and, truth to say, the book is a veritable magic carpet on which one is swiftly carried to curious lands no whit less enchanting than those fabled valleys described to King Shahryar by Shahrazade.

Professor Lowes has the skill of a Doctor Thorndyke at following clews. He tracks the Ancient Mariner across trackless seas. He knows where he went and why. He proposed to himself the task of tracing the sources of Coleridge's fantastic visions, and to this end he studied his notebooks and the notebooks of his friends as no man has ever done before. He has reconstructed not only the library, but practically all the books Coleridge ever read ; and out of it all, line by line (out of Hakluyt, Purchas, William Bartram, Frederick Martens, Thomas Burnet, Father Bourzes, Captain Cook, Erasmus Darwin, Joseph Priestley and a thousand others : books of travel, voyages of discovery, quaint accounts of strange beasts and terrifying portents rumored and gossiped from the four corners of the earth), the multitudinous images that passed through the mind of the poet into the poem are traced to their several sources.

It is difficult to speak of such an amazing work of scholarship without somehow suggesting labored dullness. The truth being the exact contrary, it might be well to make the counter-suggestion that this book has but little kinship to the campus mind. It is no ordinary critical thesis. Professor Lowes united creative to critical ability. To the interpretation of the poet's vision he brings his own imaginative sense and throughout more than six hundred pages of analysis the reader follows him as eagerly as though he were skipping through the pages of *Alice in Wonderland*.

And it is a wonderland, for, as Professor Lowes promises at the outset :

"We shall meet on the way with as strange a concourse as ever haunted the slopes of Parnassus — with alligators and albatrosses and auroras and Antichthones ; with biscuit-worms, bubbles of ice, bassoons, and breezes ; with candles, and Cain, and the Corpo Santo ; Dioclesian, king of Syria, and the daemons of the elements ; earthquakes, and the Euphrates ; frost-needles, and fog-smoke, and phosphorescent light ; gooseberries, and the Gordonia lasianthus ; haloes and hurricanes ; lightnings and Laplanders ; meteors and the Old Man of the Mountain, and stars behind the moon ; nightmares, and the sources of the Nile ; swoons, and spectres, and slimy seas ; wefts, and water-snakes, and the Wandering Jew."

One may be pardoned for asking at this point what all these adventures have to do with the study of Coleridge and his poems. That question is quickly answered. Professor Lowes is engaged in studying the creative imagination in its workshop, and, without for a moment discounting the ecstasy of genius, seeks to ascertain the origin of ideas and fancies. Having the testimony of the poet, set down a year prior to the publication of *The Ancient Mariner* — "I have read almost everything" —, he set about discovering just what he did read, and how many suggestions were therefrom derived.

To have performed this stupendous task so thoroughly was in itself enough to amaze, but to have transformed the results of these labors into a book that must inevitably give pleasure to thousands who do not care a straw for academic methods is nothing short of genius. The reader, once bored by Coleridge at school, suddenly discovers that he has been quickened into new life, and that his poems, once compact and tight, have expanded so as to include a whole new cosmos.

In my library this book now rests between Frazer's *Golden Bough* and Doughty's *Arabia Deserta :* three of the really great books of our time.

II

COLLECTING IN ENGLISH PASTURES

SOME CHRONICLERS OF THE ENGLISH SOUTHWEST

"The Moor teaches us a thing or two . . . 'tisn't only rock and heather and bog. Hear the wind huffling soft of a night and you would say 'twas a great whispering among folk. And then the heather red like spilled blood — it do seem bedecked and willing as a new bride. And see her in the rains — black and sulky and all evil temper — Oh, you'll hear her hissing like a sarpint! And then, mayhap, she's white and fresh and clean with snow and sparkling like jewels when the sun puts a glint on her. You can see her breathing if you know how to look. . . She is alive, and do sorrow and joy and suffer pains betimes — like all things living."

— Isaac the Shepherd, in *The Human Circus*,
by J. Mills Whitham

II

COLLECTING IN ENGLISH PASTURES

SOME CHRONICLERS OF THE ENGLISH SOUTHWEST

THERE is a certain poetic magic about the English countryside not to be found anywhere else in the world. It is not the mere fact that the hills and vales are lovelier than most places on the face of the earth ; not the mystic evocations of haunted Tudor cottages nor of the yet more ancient landmarks of pre-Christian peoples, standing here and there at the turn of a narrow lane or at the gate of a thatched farmhouse on the moor : these things exert a spell powerful enough to hold the sentimental American tourist, and to make any exiled son of Britain cross the world out of very homesickness ; but that is charm, not magic. The magic to which I refer is the spell that earth and air and water cast over those who have long dwelt close to that ghost-breeding soil,—upon those simple-minded pagans who have clung, unchanged, to the humble dwellings of their fathers, whilst all about them, cross and spire and rude hut-circle have been subjected to a thousand new interpretations by scientists and priests.

To a tourist the cottages of rural England are objects of delight and romance : they are, as we say, charming and quaint. The tourist is apt to carry the cottage mood with him to the downs and heaths, the tors and moorlands. But the native knows better :

51

he knows the spirit that broods on Egdon, Belstone, Wistman's Wood and Cranmere Pool ; he listens to the voices of Dart and Tavey. He has memories, associations, superstitions, if you will, that have made him personify hills and valleys that must ever be but scenery to the foreigner.

Thus it is that for us, the chroniclers of English country life, particularly those who have recorded their impressions of that slow-moving region of the southwest — Dorset, Devon and Cornwall — who have endeavoured to recreate for us the inner life of their country-folk, seem, somehow, to have deliberately overlooked the comfortable in order to exalt the cruel and to display the sinister workings of an overpowering Fate.

And yet we know that this is not true. Even the passing stranger gets some idea of Nature's little traps from the treacherous moors, where emerald-green spots on the welcoming hills turn into so many greedy mouths to swallow up the unwary ; from those down-sucking whirlpools that await the swimmer in singing brooks running southward to the sea. And if the traveler should have remained long enough in a Dorset or Devon village, conversing ever so slightly with reluctant rustics, he will have noted, despite their evident reserve, the almost inevitable fatalism that characterizes what may roughly be called their philosophy of life.

Fortunate enough to have enjoyed some days of tramping about these southern counties, to have lounged a bit in village "pubs," to have prowled along those narrow country lanes, exchanging a word, now and then, with workmen along the way, I, for one, have come to feel that those novelists who, often enough, have been charged with inventing philosophies for their rustics,— Thomas Hardy, Eden Phillpotts, John Trevena and J. Mills Whitham, to name but four of them,— have not only given us true interpretations of native thought and feeling, but have contrived to make us see Nature as she seems to the eyes of her humble children in those misty regions.

I have quite purposely linked the names of Hardy, Phillpotts, Trevena and Whitham : to me they seem to belong to one school, led by kindred impulses to the portrayal of kindred characters. One hears, now and again, of a "Hardy School." Every regional novelist, though he be so far away from Dorset as Kentucky, is fated to be compared to Hardy : and yet, in the cases of those I have just mentioned, the epithet has some justification. These writers differ widely among themselves and from Hardy. Hardy — save in the possible instance of *Jude* — was not a propagandist. Phillpotts often is, and even Mr. Whitham has been known to plead a cause. Hardy was not a mystic : John Trevena's mysticism has spoiled several of his most promising stories. None of the later writers has achieved that supreme mastery of material that was characteristic of Hardy's later work.

And yet, to one who for many years has counted among his intimate friends Hardy's *Giles Winterbourne, Gabriel Oak,* and *Michael Henchard,* Phillpotts' *Daniel Brendon* and *Nicholas Edgecombe,* Whitham's *Ned Tresillian,* and Trevena's *Peter Tavey* seem to fit quite comfortably into the same company of familiars.

The folk who live in these pages know what it is

to be pixy-led ; they struggle against and acquiesce before the same elemental forces. Nature is to them a very Person. They have the simplicity of pagan Greeks : yet they are Christians, deeply occupied by the puzzle called the-meaning-of-life, and because their older and more fundamental instincts are pagan, they arrive at quaint Christian conclusions.

These people are of the soil ; they are dominated by the earth. They are at once simple and profound. Birth, love, hate, death, and destiny make the sum of their problems. To the messages of the seasons their senses are awake. This is quite enough for the philosopher, the novelist or the poet. Mr. Phillpotts has given the essential picture in "Man's Days" (Up-along and Down-along : 1905):

A sudden wakin', a sudden weepin' ;
A li'l suckin', a li'l sleepin' ;
A cheel's full joys and a cheel's short sorrows,
Wi' a power o' faith in gert to-morrows.

Young blood red hot an' the love of a maid ;
One glorious day as'll never fade ;
Some shadows, some sunshine, some triumphs, some tears,
An' a gatherin' weight o' the flyin' years.

Then old man's talk o' the days behind 'e ;
Your darter's youngest darter to mind 'e ;
A li'l dreamin', a li'l dyin' ;
A li'l lew corner o' airth to lie in.

The philosophic novelist finds his ideal in the peasant : with him the non-essentials have already been stripped away. In Mr. Phillpotts' *Widecombe Fair*, old Coaker makes a speech that fairly reveals the secret of these ruralists : "Life goes more natural-like with us, because the better-most have built up a lot of silly nonsense round them — a whole wilderness of manners and customs, and odd funny tricks of behavior that we get along mighty well without. The higher you go, the more reality be hidden from you, and there never yet was a royal king as knew as much about the bed-rock truth of things as a working tinker. For why ? Nobody tries to hide the truth of things from a tinker. He can smell it and break his shins on it so soon as he pleases."

As if similarity of matter were not enough, these novelists of rural England are also related in manner and mood : nearly all of them are poets. Trevena, Whitham, Phillpotts, Mary Webb, and Tennyson Jesse, when they speak of the downs and dells where their creatures live and love, are alike moved to lyric eloquence. They differ in tone, true : Mr. Trevena's music is most often grim and terrible ; Mr. Phillpotts grows a bit allegorical, and Mary Webb rapturous. But they all sing.

Perhaps it is because the English southwest country reminds me of the hills and valleys of Virginia where I was born ; perhaps it is because the country folk of that region feel and think somewhat as the corn-husking rustics of the lower Shenandoah Valley. Whatever the cause, I confess to a more than sentimental fondness for the country and the books wherein it is described. For that reason I have collected with some abandon in its pastures. It has not been an expensive pastime — most of the writers I have named have not yet become collector's favorites, though they will in due time — and I commend them to such of the impecunious as may come to share my own enthusiasm.

55

FOR THE LOVE OF BOOKS

Let it be assumed, then, that what follows is but a collector's apology for his madness.

I

EDEN PHILLPOTTS

EDEN PHILLPOTTS has been writing for more than forty years. There are more than a hundred and fifty titles to his credit — poetry, drama, essays and fiction. We are accustomed to think of him as a novelist, and it seems but yesterday that his plays came to the London theatres. And yet, so long ago as 1895, his name was linked with that of Jerome K. Jerome in the production of *The Prude's Progress*, one of the scarcest of all his many books. His published verse goes back no further than 1905, but his fiction dates from 1888 — *My Adventure in the Flying Scotsman* — a novelette of the sort that English folk call the shilling shocker.

Mr. Phillpotts, one sees at a glance, is a versatile writer. The novels themselves may not be grouped under one category : there are ghost stories, stories of crime (some of these appearing under the nom-de-plume of "Harrington Hext"), stories of industrial life, historical novels, and the Dartmoor cycle.

Versatility is not always a virtue, and while Mr. Phillpotts has done some excellent "thrillers," he has not greatly distinguished himself save when writing of his beloved Devon moors.

One is compelled to record the fact that Mr. Phillpotts is an appallingly uneven craftsman : the reader who has been caught by the spell of his *Children of the Mist* (1898), or, again, by *The Secret Woman*

MY ADVENTURE

IN

THE FLYING SCOTSMAN:

A ROMANCE OF

London and North-Western Railway Shares.

BY

EDEN PHILLPOTTS.

LONDON:
JAMES HOGG AND SONS,
7 LOVELL'S COURT, PATERNOSTER ROW.
1888.

Eden Phillpotts' first published book

(1905), should be touched by a similar magic in *Brunel's Tower*, or *Old Delabole* (both of 1915); he might even expect some evidence of a greater mastery. But I dare say that had Mr. Phillpotts' novels been issued anonymously, scarcely half of them would be attributed to the creator of Will Blanchard.

For Mr. Phillpotts seems to have never quite made up his mind about his real *métier* : he is never done with making experiments. All very well for the novelist to write verse, or turn playwright : his novels should be the better for these excursions. Well, too, when a writer turns away from such melodrama as *A Deal With the Devil*, to *Down Dartmoor Way*, we feel that he is growing up. But the spectacle of a distinguished and able craftsman, who has clearly exhibited his power and understanding and skill on a stage rich with interest, turning back again and again to the vaudeville tricks of his somewhat unpromising youth, merits but little applause.

Perhaps I should not mention the work of Phillpotts' youth. Really, one should forget those early sins which most novelists strive earnestly enough to conceal. "John Trevena" tried to blot out his literary past by dropping his name : but he did more,—he abandoned childish things. There is no resemblance between the Hentyesque tales of Ernest G. Henham and the novels of John Trevena, either in matter or manner. Thus the canny novelist has at once drawn a protecting curtain over immaturity, and robbed the critic of his lash.

Not so Mr. Phillpotts. When he deserts his metaphysical rustics for the puzzles of Scotland Yard, his readers are reminded, however reluctantly, of *A Tiger's Cub*. This last was published in 1892, and reads as though it had been done in collaboration by the late Mrs. E. D. E. N. Southworth, and the author of *Mrs. Caudle's Curtain Lectures*. Sobs, sighs, shrieks, groans, ghostly deeds, maudlin sentimentalism, dull moral essays, and elephantine attempts at Victorian domestic humor are the stuff of which this unfortunate, melodramatic novel is made. No sane critic could have prophesied a happy future for the author of such a book.

True, he has long since outgrown the glaring faults of his youth. He has acquired restraint and has achieved a notable style. He has left the sentimental quite behind him, and time has given him a profound insight into human nature. But during all these years he has not overcome a taste for melodrama : he returns to "blood-and-thunder" as many a reformed toss-pot returns to strong drink.

Yet during these same years he has contrived to give delight to many thousands of readers in all parts of the world. He has been loudly, ecstatically praised by his reviewers. But at the hands of the more conservative critics he has fared rather badly. They have found him guilty of sacrificing theme to matter ; of overloading his tales of love and hate with extraneous information about the flora and fauna of the moors, about pottery and slate and mines, hut-circles and alignments, menhirs and ancient crosses of stone. He has been charged with stuffing his fictional puddings with too many plums of rustic humor ; with an inability to make his creatures other than amusing puppets,— with reducing his characters into illustrations for "types." In a word, the critics, while praising the man's powers of observation, his industry, his sincerity, his style, his wide knowledge of the antiquities and history of Devonshire, declare that he is not a novelist at all !

And these criticisms are not directed at the early work that I have mentioned, nor at the detective stories, nor at such fantasies as *Pan and the Twins*, or *Evander*, but at the Dartmoor novels : *Children of the Mist*, *The River*, and the *Whirlwind*,— the very best things that Mr. Phillpotts has done.

If one but takes the trouble to study these Dartmoor novels in the light of academic criticism, one is compelled to admit that the critics are, for the most part, right. The plots too often get their origin from the ancient triangle of passion ; the characters are obviously related by blood, and might easily be transplanted from one novel to the next without disturbing the movement of events. Nature is sometimes introduced as a dominant character, and then forgotten. The subsidiary plot sometimes runs away with its major.

But one curious thing about the standards of academic criticism is that they are so frequently trampled upon by writers whose work seems little worse for the accident. Many big men seem to have tripped over these little standards and then to have run all the better. *Don Quixote*, *Tristram Shandy*, and *Pickwick Papers* are universally held to be great books, yet, according to theory, they are pretty nearly all wrong. Balzac was reckless, and threw style to the winds. The fact is that if the creator of a book is a man of superior intelligence, with a deep understanding of his fellows and a sense of humor, the thing he writes, standards or no standards, will merit reading. And if such a man be once seized by a story that insists on being told, it is more than likely that it will give joy to many.

When, therefore, one is, on the one hand, tempted by an entertaining story, compact of good sense, delicate imagery, good humor and sincerity ; and on the other is confronted by expert testimony to the effect that the story does not obey the rules of fiction-making, what is the sensible thing to do about it ?

Why, the answer is fairly obvious, I think : tell the critic to go to the Devil.

I owe to Phillpotts fifteen years of pleasure. I have even enjoyed his second-raters. Nearly a score of his better novels I have re-read with increasing satisfaction.

A man who has done one hundred and fifty books in forty years — over three a year — has had little enough leisure in which to write even one good novel. And yet I believe that he has done a round dozen that will live to furnish pleasure to thousands, long after our contemporary critics are forgotten. Whether they are legitimate novels I leave to the captious : they are thought-provoking, joy-giving books, and that is enough.

The first book in which Phillpotts gave evidence of his power was *Lying Prophets* (1897). Here, for the first time, he revealed his fine understanding of rustic character and his real ability as a humorist. There was promise in *Down Dartmoor Way*, but here was the beginning of fulfillment. This simple tale of a self-centred artist and a fisherman's daughter, who serves first as his model and then as his mistress, unfolds no unfamiliar plot. It is rather in the treatment that we find the author's superiority.

The fisherman's daughter, Joan Tregenza, has grown up in a house of fanatic faith. Michael, her father, belongs to the "Luke Gospellers," a sect of predestinarians who in Hell see God's chiefest handiwork, and who strive, naïvely enough, to make earth-life a fitting prelude to damnation. Joan is, naturally, unhappy, and, until the appearance of the artist, John Barron, has only one hope of escape from this relentless piety : her coming marriage to Joe Noy, a simple sailor who, at the story's opening, is setting forth on a year's voyage. Joan ascends a high cliff to watch the outgoing ship and to wave farewell to her lover. Barron sees her there, a pretty, wild creature amid a tangle of flowers, and this gives him both a clue to the girl's heart and the theme for his painting. Old Michael hates artists, and the daughter has hitherto refused to pose for any of the painters who frequent the little Cornish village. But Barron, finding that the girl's fiancé is aboard the vessel she is watching, promises to make her a picture of Joe's ship, if she, in turn, will pose for him. She succumbs to the temptation, and Barron, in the weeks that follow, preaches to her a cheerful pagan gospel that, to one with her wretched background, promises freedom and joy. As day follows day the girl's affection for the absent lover wanes : the foreigner with his happy creed and gentler manners supplants the rude native. For her Barron becomes the all : to him she is but a happy incident, and when the picture is done he departs for London, having promised to send for her and make her his wife. She believes and waits. But instead of the letter of summons, she receives at last an envelope inclosing a sum of money and no word from her lover. A little later she discovers that she is pregnant.

Here, then, is an old story, an old problem demanding an honest solution. Unfortunately, Mr. Phillpotts chose, at this point, to depend on the fortuitous. Barron is an invalid, and nearly nine months after his departure he is stricken to the point of death, and writes a letter begging Joan to join him : now that death is near he is minded to marry her. This letter she receives, and is on the point of going up to London when she is overtaken by a flood and drowned. Joe returns to a world bereft of all that he has loved, and hears the story of his sweetheart's abandonment and death. He seeks out Barron to kill him, but finds that he is already dead.

Such a bare outline is quite unfair to the book. As I write it I am aware that it sounds trite and threadbare. The plot is commonplace. Where, then, does its merit lie ? It is in the treatment, the sympathetic handling of character, the fair presentation of the artist's creed, selfish though it may be, of his gods, of his relentless subordination of life to art ; in the careful study of Michael Tregenza in home and chapel, and of Joan's struggle between two equally cruel deities ; in the choice bits of unconscious peasant humor, used to lighten otherwise sombre pages, without once breaking down into the sentimental.

In nearly all the Dartmoor novels Mr. Phillpotts employs a rustic sage who watches the conflict of living forces with eyes of compassion, and who, from ripe experience, makes prophecies and offers advice that should avert disaster — though the sage usually knows full well that it will not. In the *Thief of Virtue* it

62

is Barbara Hext who plays this part: in *Lying Prophets* it is old Thomas Chirgwin, Joan's uncle, to whose home she fled after the discovery of her straitened condition. Deserted by her lover and cast off by a righteous father, the uncle tries to ease her bitterness by pointing the way to a kinder god than either of the two she has known :

"Nature's a gude working God for a selfish man, but she edn' wan for a maid, as you knaws by now. Then your father — his God do sit everlastingly alongside hell-mouth, an' laugh an' girn to see all the world a walkin' in, same as the beasts walked in the Ark. Theer' another picksher of a God for 'e ; but mark this, gal, they be lying prophets — lying prophets both !"

It matters little, then, whether the plot of the tale be old or new. There are, as we know well enough, but few plots, all of them bearing the mark of ages. The requisite of a novel, for most of us, is that it hold the attention fast. We welcome the time-worn, so be the telling of the tale is done with gusto.

The Dartmoor stories are simple enough in outline. Struggle, in those elemental regions, is limited : man's effort to get food and shelter from a land that fights back ; his fight for a mate. Along with these goes the inner struggle,— man's endeavour to reconcile himself to things as they are as against his dream of things as he thinks they ought to be. The story of the battle for food and shelter is seldom dramatic enough in itself to hold our attention to the end : the sex struggle always grips us. So also is the tale of man's effort to make himself at home in his universe, the expression of which we call his religion. It is sex and religion that come uppermost in these novels.

63

Not sex in any unpleasant or obtrusive sense : it takes
its rightful place and no more. Religion Mr. Phill-
pots leaves to be debated, in dialect, by the yokelry. It
is in these discussions — most often the forum is the
bar of some village pub — that Mr. Phillpotts has
shown himself to be one of the most delightful
humorists of our time.

The sex situation, in the Dartmoor novels, is
usually, as already noted, triangular, though not always nor often the conventional domestic triangle :
now and again it becomes quadrangular. A few years
ago Mr. H. C. Duffin, in an admirable study of
Thomas Hardy's novels, made a graphic representation
of the relations of the principal characters in six of the
Wessex novels, in which one woman is loved by two
or more men, or, *per contra*, one man by two or more
women. Nearly all of Hardy's plots take their origin
from some such situation. If we should apply the
same test to Phillpotts the result would be similar. In
Children of the Mist, Phoebe Lyddon is loved by Will
Blanchard and John Grimbal ; in *The Secret Woman*,
Anthony Redvers is loved by his wife and by Salome
Westaways, while Salome is loved by Anthony and by
his son, Jesse ; in *The Portreeve*, Ilet Yelland is
loved by Abel Pierce and Dodd Wolferstan, while the
latter is desired by Primrose Horn ; in *The Whirlwind*, Sarah Jane Friend is loved by Jarratt Weeks,
Daniel Brendon and Hilary Woodrow ; in *The Thief
of Virtue*, Philip Ouldsbroom and Henry Birdwood
love Unity Crymes ; in *The River*, Nicholas Edgecombe and Timothy Oldreeve love Hannah Bradridge,
while Nicholas is loved by Mary Merle. Out of such
situations grow the plots of most all the Dartmoor
cycle.

Perhaps one should note here that *The Secret Woman* may not be dismissed so easily as the others I have just named. There we have a more complex situation leading to a tragedy that is manifold. The plot grows, primarily, out of the love of Anthony Redvers for Salome Westaway; it is complicated by his son's falling in love with the same woman, and by the fact that his other son, Michael, is cool to his father, but is passionately devoted to his mother. The book opens with the wife's discovery that her husband has a mistress. The wife, in a moment of blind rage, kills her husband. The sons are witnesses to the deed, and a long feud between the two results. One is for having the mother take her punishment, the other for keeping it a secret. The identity of the mistress is not revealed until the end of the story where she learns that her lover has been killed by his wife.

The Secret Woman is perhaps Mr. Phillpotts' finest and most powerful novel. The wife and mistress, as he paints them in clean, bold strokes, acquire the dignity of figures in a Greek tragedy. Nowhere is there a smear or sordidness or shame. His work shows both intensity and reserve. When we lay the book aside the only emotion that we know is pity.

In *Knock at a Venture,* a volume of short stories, done some years before *The Secret Woman,* we are given the picture of a woman, Sarah Belworthy, whose heart is rent by the love of two men, John Aggett and Timothy Chave. She turns first to one, then to the other, with the result that the two men take turns at playing Hell and Heaven, and at last one tires of the game and makes away with his life. Here, however, it is made clear enough that Sarah's love for Aggett had long since turned to mere pity. It is a slight story, rising nowhere to the clear heights attained in *The Secret Woman.*

Again, in *Sons of the Morning*, we are permitted to study the hesitant woman. Honor Endicott loves both Christopher Yeoland and her cousin, Myles Stapledon, spoiling the lives of all three.

In *The Whirlwind* occurs the more usual domestic triangle. Sarah Jane, married to Daniel Brendon, is persuaded to sell herself to Hilary Woodrow, her husband's master, who tells her that he has but little time to live, and that in return for her favors, he will advance Brendon and deed to him the farm whereon he now works as an hireling. The woman's acceptance of this offer rather strains credulity, for there is no indication that she does not love her husband. It is made clear, however, that her husband's narrow piety is foreign to her nature, and that she is frequently exasperated by his preachments. Woodrow is a nonbeliever, and has little enough difficulty in persuading her of the fallacies in Brendon's teaching and in pointing out that morality is a matter of time and place. Having a healthy mind in a strong body, she accepts the new philosophy, and having done so, is at peace with her world. But Woodrow, as death draws near, turns to Christianity and wants to confess to the woman's husband. Sarah despises him for his weakness.

Here we have *Jude the Obscure* turned topsy-turvy. In Hardy's novel it was the woman, Sue Bridehead, who taught pagan freedom until social chastisement weakened her mind and brought her trembling before the Ten Commandments. Hardy's story is incomparably greater, but it is interesting to note that both novelists were led to study the same psychological problem.

Mr. Phillpotts is not misled by apparent simplicity or naïveté. The heart affairs of these peasant folk are troubled with subtle complexities. Nowhere does love move in unbroken lines. He has studied his people with meticulous care and has written of them with sympathy and sincerity. His eyes have been open upon both beauty and ugliness, and whilst he has been moved to tenderness by the loveliness of Nature on the moors, he has not been unmindful of the unlovely fact that beauty is also a trap. The Nature that inspires us to lift our faces in praise, may, in a twinkling, call forth our imprecations or plunge us into despair. We may think to have plucked a flower from her bosom only to find that it is a thorn. Eden Phillpotts has even suggested that Nature resembles a cat :

> " 'Life's a cat with nine sharp tails' :
> Loud laments the man who fails.
> 'Life's a cat with nine good lives'
> Answers him the man who thrives.
> Good or ill their fate may be,
> Life's a cat they both agree ;
> Let what fortune haunt the house,
> Life's a cat and man's a mouse."

More than enough has been written in praise of Mr. Phillpotts' description of Dartmoor. Were the rank of a novelist determined by his ability as landscape artist, few indeed could claim to merit so high a place as he. He seems to know and love every flower and shrub, every rivulet and hill in all Devon, and he makes his reader love them as well. And he has a way of opening each of his novels with a description of some aspect of the moor, leading the reader to believe that he is being given the theme of all that is to follow. Is the sky frowning? Are the clouds lowering and dark? Does a sly adder steal across the foreground? Surely, then, a tragedy is a-brewing, and the tiny figures of hero and heroine whom we shall presently see emerge from thickets of gorse are already doomed. But one cannot be sure of this; frequently the theme of the prelude is abandoned altogether. Moreover, the human figures are not always fitted to the background. Often they seem to have been painted quite independently, and then superimposed upon the larger canvas. Honor Endicott, for example, seems entirely out of key with the granite and heather against which she is shown to us in *Sons of the Morning*. In *Children of the Mist*, on the other hand, Will Blanchard and Phoebe Lyddon are just the figures we would expect to see by the misty water of the Teign, or amongst the grey stones of Pixie's Parlor. In general, however, these fine descriptions must be taken for what they are in themselves,— little prose-poems, related, but seldom essential to the work of which they form a part.

One secret of Mr. Phillpotts' great charm lies in the humor of his rustics,— Billy Blee, Abner Barkell, Sorrow Scobhull, Daniel Sweetland, and all that company of delightful old men who gather at the wayside inns of an evening to gossip and moralize over mugs of rich brown ale. And, as already noted, the quality of this humor is richest when the theme has to do with sacred subjects. Not that the peasant philosopher is given to blasphemy. On the contrary, it is precisely his faith, his assured familiarity with the ways of

Providence, his quaint heathen-Christian theology that makes him amusing to the more sophisticated. Unlike the Latin, who is a believer, and thus feels free to jest with heavenly powers that are as real to him as his own mother, the respectable Anglo-Saxon takes his religion without the salt of humor. Only in remote places and among the lowly are the gods permitted to relax. The "children of the mist," in England, and the negroes of the South, are alike in that they have contrived to inject some elements of comedy into an otherwise appalling theology.

The Devon yokel is not trying to be funny, nor is Mr. Phillpotts, rationalist that he is, using him as a mouthpiece for ridicule. One is made to feel, somehow, that the author is setting down bits of dialogue that he has actually overheard, and that, throughout, he is giving the reader a sympathetic interpretation of Dartmoor theology.

I hope I have not conveyed an impression that these amusing skits have but a local significance. The joy of them is that they are universal. That which befuddles the yokel mind has proved a stumbling-block to pretty nearly all mankind.

In *Children of the Mist* one comes upon an excellent example of pragmatic reasoning, done by Billy Blee, who knows what a god is for, and expects him to live up to his reputation for benevolence. Billy and old Gaffer Lezzard are competing for the hand of the widow Coomstock who, according to rumor, has been left a tidy fortune. Each of the old men finds the other's courtship highly ridiculous, and each is happily unaware of his own frosted hair and furrowed face.

When old Blee finally mustered up enough cour-

age to ask the hand of the widow Coomstock and received her solemn if slightly gin-muddled affirmative,
he praised the Lord and looked to the future more
hopefully than most lovers of threescore and over ever
dare. It was then with some amazement and discomfiture that he heard, a few days later, that old Gaffer
Lezzard had likewise been accepted on the very afternoon of his own brave adventure,— and by the same
woman ! In some heat he went to her and demanded
an explanation. The wily widow had heard that
Gaffer Lezzard was wealthier by some hundred
pounds than Billy, and was firm in her intention to
marry him. In point of fact, she had been a bit
bosky-eyed on the afternoon of the two proposals,
and had been vague as to her preferences. Billy
marched home trembling. Asked as to the matter
he cried :

"Matter ? Tchut — Tchut — Theer ban't no God —
that's what's the matter. . . She'm gwaine to marry t'other
arter all ! From her awn lips I've heard it ! That's what
I get for being a church member from the womb ! That's
my reward ! God, indeed ! Be them the ways o' a plain-
dealin' God, who knaws what's doin' in human hearts ?
No fay ! Bunkum an' rot ! I'll never lift my voice in
hymn nor psalm no more, nor pray a line o' prayer again.
Who be I to be treated like that ? Drunken auld cat ! I
cussed her — I cussed her ! Wouldn't marry her now if
she axed me wi' her mouth in the dirt. Wheer's justice
to ? Tell me that. Me in church, keepin' order 'mong
the damn boys generation arter generation, and him never
inside the door since he buried his wife."

Then, within the space of a few months after her
marriage with Lezzard, the poor woman died of de-
lirium tremens. She had found, to her sorrow, that

her husband had lied about his money ; he was a
pauper. And while his wife lay dying, old Lezzard's
mind dwelt upon his future of ease and comfort.
This dream also was to end in futility : the widow was
possessed of nought save an annuity and a host of
debts. When the will was read the old man found
that, in the stead of ease, he must content himself
with the almshouse. That night Billy Blee was in
high fettle :

"Be gormed if it ban't a 'mazin' world ! She've left
nought — Dammy — less than nought, for the house be
mortgaged sea deep to Doctor, an' theer's other debts. Not
a penny for nobody — nothin' but empty bottles — an' to
think as I thought so poor o' God as to say theer weren't
none ! . . . An' Lezzard left at the work'us door — poor auld
zawk ! . . . Awnly for the watchin' Lard, I'd been fixed
in the hole myself. Just picture it ! Me a cussin' o' Christ
to blazes an' lettin' on theer wasn't no such Pusson ; an'
Him, wide awake, a keepin' me out o' harm's way even
arter the banns was called ! Theer's a God for 'e !
Watchin' day an' night to see as I comed by no harm !
That's what 'tis to have laid by a tidy mort o' righteous-
ness 'gainst a evil hour. . . I misjudged the Lard shocking,
an' I'm man enough to up and say it, thank God. He was
right an' I was wrong ; an' lookin' back, I sees it. So I'll
come back to the fold, like the piece of silver what was
lost ; an' theer'll be joy in heaven, as well theer may be.
Burnish it all ! I'll go along to church 'fore all men's eyes
next Lard's Day ever is."

If the rustics demand a god who cares for their
needs in this world they are scarcely less concerned
about his providence in the world to come. As among
more learned theologians, there are some who hold for
a material resurrection, while others believe in pure

spirit.   In *The Portreeve*, Abner Barkell upholds the latter against his friend, Mr. Perryman :

"To be an airy sort of creation is a very comforting thought to me," declared Abner ; "for 'tis clear that a heavenly angel, such as I shall be, can't feel a twinge. I shall say 'good-bye' to my bones with a light heart ; for, to tell truth, bones and rheumatics have been one an' the same to me any time this thirty year. An' after the doings I've had with 'em, I should never trust 'em no more — not even in Heaven — but expect the stab of 'em every morning, so soon as I drawed my waking breath."

"We shall be raised in our own flesh, however, whether you like it or not," argued Mr. Perryman. "An' a good thing too, sez I. What's the sense of having no more body to you than a shirt drying on a clothes line ? A very ondacent thought, if you ax me. We'm accustomed to live in our flesh an' bones ; an' I shouldn't expect no lasting happiness outside 'em. . . What's the good of golden streets if us shan't have no solid feet to tramp 'em ; or of golden thrones if us ban't going to have no sit-downs to put on 'em ? You oughn't to let rheumatics drive you into such Godless thoughts, I'm sure. An' wi' all the singing, ban't there going to be no drinking ? Answer that !"

Not all the country folk are models of piety. In *The River* when Mr. Trout was criticised for begetting eleven children to grow up in the direst poverty, he replied :

" 'Twas like this," explained Mark Trout fretfully. "Us was set on a man child from the first ; an' us had to fill the house to get un. Yess, us had the house full 'fore a bwoy comed. Cheel after cheel 'twas — five maids running in fact ; then my old woman lost heart an' beginned to talk 'bout Providence, as females will do when the'm crossed. So I comforted her with the bravery of a man.

'Damn Providence !' I said to her in my courageous way ; an' be blessed if the next wasn't a bwoy ! So it went on."

And, as in other places, family life is sometimes made uneasy by doctrinal insistence. Joan Tregenza had rebelled against her father's dogmas, and even her step-mother, not nearly so bold, finds the creed a bit irksome :

"Luke Gosp'ling's a mighty uncomfortable business, though I lay Tregenza'd most kill me if he heard the word. 'Tedn' stomachable to all. I tell you, in your ear awnly, that Luke Gosp'lers graw ferocious like along o' the wickedness o' the airth. Take Michael, as walks wi' the Lard, same as Moses done ; an' the more he do, the ferociouser he do get. Religion ! He stinks o' religion worse than ever Newlyn stinks o' feesh ; he goes in fear o' God to his marrow ; and yet 'tis uncomfortable, now and then, to live wi' such a righteous member."

Mr. Phillpotts is a realist of the older school. He views life objectively, and lets us see both the virtuous and the vicious : where action follows a thesis, the arguments on both sides are presented fairly. If the creatures of his making frequently experience failure and suffer disaster, we are made to feel — save in a few cases where mere mischance is allowed to meddle — that the end was inevitable from the beginning.

I have put it down — somewhat rashly I fear — that there are twelve of the Dartmoor novels that will be long remembered. There is no apostolic significance to the number, and perhaps I am guided by no surer rule than my own preferences. I have tried to grade them in order of structure, style and humanity. Here, then, is my own list :

The Secret Woman ; Children of the Mist ; Wide-

combe Fair ; The River ; The Mother ; Orphan Dinah ; The Beacon ; The Thief of Virtue ; The Children of Men ; The Three Brothers ; The Portreeve ; The Whirlwind.

I place *The Secret Woman* first for the reason that in structure, characterization and dignity it seems the most nearly perfect thing that Mr. Phillpotts has written.   There is closer knitting and less digression than in any book of the Cycle.   *Children of the Mist,* most popular of all his books, gets second place purely by reason of its great beauty and profound human sympathy.   In structure several of the lesser novels surpass it.   *The Portreeve* and *Children of Men,* some will say, should be given higher rank.   They both have power, and even approach greatness.   But in the first, Primrose Horn, the villainess of the piece, exercises such pertinacious, such persistent malignity in prosecuting her revenge that the reader is inspired to actual hatred for the woman.   Moreover, she is made to take the place of Fate in the destruction of Dodd Wolferstan, the hero, so that his own weaknesses do not play a significant part in the resulting tragedy.   In *Children of Men,* Mrs. Huxam is so thoroughly mean that we lose sight of the not inconsiderable faults of her son-in-law, and again the villainess takes stage and footlights while the audience in its rage forgets to pity the hero.

The Whirlwind I have placed last in the face of able critics who would accord it at least a second place.   But the sale of the wife in that otherwise excellent novel, is not made convincing.   I am well aware that both husbands and wives, on occasion, have sold themselves for money, and that the onlooker may or may not be able to comprehend the reason for the bargain. But in a work of fiction the reader requires somewhat more than a statement. Sarah Jane is represented to us as a normal, loving wife. Her family is provided for, she does not long for finery : the sacrifice is made, we are told, that her husband may inherit the master's farm. But Mr. Phillpotts has not made that kind of a woman. To convince us he should have made her a creature of ambition. As it is, the reader is bewildered.

Demeter's Daughter I have excluded from this list with reluctance, for it is an interesting book, and Alison Cleave is a noble figure. But there is an excess of unmerited misfortune hurled at her head ; and an excess of misfortune may almost turn tragedy into farce. Most of her sorrows come from her husband, and he, poor wretch, is a figure better fitted for a comic opera than a serious novel.

Green Alleys, The Judge's Chair, A Virgin in Judgment, Cheat-the-Boys, and *The Forest on the Hill,* all have their champions, and all merit praise, but they seem to me to lack any enduring distinction. *Sons of the Morning* has descriptive passages and many humorous incidents in which Mr. Phillpotts is at his best : but the sudden return of a husband, supposed to be dead and decently buried, to a wife already remarried, converts a work of art into fiction for the backstairs.

But, for all his structural faults, Mr. Phillpotts remains one of the most remarkable writers of our time. For he has packed his books with wisdom and with kindness, and has made his people so real and so lovable that when we are too long away from them we grow lonely and long for them as for departed friends. He has been given to know the ancient magic of the moors, and because of his enchanted pages men in far-away lands have been vouchsafed to see the pixies playing in the moonlight, and to hear again the elfin music that is played before the dawn.

In a preface to *Children of Men* (which he calls the last (?) of the Dartmoor Cycle), Mr. Phillpotts has stated his modest creed, and in a paragraph has told us somewhat of his purposes. I shall let his words make my own conclusion :

"As a man's footsteps in the dew of the morning are the labours of the minor artist ; but if he challenge surer feet and greater strength to pursue his quest before the dews are dried and his passing forgotten, then he also has played a part. The masters flash lightning through our clouds of human passion, ignorance and error, or hang rainbows of promise upon their gloom ; but for us of the rank and file, it is enough that we make happy such as have only heard of happiness and waken the dayspring of courage in fearful hearts ; it is enough if we kindle one valley mist with a gleam of beauty, or pour some few, pure drops of hope into the thirsty and percipient soul."

II

MARY WEBB

SHROPSHIRE, lying on the border of Wales, is, like Devon, a pixy-breeding ground, rich in legend-studded hills that look down into the weedy depths of haunted meres. Its people have not yet been spoiled by progress and its valleys remain quiet and sweet, inviting those who would rest and dream and forget the cheap tin trays of a mechanized world.

The dialect and lore of this charming country are

not the dialect and lore of Devon or Dorset, and I dare say that to a native its people would seem to be very different from their southern neighbors. But to a country-bred American, John Arden, of Mary Webb's *Golden Arrow*, might very well be a double cousin to Gabriel Oak, of Hardy's *Far From the Madding Crowd*. Mary Webb's Salopians share that inevitable tendency to philosophic brooding that has made the Devonians of Eden Phillpotts a delight to so many readers. Indeed, I venture to assert that any reader who really enjoys the companionship of the folk who promenade the pages of either Hardy or Phillpotts will find himself thoroughly at home with the Shropshire lads and lassies immortalized by Mary Webb.

Mary Webb has no bad novels registered against her name. From the first she wrote with simplicity, dignity, beauty and power. Her novels are not padded with the inconsequential, nor dated by the passing fads of literary cliques. She founded her themes upon verihood ; and in the shaping of her creatures she omitted the insignificant and cast aside the irrelevant. She wrote from the heart, but she was never a sentimentalist. She saw the drama of life with clear eyes, but when she wrote of the tragic it was with tenderness. Ugliness and pain she recorded faithfully, but in her pages they are lighted by understanding. One is not surprised on learning that the late Thomas Hardy found in her novels a source of pleasure and satisfaction.

Mary Webb's first book, *The Golden Arrow*, appeared in 1916. Her next novel, *Gone to Earth*, was issued the following year, but did not reach America until 1918. Mary Webb was, naturally, unknown

77

and unheralded, and I viewed the book with suspicion. Then I read a bit about Hazel Woodus and her father Abel, a bee-keeper who made coffins and played on both harp and harmonica, a man without great ambition and untroubled by convention. The Wooduses interested me, and I bought the book. Two days later I sent to England for a first edition of Mary Webb's second novel. Beautiful prose ; characters that live ; open-eyed wisdom ; sentiment without sobs. I congratulate myself that I began collecting Mary Webb before Mr. Stanley Baldwin's testimony sent her first editions skyward !

Mary Webb died in 1928. She wrote but six novels, the last (*Armour Wherein He Trusted*) being but a fragment. Of the five finished novels I find it difficult to pick my favorite. *Precious Bane* has, perhaps, been accorded more praise than the others. This story of a noble woman, in the making of whose body but a single feature was marred ; the record of her humility, her strength, her loyalty, and her undying love, will live long after many of the "significant" novels of the period are forgotten. The character of Prue Sarn could not have been created by other than a genius. I mean precisely what I say. Prue Sarn lives and breathes, and remains a living, vital creature long after one has put aside the book of her life. Cleverness does well in making what Arthur Machen calls "reading matter" : clever people put amusing imitations of living creatures in their books, but when these creatures try to dance one hears the crackling of their paper masks. When we are parted from them we are left with no feeling of loneliness. Unreal, they leave behind no impress of reality. With Mary Webb's creatures one shares joy and sorrow as if they were our living friends.

I commend *Precious Bane* to those who still believe that life is somewhat more profound and solemn than jazz and radio would seem to suggest, a bit more tragic and painful than our official spokesmen would allow, fuller of significance and dignity, than the chronicles of Theodore Dreiser, Sinclair Lewis and William Faulkner have it : to those who still feel that one of the functions of prose writing is the communication of intelligible ideas or communicable moods in a coherent and intelligible manner, that a nice selectivity is the mark of an honest craftsman, that distinction is not snobbery, and that Wisdom, Love and Beauty may be choice companions even for a venture into the Land of Make-Believe. Such readers will understand and joy in the story of Prue Sarn, and will know why it is that had not Prue been grievously afflicted she could "never have known the glory that came from the other side of silence" ; why it was that Kester Woodseaves, the weaver, came to love her as he did, seeing at once her beauty and her virtue. They will understand how it was that Gideon Sarn's single-hearted lust for power cost him love, wealth and life, whilst his sister, who gave all that she had out of love and loyalty, got all that is ever worth having.

The Victorian, taking such a theme, was apt to sob and sprinkle his pages with tears. He overemphasized sentimentality. The post-war novelist is apt to resort to sneers, and to overemphasize brutality. Mary Webb had the taste and the good sense to balance the accounts.

To the making of her books Mary Webb brought rare bits of knowledge, patiently gleaned from Shropshire history and folk-lore. The writer of *The Golden Arrow* was not unread in the ways of witches

79

and of those wise old women who were used to brew strange mixtures during the dark of the moon. The maker of *Precious Bane* knew the intimate history of her county, its superstitious fear of harelip and evil eye, nor was she unfamiliar with the encyclopedic gleanings of *The Golden Bough*. But this knowledge, however interesting in itself, was never permitted to intrude upon her story : it was hidden in the background, to be fetched forth at the proper time for the greater enhancement of her narrative.

In the portrayal of love what modern writer has shown such insight, such wisdom, as Mary Webb ? She knows the flesh and does not belittle nor despise it. She knows what, for want of a better word, we call the spiritual, and she exalts it without growing vaporous or melting into metaphysical nonsense. She is neither nasty nor nasty-nice. She values beauty, but knows that understanding will go farther along the pleasant ways of love. Prue Sarn and Amber Dark (the latter of *The House in Dormer Forest*), win their happiness because they have learned to give and to know the heart-secrets of others. Robert Rideout (of *Seven for a Secret*), is not cast down when his giddy sweetheart flies to the arms of Ralph Elmer. He knows that she loves him, and why she loves him ; knows also that she will soon realize the quality and value of his love for her. He has the insight to know that she really belongs to him. He can, therefore, wait without worry, so assured is he that the girl's temporary unfaithfulness of the flesh is of no moment whatever in his scheme of things.

In *Gone to Earth*, Edward Marston is unable to see that the girl he has married is a woman, hungering for somewhat more than spiritual devotion. The girl

80

loves him and fancies that physical love is a thing quite apart from a being so noble as her husband. When Jack Reddin, speaking to her instincts, overpowers her, she comes to desire him, not as Jack Reddin, but as a poor substitute for the husband who has denied her body. She wants her husband to remain the tender, sympathetic friend and companion (which Reddin is not), sacrificing none of his fineness. She likewise wants him to desire her as Reddin does. The tale of Marston's failure to comprehend all this, and of how the light finally dawns upon him only at the last tragic moment of her life, makes one of the loveliest and most poignant stories in our language. A craftsman with less skill and understanding would have made it either silly or obscene. Mary Webb turned it into a thing of beauty.

I need say no more. Mary Webb's novels are already heralded afar, and I am too well assured that they will continue to be collected, read and loved by those for whom they were written,— the simple folk who know quite well how much better it is to dwell among willows and wild hyacinths than in "centres of culture," who have found the "soul that haunts the depths of the forest," and who

"... follow a secret highway
Hardly a traveller knows."

III

"JOHN TREVENA"

JOHN TREVENA is a man of mystery. Concerning his books critics have debated for more than thirty years, but, beyond the facts that his real name is Ernest G. Henham, that he lives somewhere in Devonshire, and that before taking refuge in pseudonymity he had produced six extremely bad novels, few know anything about the man. A portrait, used as a frontispiece to *Bracken* (1910), shows that he is, or was, a handsome fellow, and not the monster that some of his critics imagined. The rest is surmise. One fancies that he is a University man, born in Cornwall; that he spent a few years in Canada, possibly as a clergyman; that he suffered from incipient tuberculosis, and took to the heights of Dartmoor in search of health. It is an impertinence, however, to hazard guesses. But whatever his objective life may be, his books show us a man of singularly tormented genius. I dare say that a real "analysis" of John Trevena would reveal to us one of the most painfully interesting figures of this century. Idealism, mysticism, realism; cruelty, fear, tenderness : these moods seize upon him at will. One cannot say that he has a philosophy; it is all a matter of mood. When he masters his moods and his matter, as he did in *Furze the Cruel,* there is scarcely a man living who can write with such power. When the mood is his master he can be almost as chaotic as James Joyce : and Joyce himself is not more fervid in his hatreds.

Anything that Eden Phillpotts could do well, Trevena could do better. His descriptions of Dartmoor are more varied and colorful; his characterizations more vivid and less typified; his humor more spontaneous. *"Business is Business"* (This short story is one of a collection published under the title, *Written in the Rain,* 1910), remains one of the most delightful bits of English humor ever written, and Peter Tavey is more than a match for any of the comic rustics of Eden Phillpotts.

COLLECTING IN ENGLISH PASTURES

I began collecting Trevena's books more than fifteen years ago, and my faith in him rests on the foundations he laid in one of the most remarkable trilogies of this century : *Furze the Cruel, Heather,* and *Granite.* The power that went into the making of Farmer Pendoggat and Will Yeo, the droll humor that created Willum and Ann Cobbledick, or the tender pity that clothes pedlar Brightly, have somehow compelled me to the buying and reading of his twenty-five rather formidable volumes.

And the reading has sometimes proven a perilous adventure. I pass hastily over those early novels in which the young Englishman looks at Canada with unfamiliar (and sometimes unfriendly) eyes, and attempts to make a foreign land the background for Algeresque thrillers. The collector in me forces me to point out, however, that these poor things are very scarce and are quite apt to become "rare." Reading these fictions, one is not likely to be drugged by monotony : one moves from the fantastic humors of *The Dartmoor House that Jack Built,* or *A Drake by George,* to the almost inconceivably silly idealism of *No Place Like Home,* or the utter madness of *Sleeping Waters ;* from the charming whimsy of the *Pixy in Petticoats,* to the pointless propagandistic *Reign of the Saints ;* from the curiously depressing symbolism of *Bracken* to the cheerful objectivity of *The Vanished Moor.*

Sometimes Trevena's clergymen clutter up too many of his pages. Usually they are either bumptious, opinionated asses or raving mystics. But when they are conveniently out of the way, when abandoned harlot sisters are left behind, and when the author forgets to be missionary or reformer, and when, losing himself on the great moors, he becomes the sympathetic observer and the ironic humorist, Trevena is a master whom even a Hardy could not despise.

Trevena is not for the tired business man nor the timid optimist (though the short story named above might well delight any man in any mood). At his best he celebrates the cruelty, the remorseless grind of Nature, rending her creatures with reckless impartiality. He gives us at once a picture of beauty and brutality ; and he despises sham of every sort. Trevena is a student's novelist. I think it might almost be said that he has made a source library for novelists.

Symbolism has been one of his weaknesses : most often it has used him to his great disadvantage. But in his trilogy the craftsman was master of the tool. Looking about Dartmoor he saw on every hand furze, heather and granite. To him they became symbols of cruelty, endurance and strength. "The Furze," said he, "is destroyed by fire, but grows again ; the Heather is torn by winds, but blossoms again ; the Granite is worn away imperceptibly by the rain." *Furze the Cruel* is far and away the best thing that Mr. Trevena has done. To have written that one book gives him a place among the best novelists of our time.

It is impossible to make a summary of *Furze*. It is no simple fiction of events. Farmer Pendoggat's inhumanly brutal career and his justly earned punishment ; Brightly's sad misfortunes ; the grotesque exploits of the delectable Taveys, the trivial love affairs of one Boodles and her mannikin, Aubrey ; the minor iniquities of Parson Pezzack, the indelicate downfall of Thomasine, the tale of Saint Goose and Farmer

84

Chegwidden's mysterious accident, are but incidents in this moving novel of Dartmoor life which, despite its spice of humor and a certain vein of adolescent nonsense, is a closely-knit chronicle of cruelty, illumined by bits of sage philosophy and descriptive paragraphs that are a joy to read.

For a time (1906-1910), it seemed likely that Mr. Trevena was about to adopt a definite formula for his Dartmoor stories. In at least six of his books one met the invalid who had been driven to the wind-swept hills for his health, who was the object of native suspicion, and who attempted, in one way or another, to meddle with the morals and manners of the frowning rustics. His comics were cut from the same pattern : Willum and Ann Cobbledick being but new names for Peter and Mary Tavey. In all of his novels of this period the critic dominated the observer, and one might fancy that all of them were written by an alien invalid.

Since 1910 the formula has been abandoned. *Moyle Church Town*, *The Custom of the Manor*, and *Off the Beaten Track*, have little or nothing in common with the earlier books. Historical novels, stories of madness, humorous stories, tales of double personality, have followed, and along with the formula went the power that promised so much. His books are always interesting and studded with bits of rare beauty, but clarity of vision seems to have been lost.

And yet I would not part with my Trevena collection. Was there ever a novelist whose every tale gave content and joy ? And have not those half-successes of great men, nay, their very failures, thrown some light upon their masterpieces ? I do not delight in the minor pieces of Cervantes, but they tell me

somewhat of the creator of *Don Quixote*, and I
return to the great book with greater understanding.
I may be embarrassed if you mention *The Reign of
the Saints*, but I am willing to match *Furze the Cruel*
with any regional novel you may care to name, and
as for *Business is Business*, I'll swear that by all odds
it is a more amusing thing than any yarn that Mark
Twain ever told.

Trevena items are not, at the date of this writing,
very expensive : I shall avoid the folly of quoting
figures. The seven books credited to Ernest G. Henham are rather scarce, and it took years and patience
to complete my collection. The anonymous *Pixy in
Petticoats* is not too easily obtained, and it is a bit
difficult to lay hold of *Heather*, containing the loose
"Appeal" slip in which Mr. Trevena confessed that
Brightly of *Furze* was drawn from life, and solicited
funds for lightening that poor creature's burden of
misfortune. The trilogy is going to be as difficult to
obtain five years from now as Phillpotts' *Children of
the Mist*. Five years ago the Phillpotts novel could
have been bought for five dollars. The last catalogue
price I saw was something over three hundred dollars !
Pardon the egotism of a very minor prophet !

IV

F. TENNYSON JESSE

Secret Bread, I may as well confess at the outset,
is one of my favorite novels. In my own library it
occupies a place very near to Hardy's *Woodlanders*.
Certainly no account of the regional novels of the
English southwest would be complete without some
mention of this beautiful book.

Tennyson Jesse's other novels leave me indifferent : I cannot think that they are important, and I am not interested. It is no matter. *Secret Bread* has enough of wisdom and grace to illumine a very long shelf of ordinary novels.

I fancy that this book was a long time in the making. It has a mellowness and depth absent from the work of the book-a-year-or-be-damned hacks. When I speak of its mellowness I am not unmindful of the fact that the first American edition (back in 1917) was suppressed on the ground that it was more than mellow. After a fourth reading (1931) it seems incredible that even the most loyal subject of Queen Victoria could have found an offensive passage in so rarely fine a book.

In *Secret Bread* we are at the tip of Cornwall from about 1840 until the end of the first decade of the twentieth century. We are given the full life-history of Ishmael Ruan from the sorrowful day of his birth until, after having won a goodly store of successes and a full measure of peace, he rounds out his threescore and ten. Ishmael was the only legitimate son of old James Ruan, all of whose elder children were born out of wedlock. On his deathbed, just prior to the birth of Ishmael, old James is married to Anne Begoe, his slatternly and ignorant mistress, leaving to his unborn son not only the broad acres and ancient Manor of Cloom, but likewise a vast heritage of jealousy and hate.

How Ishmael endeavors to deal justly with his illegitimate brothers and sisters, how he lives down the sins of his father and redeems his estate from ruin, how he strives to make his own life into something fine and enduring, whilst his oldest brother plots to destroy his happiness, would provide a generous theme for a good novel. But the heart of the story lies in Ishmael's constant search after the secret bread of life,—the thing that men really live by.

All the love of Ishmael's mother went to her first born, Archelaus, a great, hulking fellow, ignorant, embittered by the fate that forever was to deprive him of a fine estate, and had it not been for the wisdom and love of his guardian and tutor, Father Boase, rector of the village church, the boy's life might easily have been spoiled. But through Father Boase there was implanted in him a desire to be all that his father was not, to build up his inheritance and be indeed the benevolent Squire, the kind master, the responsible citizen and servant of his fellow men. To this end he bends his energies at school and on the farm. His father's misconduct has brought suffering : his own life shall be devoted to kindness and service.

Archelaus is his devil. Every important event in his life is spoiled through the undying wrath of the older brother : his birthday dinner on the day he came of age ; his first reception of his chum, Killegrew, when, attempting to restrain his brother from unwonted acts of cruelty, Archelaus attacks and very nearly kills him. The girl he is to marry is seduced, and finally, in his old age he is faced by the terrible fact that his son, inheritor of Cloom acres, is, in reality, the son of Archelaus, begotten not of passion, but of hate for his more fortunate brother. In his heir, Archelaus will hold sway over Cloom when Ishmael is laid away.

This that I have written gives but the outer husk of the story. The kernel lies in Ishmael's inner victories. For, after all his triumphs in the phenomenal,

Archelaus loses in the real world. Ishmael had provided for himself places of refuge concerning which his brother had no knowledge. His spirit had been severely wounded, but remained triumphant at the last. For :

"In his childhood he had lived for what would happen in a far golden future ; in his youth by what might happen any dawning day ; but in his years of manhood . . . he had lived by what he did" : when sorrow came, there was the determination to make the best of things, to get the best out of everything. But no, there had been more than that. "Beauty, the actual joy of the world, that had been feeding his soul all the time, giving him those moments of ecstasy without which . . . the soul could not be saved alive." He had stood upon the hill and prayed : "Let beauty not die for me. . . May dawn and sunset, twilight and storm, hold their thrill to the last ; may the young moon still cradle magic and the old moon image peace ; may the wind never fail to blow freedom into my nostrils, and the sunlight strike to my heart until I die. And if colour, light, shadow, and the sound of birds' calling all fall away from my failing senses, at least let the touch of earth be sweet to my fingers and the air to my eyelids."
Then, in the last years, his strength of body swiftly declining, "He had lived by the knowledge of death, by the blessed certainty that life could not go on forever, that there must be an end to all the wanderings and pain, to all the dullness and . . . driftings, to all the joys that would otherwise fall upon sluggishness or cloy themselves. This it was that gave its fine edge to pleasure, its sweet sharpness to happiness, and their possible solace to pain and grief. He had lived, as all men do, knowingly or not, by death. This was the secret bread that all men shared."

So it was that Ishmael Ruan, for all the cruel tragedy he had known, had known also the wonder of the world, and despite the last cowardly blow, dealt by his life-long enemy, had found the gift of peace. Moreover, his enemy had been vanquished, for while the future heir of Cloom was indeed begotten of Archelaus, he had been trained by Ishmael, and Ishmael's soul it was that lived in the son of Archelaus.

Secret Bread is not sentimental, but it is dominated by a fine sentiment and a reverence for the permanent values of life so sadly lacking in many modern books. It is whole, sound, well knit, flavored with an honest bitterness that is finally purged away. Perhaps it lacks the genius that inspired Trevena's *Furze the Cruel,* but there is more sanity in it.

The first edition of *Secret Bread,* clumsy and thick in its red covers, shall remain high on my shelves but not out of reach. Let the silly speculators rave about modern "high points" in fiction : this rare book will be prized in a day when many of its more loudly applauded contemporaries have accommodated themselves to the italics of period footnotes.

V

J. MILLS WHITHAM

J. MILLS WHITHAM is one of the most capable, consistent and sympathetic of present-day regional novelists. He knows and loves the North Devon country, interprets its peasant character without either affectation or artifice, is enough of a poet to have an imaginative sense of life, and enough of a realist to avoid sentimental banalities. He writes clearly, beautifully, and, in at least three of his novels, with great power. His is not the erratic, brilliant genius of John Trevena : he has none of Phillpotts' delightful sense of humor.

But he is far more reliable than either of the older chroniclers of Dartmoor.

If reliability is to be associated with dullness, as it commonly is, it would be truer to say that Mr. Whitham manages to keep the level of his writing up to a standard that his readers have come to expect of him ; for he is never dull.

Since 1895 enthusiastic reviewers have been engaged in the happy pastime of picking a fit successor to the late Thomas Hardy. Should a book contain a bit of dialect, a modicum of folk-lore ; should it chance to be ornamented by a few passages descriptive of Nature ; should it chronicle the death of a farmer, or the betrayal of a country maid ; above all, should it come to an end on a note of melancholy, then must the writer be, perforce, a successor of Thomas Hardy. Thus Sheila Kaye-Smith, the Powys brothers, Henry Williamson, and a score of others, have, at one time or another, been awarded the somewhat tattered mantle of the great master.

Very well, I, too, will play the game, and, conscious of all the hazards, name my candidate for the honor. For ten years I have had the itch to enter Mr. Whitham's name in this list. I am aware that English critics have not been unmindful of him in this connection : for aught I know to the contrary he may have been heralded over here. But he has never received the acclaim he deserves, and the nine novels bearing his name contain within their covers sufficient of wisdom and beauty to warrant giving their creator a high place among those who carry on, intentionally or not, the Wessex spirit.

One is never quite safe in making predictions, and it is vain to foretell the futures of the living. They may give the lie to all that one has prophesied. The regional novelist of today may tomorrow turn cosmopolite. The young chap who set out on the road Stevensonian may desert to Tolstoi. Mr. Whitham has published no fiction during the past five years. His novels began to be issued in 1912, and since 1925, he, for some reason, turned editor and translator. One feels sure, however, that the man who wrote *Starveacre* and *The Windlestraw* will not desert for long the road on which he so bravely set forth.

All of Mr. Whitham's stories have to do with North Devon. All of them are simple in their plots, and none were made to create a "sensation." One feels that Mr. Whitham takes his time. He does not write for the summer excursionist. He is philosophic, calm, dispassionate, intensely interested in the development of character as it is played upon by both internal and external influences, and, once a theme gets possession of him, he refuses to let himself be diverted by any minor issue. In brief, the man knows human nature, the country he has chosen for a background, and has a genuine respect for form. His themes, with two exceptions, are timeless.

The first of his books to win any considerable popularity was *The Human Circus,* his fifth novel. As one might expect, it is not Mr. Whitham's best work. It has a rather time-worn plot which, for all its age, seldom fails to appeal, being the story of a runaway Cinderella — in this case the natural daughter of a young nobleman by a gipsy woman who, after the birth of the child, drowns herself. The child, Zillah, is given into the not too tender hands of Devon farm folk, from whom, after years of torment, she escapes to join a travelling circus. The men she loves lack courage : Nat, the playmate of her childhood, loves her, but is afraid to run away ; Dilberry, a gentleman-gipsy of independent means who has her heart all along, fears that he is too old. But Dilberry sees that she has golden gifts, and finally persuades the girl to leave the circus and study for the stage. Success follows, but the girl is a child of the moors and longs for the vans on the road, and after her father, now an old rake who hovers hopefully around stage doors, makes love to her, she throws away a career for a Devon cottage. A hackneyed tale this, but surprisingly well told : a slight thing, but beautiful.

Of a different sort is *The Heretic*, a rather thinly disguised biographical study of a well-known London surgeon, whose professional heterodoxies won him the hatred of his colleagues. Raymon Verne, who left the moor for London, is an heroic if slightly quixotic figure, a bit too noble, perhaps, to be convincing. The story of his life is ably and entertainingly told, though one may be allowed to observe that Mr. Whitham's men and women thrive but poorly in London air : they breathe more freely on their native hills.

Fruit of Earth, *Sinful Saints*, and *Wolfang* have, all of them, won friends. All of them show power and understanding ; all of them are studies of rather exceptional people. The curious, unearthy idealists of *Sinful Saints*, and the timid, self-distrusting artist in *Fruit of Earth* have much in common. Now the sorrows of the saints have ever been of interest to healthy sinners. But the sinner is not profoundly moved by tragic situations from which his own blunt common sense must ever protect him. He is curious, but feels no intense pity. Mr. Whitham's saints pay a high price for their devotion to a somewhat uncon-

ventional ideal : Ingleberry, in *Fruit of Earth*, is sorely
punished for his scruples. Well, Mr. Whitham
seems to say, people who entertain ideals and scruples
in a world like this, must expect to pay for the luxury.
Wolfang contrasts the idealist with utter brutes. It
is a chronicle of violence, hate and cruelty. Puritan-
ism and profligacy come face to face, and both sides
refuse to surrender. A Hamletesque artist and his
faithful mistress are destroyed in the fray. The book
shudders with brutality. A brutality, however, that
calls to mind those tortured souls in *Wuthering
Heights*.

There are three books that demand more extended
notice : *Silas Braunton*, *The Windlestraw*, and *Starveacre*. Here the moor takes on personality, and, from
being a mere starting point, becomes the whole background of tragedy.

Silas Braunton is Nietzsche bravely striving to practice his own inflexible precepts ; trying to "be hard,"
and perishing in the attempt.

Silas was at heart a dreamer, a sensitive fellow with
a bit of the poet in him, but terrible things had happened to him, and to hide his pain he made for himself
a grim mask. "Behold !" he cried. "There is no
weakness here !" It became necessary to pattern his
life after the mask, and to assume a brutally practical
role that was not always as jolly as it seemed. For
Silas could create a mask more easily than he could
destroy his soul.

The things that had spoiled the real Braunton had
been bad enough : his father had been hard to the point
of cruelty, and had wound up bankrupt and a suicide ;
his mother, a meek, patient, woman, had died when
the boy was in his 'teens, and people had not hesitated

94

to whisper that old Braunton was responsible for her death. His fellows had shunned the son of "Cut-throat-Braunton," and he had known a long period of loneliness and humiliation. Then the girl he had loved was taken from him by her mother — the son of such a father was unfit for a husband. To ease this last blow he had married a poor creature who had likewise suffered from a cruel world, but who was by no reckoning fitted to be his mate. And, finally, he had hired out to a master — Farmer Hickory — who was by instinct the hard, unfeeling, practical man Braunton strove to imitate.

These, then, were the forces that made Silas Braunton the creature he seemed. They made him hard enough to succeed in a material way — and to merit enemies. And he might have won a kind of contentment playing his part, had there not been opposing forces.

A marriage made on the rebound from a real emotional attachment is not apt to yield satisfaction for long, and Silas had soon grown to despise the woman he had taken ; and when his master showed in every way his own active dislike of the woman, and offered to make Silas his heir on the condition that he get rid of her, his tolerance of the poor creature was not thereby increased. She was weak and will-less, and the strong have no room for such in their world. And yet he would have never gained the courage to put the woman away without a conventional excuse.

The excuse might have been forever lacking had it not been for the diabolical cunning of old farmer Hickory, who arranged it so that Minna seemed to be involved with Nathan Dart, one of his meaner hirelings. Before her accusers Minna was like a poor, dumb animal : Dart, a miserable egoist, was more flattered than hurt by the charge ; and Braunton, with a great show of self-control, drove the bewildered couple from his door.

The story of Minna Braunton is told with great power : Tess Durbeyfield, if a nobler, is not a more convincing or pathetic figure. But the tragedy of Minna is not permitted to hold our attention longer than is strictly necessary to Mr. Whitham's purpose, which is to show the ultimate effect of that tragedy upon the character of Silas.

With Minna gone, Nightcott Farm seemed rid of every weakness. Silas went his way, casting off the old and feeble, demanding his due of every man, and making himself both hated and feared. And he felt himself wholly righteous and quite justified in all that he did. One comes to feel, however, that even as many another would-be Nietzschean soul, he depended upon his master for strength : and when old Hickory died, and Silas was lord of Nightcott, the dreams of his youth began, ever so timidly, to assail him, and he began to question his own philosophy. Minna had never been a reality, but his dreams had once been bread sweet to the taste.

And yet Minna would not down. A child was born to her, and after the bitter hardships of the road and the brutal neglect of Nathan Dart, ill and dying she crept back to beg for her little girl a home. That done, she died — well rid of a world that had no place for gentleness.

To the dead woman Silas gave scarcely a thought : she was to be buried, and that was the end of the matter. And, at the outset, he determined to rid himself of the bastard child. But here his determination did not prove equal to that of his housekeeper. It was the first sign of the breaking.

How this unwanted little girl stole her way into Braunton's life and awakened a love that made all else seem trivial ; how she made him doubt his own philosophy and take an accounting of his values ; how she smashed his universe, in fact, fills the last third of Mr. Whitham's book. The reader may begin to fear that after all *Silas Braunton* is but another sentimental fiction in which the villain is to be redeemed by a little child : the terrible stuff of the Nineties. But it is not so.

Nathan Dart, the girl's father, was to be reckoned with : he still lived and nourished an ancient hate. Had not Braunton scorned him, and cast him off ? Very well, he would pay. The weak may also have their vengeance. And Braunton was in his power : to his storehouse Dart was provided with a key. To crush the man he hated he would need but to take the child.

Perhaps the end of this tale is a trifle melodramatic and brutal, but the seeds of violence were sown in its beginning. There is about it an inevitability and a justice that is satisfying to the taste. Mr. Whitham has here written a moving and mighty story, dominated at its climax by the Furies and at its close by the Pities. It is a story that deserves a place quite close to *The Mayor of Casterbridge*, and that is saying a great deal.

The Windlestraw is a chronicle of failure : it opens and closes on a note of futility. Ranley Hibbertson's father stumbles out of a storm-drenched night, bearing in his arms a child. That is the opening of the story, and it marks the end of Ranley's father, whose name

97

and origin are never revealed. But the doctor who had been summoned to the bed of the dying man found, among his patient's meagre possessions, a battered copy of Pascal's *Pensées*, on a flyleaf of which was written the name of "Cuthbert Hibbertson," and bending over the dying man he heard him whisper the word "Ranley," and the name of the doctor's own college. This good man, therefore, concluded that Ranley Hibbertson was the proper name of the boy, and, being a man of sentiment, he wished to help smooth the path for the waif. Having no child of his own, he determined to see that, when the time came, the boy should receive an education befitting the son of a Magdalen man.

Thus it was that after a calamitous beginning Ranley Hibbertson secured for himself a patron. And he had done more : the village baker and his wife fancied they saw in the child a resemblance to a little son who had died, and, being poor folk, they welcomed him as one of their own children.

All of which, fortunate as it seemed, was quite unfortunate. For while his foster parents fitted him for a life of simple piety, his education gave him a taste for something quite different. His was a house divided against itself, and the result was a fear of living that foredoomed him to failure. He could not adjust himself at either extreme of the social scale. He married a woman for whose fellowship the University had fitted him, but he was too much the rustic for her ; his lack of ambition drove her away from him. In a mood of reaction he returned to the home of his childhood, married his foster sister and began to play at farming. But he was by now too much of a theorist and his ideas of life were revolting to the

98

Methodist wife : in her turn she left him. In the end, a transient farm laborer, under an assumed name, he died unknown, even as his father, leaving behind him a journal wherein he recorded his failures, and some odd volumes for the puzzlement of men who understood him not. The meaning of life? Futility. Its process? Repetition.

Windlestraw is the chronicle of a soul ; the soul of a man whose objective life was a complete failure, but who, throughout, maintains dignity and a certain greatness. Hibbertson's greatness rises almost to the point of genius in the closing days of his life when he voluntarily chooses the paths of torture, and renounces a relief that could only be secured by an affront to his soul. Mr. Whitham understands these pathetic creatures who are predestined to suffering, who stand mute whilst eagles pounce and chattering social magpies make the air vocal with vociferous protest and endless explanation. He is the spokesman for the hesitant and the weak.

To me, *Starveacre* is the most appealing and powerful of Mr. Whitham's books. In style, characterization, plot, and (may I be forgiven the use of this maimed and now meaningless word !), psychology, it stands among the best of modern English novels. Here the frowning moor justifies its evil reputation, and enters as an active participant in a heart-breaking drama. Here, too, the Furies have their fling, and the sheeted dead move about unquiet until wrongs avenged permit them at last to find repose.

Let me not mislead some poor, hysterical seeker after "ouija" wrigglers : this is no novel for mystics of the modern sort. It is a tale of flesh and blood : what spirits are therein named are of the Earth.

It is a story of struggle and strife, wherein, as usual, the thing called love makes a sorry mess of life. Brenda Tressillian really loves her husband, but association with Bert Raikes, hard-drinking, hard-fighting master of Starveacre, makes Ned seem a bit flat and stale. Tressillian is a gentle man, quiet, unmoved by passion, and ungiven to extravagant dreams. Unfortunately, like so many of Mr. Whitham's heroes, he doubts his own values. Raikes is not so afflicted : he makes his way by dint of cyclonic energy and very competent fists. Being handsome and reckless he attracts many women and repels nearly all sober men.

That Raikes will take Brenda from her husband is obvious from the first meeting of the couple. It is equally obvious that she will reap misery, and regret the step. But Mr. Whitham has an art of transforming the obvious and trite into the tremendous. It is his skill in setting forth the inner struggles, the loyalties and disloyalties, the fears and hopes and doubts of the parties to this triangle that commands our respect and holds our interest. We are given to see the pride that drives its victims to the unwanted, and the pride that bids them hold their peace. We see those who are destroyed by their inhibitions, and those who fall for the lack of them. The hell of Raikes and the hell of Tressillian seem leagues apart, but both are places of torment. And what with Raikes snatching what he wants and Tressillian standing aloof in sad silence, Brenda suffers in yet a third hell more horrible than either.

Meantime, while this human drama is being played, one senses the play of ghosts. The moor is hungry for a victim, and is only waiting to destroy what the impetuous farmer strives to take. Mother Meldon is waiting to avenge her children. And when the curtain falls one feels that for all the terrible tragedy, justice has been fully satisfied: the Pities cry aloud, but Nature smiles her old, familiar, and somewhat cynical smile.

Mr. Whitham, it will be seen, is a serious writer. His pages are not enlivened by irrelevant bits of peasant humor, nor lightened by epigram. His admirers will not readily find the clever sentence by which to bait the indifferent. A Whitham book must be judged as an artistic whole : its merits will be found to consist in completeness, balance, coördination and a steady movement to a conclusion that will seem, by reason of both internal and external forces, inevitable. True, the men and women who live in these thought-provoking pages are not the robust creatures that one commonly associates with the rugged moorlands. Mr. Whitham has quite deliberately, and wisely, circumscribed his field. What he has, thereby, lost in scope, his art has gained in beauty and intensity.

VI

THE POWYS BROTHERS

THREE brothers of Dorsetshire — all country-bred, all country-wise ; all introspective, and all novelists.

One thinks of the Brontë sisters. Literary families are not unknown to history ; we call to mind the Benson brothers. The writing urge often persists from generation to generation, as with the Huxleys. But it is no common thing for a single family, in one generation, to breed three such distinguished writers as John Cowper, Theodore Francis, and Llewelyn Powys.

The family likeness persists in their books as in their faces. They share an almost caressing tenderness for wild flowers and for the harmless beasts that hide along hedge-rows : in common they seem to hate all men of sound digestion and those who live in large houses : all three are preoccupied with a half-Christian, half-pagan mysticism. All the Powys novels are touched by the magic of ecstasy.

They differ. Llewelyn has more humor than his brothers, and is a truer child of earth,— unashamed before Pan or Priapus. There are times when he writes in the golden manner of the late Elizabethans.

Theodore, with his terse sentences, clipped paragraphs and simple Anglo-Saxon words, reminds one of Bunyan. No one knows so well the malignant cruelty of those thwarted, inhibited little people, caught fast in the everlasting monotony of a village existence. He has laid bare their secret lusts, and all their pathetic, wistful hopes. He is a strange, hermit-like philosopher who, free of the conventional gestures of piety, has used his English Bible to a noble purpose. Breedy solitudes have begotten in him a manner that sets him quite apart from his fellows.

JOHN COWPER POWYS has been touched by many cultures, and chameleon-like, he has taken hue from all. But while lacking, perhaps, the curious originality of Theodore, and the quaint humor of his younger brother, he writes with more power and spontaneity than either. He has none of Theodore's restraint : his vocabulary is enormous, and his flow of adjectives, when he is moved, torrential.

Wood and Stone — the first novel by John Cowper Powys — is a remarkably fine book : a roomy, com-

fortable volume, in which one gets a sense of spacious-
ness and the leisure in which to form an intimate and
lingering acquaintance with the people who are brought
to life in its pages. Let it be said at once, however,
that these people are not comfortable, normal human
beings. Mr. Powys has called this book a romance
(and it is), but it lacks what is usually termed the romantic outlook. It is what may be called a psychological novel, concerned with the struggle between
"the well-constituted" and the "ill-constituted" : the
problem of the will to power against the will to love ;
and the author, in his preface —'tis a bold novelist who
in this century dares a preface — wonders whether the
vanquished of this world are not really the victors,
seeing that the secret of this our universe is not self-
assertion, but self-abandonment. For the answer he
trusts to art rather than science.

In *Wood and Stone* we have Mortimer Romer and
his daughter Gladys, both relentless, hard and determined to have what they want : we have Lacrima
Traffio and Maurice Quincunx, timid, shrinking souls
who bend with the wind and yet are destined to exert
a force of their own ; James Anderson and his brother
Luke, stone-cutters and dabblers in the philosophy of
Nietzsche ; Mr. Taxeter, a Catholic whose philosophic
tolerance enables him to steer a middle path in a world
of extremes ; Mr. Wone, who mouths Christian
socialism with pious unction, and John Goring, a stupid
brute to whom Romer intends giving Lacrima perforce. These, with an American artist, Ralph
Dangelis — a sort of *deus ex machina* — are the principal persons of this undramatic struggle.

But there is no final answer to the question, no solution to the conflict. For each individual there is a

different answer, proving nothing. Lacrima escapes John Goring and the leonine Mr. Romer, and, aided by Dangelis — who has slipped from the feline claws of Gladys Romer — goes away with the book-loving esthete, Maurice Quincunx. James Anderson, unable to win Lacrima's love, dies: Luke, with an amused gesture, marries. Wood may ultimately split the stone, but some must inevitably be crushed in the downfall that follows.

Mr. Powys is content to record what he sees, and while his own curious predilections lead him to study more intently the maimed and suffering, he does not take sides. Perhaps, indeed, the will-less and meek may inherit the earth: perhaps not. But at all events they may be as intensely interesting in their inarticulate sufferings and fears as are the fat-paunched protagonists of success.

Rodmoor, which followed closely on the heels of the first novel, I pass by. It has no place among these country chronicles. Moreover it seems to me a thin, shrill book, a slight thing in which neurotic symptomatology is quite overdone.

Ducdame is a sounder book. The problem of the Ashovers is the old one of perpetuation. The family must go on. Mother Ashover is frantically anxious for a grandson. Her two sons, Rook and Lexie, seem indifferent, though both are ready enough to mate for an hour with any wench of the countryside. Lexie, the younger, is ill and unfitted for marriage. Rook has a mistress, Netta Page, whom he loves after a fashion and would marry in the event of her pregnancy. Mother Ashover despises Netta and prays that Rook may get rid of her and marry his cousin, Lady Ann. Rook and Ann have always loved one another, and it requires but little effort on the part of Mrs. Ashover to enlist her aid in solving the family difficulty. Snubs from the mother, and Machiavellian advice from Ann soon reduce this noble girl to a state of utter misery, and, as part of a set program of deliberate renunciation, Netta is persuaded to act the drunken slut, and shame Rook before his friends.   But when all seems to have worked together for success, and the head of the Ashovers has been securely married to his cousin (Netta hiding herself betimes in a London apartment), Rook wakes to the realization that he cannot live without his mistress, and flies off in frantic search of her.   But here he is helpless.   The only person to whom Netta has confided the secret of her hiding-place is the mad parish priest, William Hastings, who symbolizes the will-to-extinction, and who has spent the better part of his life in writing a book on the vanity of life.   This priest hates the persistent life-hunger of the Ashovers, and takes a malicious satisfaction in preventing Rook from joining his mistress until after she had found a kind of peace in a religious sisterhood.   It is this same priest who, at the last, in a fit of madness, sends Rook to his death at the very moment when his son, heir to the Ashover domain, is being introduced into this unhappy world.

Thus Ashover triumphs alike in its new-born infant and its new-made grave.   For Lady Ann the victory turns to dust and ashes : it remains for Netta to moisten the grave of her lover with her tears, and to whisper words of pity to his clay.

Fittingly enough *Ducdame* is dedicated to the great Kwang-Tse, who, as Mr. Powys says, combined reverence for his forebears with a philosophy of acquiescence.   He was "at once respectful to his spirit-like ancestors and indulgent to those who, like the protagonist of this book, go where they are pushed, follow where they are led, like a whirling wind, like a feather tossed about, like a revolving grindstone."

That was the philosophy of Rook Ashover : perhaps it is the secret of all those wind-driven souls concerning whom John Cowper Powys writes.

Ducdame is beautifully written, saturate with an intimate knowledge of Nature and her creatures. Comfortable, these forest and meadow meditations of the Dorset-bred writer : but he superimposes upon them an astrologic-metaphysical symbology that sends chills of terror up one's spine. Perhaps I exaggerate, but just now I am firmly convinced that in the Reverend William Hastings Mr. Powys has created one of the most suggestive and sinister figures in modern fiction.

Wolf Solent is the natural, the legitimate successor of *Wood and Stone*. All the literary children of the Powys family bear evidences of a sort of consanguinity, and J. C. P. has an unmistakable touch. One finds the same point of outlook, the same "mythologizing," the same personifications, the familiar mystic animism, the meticulous attention to the more fleeting moods of the spirit and to those particular aspects of Nature that made *Ducdame* at once a handbook of pantheism and a guide to the botany of Dorset.

Wolf Solent's father had been a teacher of history at Ramsgard years before this story opens, and his amours and ultimate disgrace had driven his not-too-virtuous widow and her son to London, where, after University, Wolf, also, became a teacher of history and literature, until, driven to a "malice-dance" against the fatality of a machine age, he, too, lost his position.

The story proper begins with Wolf's boarding a train at Waterloo Station bound for Ramsgard, where he is to collaborate with Squire John Urquart in writing a somewhat scandalous history of Dorset. At the very moment when he is most elated by his new opportunity he chances to see the haggard, miserable face of one of those whitened London starvelings, looking its rebuke to every form of affluence and success. This "face at Waterloo" becomes the symbol of outraged suffering, and recurs again and again throughout Solent's life.

Once in Ramsgard (Yeovil), the living son and his dead father meet. In company with Selena Gault, once mistress to the elder Solent, he visits the grave of that voluptuary, whose last words,— "Christ! I've enjoyed my life!" — revealed a robust vigor wholly incomprehensible to his bewildered son.

Wolf Solent is a novel of inner strife, a chronicle of the unending malice and trickery of women ; of the irresponsible and lecherous philandering of sex-driven men. The woman-sweet, malignant bitterness of Wolf's mother : Selena Gault's hoarded jealousy that survives the grave : John Urquart's curious lust after entombed salacity : the haunting spectre of Mr. Redfern, Wolf's immediate predecessor, concerning whose death so many consciences are troubled : Mr. Malakite, the incestuous bibliopole : T. E. Valley, the drunken rector : Jason Ottor, the fear-ridden poet, and his brother Darnley, who tastes waters from some *well of loneliness :* Smith, the hatter, whose daughter Mattie proved to be an illegitimate half-sister to Wolf : Christie Malakite, the wraith-like, unattainable, spiritual mate to Wolf's highest moods, and Gerda Thorpe, stone-cutter's daughter, a wild,

pagan whistling-blackbird who becomes at once Solent's wife and mistress to the parish — these weird
creatures march before a sombre background of muttering hills over which there hangs a brooding sky.
Poor victims of inner compulsion, they sacrifice and
are sacrificed ; now on the rude stones of pagan Celts,
and now before the high altar of the Lord Christ.

Nature, hereditary forces, passions dominate :
thought rises in thin, vaporous spirals, like some filmy
incense, only to be blown away by the winds of primi-
tive mood.

But, for all the lowering clouds, it is Nature that
provides the beauty of this wayward novel. Out on
the downs, the poet masters the psychoanalyst : within
four walls Krafft-Ebing runs amuck. Indoors men
brood and stew in their own acids ; along their narrow
village streets they sneak and spy upon one another,
anxious to uncover some unutterable depravity of
brutal lust : venom-tongued women, unwashed by the
sky, seek to probe the ulcers of the soul.

Throughout all this riot of madness, Solent discovers not one universe, but many, "one inside the
other, like Chinese boxes." He finds nothing stable.
Christie Malakite leaves him ; his mother's love is for
others ; his friend Darnley marries ; his wife is un-
faithful with the greengrocer. He turns to his
father's grave and cries aloud to the mocking skull beneath the soil :

"There is no reality but what the mind fashions out of
itself. There is nothing but a mirror opposite a mirror,
and a round crystal opposite a round crystal, and a sky in
water opposite water in a sky."

"Ho ! Ho ! You worm of my folly," laughed the
hollow skull, "I am alive still, though I am dead ; and

you are dead, though you're alive. For life is beyond your mirrors and your waters. It's at the bottom of your pond ; it's in the body of your sun ; it's in the dust of your star-spaces ; it's in the eyes of weasels and the noses of rats and the pricks of nettles and the tongues of vipers and the spawn of frogs and the slime of snails. Life's in me still, you worm of my folly, and girl's flesh is sweet forever and ever."

But his son answers : "You lie to yourself ! You lie with the old, hot, shuffling, fever-smitten lie. It's the foam-bubbles of your life-mania that you think is so real. They're no more real than the dreams of the plantains that grow over your grave !"

At the last, stripped of all the outward show of things, the poet learns that ripeness is all ; that he must endure and even welcome loneliness, must learn to enjoy and forget ; learn to endure, or escape this crazy-patch of life.

Wolf Solent is not one of the great novels of the world, but it is alive with interest and a worthy twentieth-century companion to *Wuthering Heights ;* full of beautiful writing, interrupted often by passages of painfully profound psychological analysis ; dominated, now and again, by a rapturous mysticism.

For comparisons one must look, not to Hardy, but to Emily Brontë, to John Trevena, and, oddly enough, to Henry James. The subjective method employed by Mr. Powys was not sired by James Joyce, but by the sly, American-Englishman who was the analyst of the drawing-room. If one could imagine a soul compact half Brontë, half Dostoievski, made to exercise its terrible moods over the subtle hand of a modern Henry James, now exiled from polite parlors and rudely thrust into a Dorset cottage somewhere near

Cerne Abbas, one might very nearly conceive of the forces that made this pathetically beautiful book. But in the last analysis one is compelled to confess that there could be in all the world but one "onlie begetter" of *Wolf Solent*, the unmistakable and utterly characteristic creation of John Cowper Powys : only his mind could have imagined such things.

LLEWELYN POWYS has written but one novel — *Apples Be Ripe* — a delectably sad story of a carefree lover and his loves. Chris Holbech is a modern Casanova grown introspective and a bit more tender. Far from acting as a deterrent to Holbech's love affairs, however, this fond self-examination but adds to his pleasures and to the sum of his charms.

Holbech engages one's sympathy from the outset. None of your dirty, conventional philanderers or whoremongers, he is a healthy chap with a genius for winning love from the loving. His marriage to Adela Manners is doomed from the beginning. Adela is prismatic, practical and cold : to her mind even married love is a bit nasty and sinful. Holbech's career is likewise doomed. He is too human, too free-and-easy to fit well the little mould required for an English country school master. Career and marriage together come to disaster on a night when the headmaster — Adela's uncle — discovers the quixotic young teacher beneath the untidy bed of a housemaid, who, on that very day, had received a sharp dismissal by reason of an unpremeditated, unhallowed, but unmistakable pregnancy. The irony of the situation lay in the fact that Chris had gone to the girl's room, not for a deed of kind, but for a deed of kindness, being unable to endure the thought of her helpless

tears over a brutally cold sentence. The head-master
could add two-and-two as well as any, but in this case,
unable to see the correct figures, his results and conclusions were unfortunate. Explanation was impossible : the master was enraged, so Holbech and the
miserable girl left the house together.

This chronicle of Chris Holbech's life as wandering farm-hand and lover ; his idyllic mating with
Nelly Giles, and his mad flight with Flora Hustings,
makes excellent reading ; slight, perhaps, but delicate,
whimsical and withal convincing. Good, honest
prose is here, and fine feeling. Drawing-room passion and the heavy-scented lusts of curtained boudoirs
make no appeal to this vigorous writer. Out in the
hawthorn hedges and on the haycocks where the air
is sweet and the night breezes blow, and the imper-
turbable stars look down in cool indifference, the mating of boys and girls takes its natural place. Love was
discovered out-of-doors : dirty thoughts festered into
being within the unaired chambers of the dyspeptic.
Apples Be Ripe is earthy and clean.

THEODORE FRANCIS POWYS sets forth his distinctions
between good and evil with a sharpness that is distinctly unmodern, being much more akin to that
ancient with whose work his own has often been
compared, John Bunyan. His good people are *fools
in Christ* — gentle, dreaming mystics, impractical and
ever imposed upon by the evil sort who are wholly
occupied by greed, lust for power, cruelty and hate.
Theodore Powys does not interest himself in, nor
make interesting, those of the middle sort : they are
inconsequent, and rather to be despised. This point
of outlook is familiar enough to readers of *Pilgrim's*

Progress, where one is either on the narrow, upward path that leads to Mount Zion, or the broad, descending road to eternal ruin. Christian and Hopeful are worthy : Apollyon and the Giant of Despair are formidable ; but By-ends and Slothful are nobodies.

Mr. Powys' terminology is slightly more modern, and his devils have this of modernity that they are not infrequently parsons or deacons, whose pious phrases ever belie their evil hearts, but the distinctions are quite as sharp as in Bunyan. Mr. Tasker, Farmer Mew, and James Andrews are excellent examples of his fiends : they rob widows and orphans, rape the village maids, beat the weak and helpless, are cruel to animals, clutch for wealth, and destroy beauty everywhere. They possess no amiable inconsistencies, and are damned without qualification. Manners have changed with the times, and the evil ones that were wont, in Bunyan, to loiter about the aisles of an established church are here as free in the chapels. Mr. Tasker is so sanctimonious that his father's tippling offends his sense of decency, but he thinks it fit that his pigs fatten on the old man's flesh, and that his bones should rot beneath their ordure. Mr. Tasker, churchman and worshipper of pigs, is a very unbeautiful devil.

On the other hand the saints, while unqualifiedly good, are not without humor, nor does their holiness interfere with a wholesome enjoyment of harmless pleasure. The Reverend Silas Dottery, perhaps the most charming of Mr. Powys' characters, has a nose for wine and is not unmindful, in a perfectly proper way, of girlish grace : even Mr. Weston is not without sympathy for calls of the flesh. To his saints, then, Mr. Powys has added an increment of benevolent naughtiness that, without detracting from their sanctity, contributes in no small measure to their convincingness. Perhaps it is unfair, in an age to which Bunyan is utterly alien, to associate these amazingly original stories with even the name of *Pilgrim's Progress*. For Bunyan is probably a synonym for boredom to young moderns, while T. F. Powys, by reason of his surprising mental agility, his uncanny insight and his spiritual heterodoxies is the very antithesis of dullness. (Nor would it remedy matters, I fear, for me to reassert the truth that *Pilgrim's Progress* is one of the world's most entertaining books!) And yet Bunyan must be mentioned in this connection. One cannot read *Mockery Gap*, *The White Paternoster*, or *Mr. Weston's Good Wine* without being constantly reminded of the mighty pen of the old Puritan. But if Bunyan comes first in the point of influence upon Mr. Powys' style, the English Bible is a close second,—and, if one will but take some notice, it is not difficult to discover little patches of prose inspired by that other odd old man of the 17th century, Robert Burton, a text from whom stands at the head of that story of "Abraham Men" in *The Left Leg*.

But one must be careful. T. F. Powys is an original. He dwells within himself and creates his own unique world. He recalls, here and there, the manner of the English Bible, Democritus Junior, Thomas Fuller, or Jeremy Taylor ; he is steeped in the spirit of the traveling tinker : but through it all he is himself and has achieved his own style, quite unlike anything that is being written by his contemporaries. His people do not dwell in Dorsetshire as do most of Thomas Hardy's men and maidens, even unto this day.

They are country folk, village folk, speaking the local dialect, and in a certain sense they are true to Dorset life : they are living, breathing people : but their real locale is in the curiously convoluted brain of Theodore Powys.

One meets with strange sentences and fantastic folk in these stories of his. Mr. Pring, in "Abraham Men," is said to have "looked like a person who expects to hear a voice walking in the darkness." Elsewhere in *The Left Leg* we read that "Every little bird in Madder thought that there was no place like its own nest ; so did the hills ; so did Mrs. Patch, for her name was Ann."

But it is not enough to say of this recluse that he is original and curious. He is a man who writes with sincerity and passion. He is saturate with both loves and hates. He hates cruelty and greed ; he loves the meek and humble. He likes to read "the humble writings writ in the mud by the terrible one who stoops to write in the crust of the earth."

It is easy to see that T. F. Powys will never appeal to a large company of readers. *Mr. Tasker's Gods* is really rather brutal, a cruel book, and for all its excellence, repellent to most. *Mark Only* is nearly as full of unpleasant suggestion. *Mr. Weston's Good Wine* is a great book, filled with pity and terror, an allegory of life with God for leading character ; a holy book, but for all its beauty and tenderness many people will be repelled by the ways of Folly Down, true though they are. There is something blunt and forthright and savage about this mystic that will ever make the tender wince. For while men like well enough Mr. Weston's light wines, they shudder before the darker drink. The pleasant ironies of Mr. Gunter's life will escape the notice of those who are stricken by the vileness of Mrs. Vosper and the callous cruelties of farmer Mumby's sons.

But bother these delicate people ! *Mr. Weston's Good Wine* is for those who know somewhat of love and who realize that without death there could be no love at all. It is not a book of joy, but of wisdom.

Kindness in a Corner may prove more palatable, for it *is* a book of both joy and wisdom. Here the Reverend Silas Dottery, who has played a modest role in Mr. Powys' earlier stories, is, so to say, hero. And surely there never was a more lovable clergyman in all fiction. Utterly irresponsible, neglecting Christian homiletics for pagan classics, forgetting holy festivals, pampering his palate, he is the very symbol of benign grace and abounding love. He is beyond good and evil, and guile is a stranger to him and his ways. To the suspicions of Canon Dibben and his wife as to the amorous caprices of Lottie Truggin he is utterly immune. Against the designs of the Evil One he wears an impenetrable armor of innocence, and from every trap and pitfall he is saved by a miracle. But the sinister spirits that walk in the nighttime are happily here absent. For the moment Mr. Powys has mellowed a bit, and without forgetting the austere sanctities, has permitted his reader to smile for a time at the human comedy and to remember that sometimes "he that sitteth in the heaven shall laugh."

III

PICK AND CHOOSE

"The happiest [book] hunter is he who stalks and tracks down what he likes best and what he can read and enjoy."
— *Holbrook Jackson*

III

PICK AND CHOOSE

I PREFER great books to great sets. Sets, "The Collected Works of . . . ," more often than not are a nuisance. They occupy space that might be better filled, and they suggest anything but reading. One's favorite novelist must ever be excepted, though even there the question is worth pondering. For example I want my complete sets of Hardy and Anatole France. The collector in me would like them all in first editions, but, purse forbidding, I satisfy myself with outstanding favorites — *L'île des Pingouins*, and the three green volumes of *The Woodlanders*, and a few odds and ends enriched by some pen stroke of association : the reader in me makes compromise, and I complete my authors with an early collected edition. Here I confess that cost has been the collector's undoing : whim would lead me to order every book of these writers in prime first state.

For most writers, fortunately, one does not have an all-embracing affection. In the case of Charles Dickens, as much as I have loved his novels from boyhood upward, I'd be content with a well-bound copy of the first *Pickwick*, with "Veller" title and all the plates in what is supposed to be their first state. For, to me, *Pickwick* is not merely the rarest of the great Victorian's works : it is the one book of his that bears the unmistakable stamp of genius, one that is an inexhaustible source of delight. And I want it bound up from parts for the reason that those fragile, pale-green originals seem to me but magazinelets, and I should hate to touch them. If books are not to be handled and read, let them by all means be placed in a museum. Even the greatest author seldom creates more than one great book. Give me *The Egoist*, and you may do as you will with Meredith.

Why, then, should not the collector of modest means confine himself to the world's greatest books, or, what amounts to the same thing, the books he thinks are great? Why should I accumulate a twenty-foot shelf of Mark Twain's hideous firsts, when *The Jumping Frog*, *Huckleberry Finn*, *Tom Sawyer*, and *The Mysterious Stranger* are all I care to read or preserve? The average lover of books, who cares not a fig for firsts, is sensible enough in this particular. He reads first at the public library, and then buys only what he loves. Why may not the impecunious collector follow his wise example?

The case of Claude Tillier comes to mind. Tillier (1801-44), the French soldier, schoolmaster, political pamphleteer, poet and novelist. He was unknown in this country until, in 1890, the late Benjamin R. Tucker translated and published his *Mon Oncle Benjamin*, which had first appeared in 1843. Since 1890 many Americans, following the lead of the Germans, who were first to hail the author as the greatest of French writers, have been ardent admirers of this unique writer. But the fact remains that Tillier's pamphlets and poems make dull reading for this age, and his one other translated novel — *Belle-Plante and Cornelius* — is but sentimental tosh. The man is not worth collecting.

PICK AND CHOOSE

But *My Uncle Benjamin* is a book to treasure
against a day of lost illusions : walls paneled in ancient
oak, made fragrant with honest pipe tobacco for an
hundred years ; a tankard of rich brown ale ; a cob-
webby bottle of château Margaux, and the best of
hearty companions.

Uncle Benjamin — Dr. Benjamin Rathery — had
never a shred of greed, thrift, or ambition : he wished
but to drink, eat and be kind. He gave but little
medicine to his patients, his chief purpose in visiting
the sick being to inspire them with laughter and hope.
He seldom collected and rarely paid. The devices
by which this genial doctor tries to satisfy his creditors ;
the tales of his drinking bouts, his conversations with
his family who are eager to have him tied in marriage to a practical woman ; his mild heresies, catholic
philosophy, and, above all, his exploit in compelling the
Marquis de Cambyse to satisfy a curious debt of honor,
make Benjamin forever welcome at any fireside
around which are gathered such gallant gentlemen as
Pickwick, John Falstaff, and Shandy's Uncle Toby.

Therefore it is that while I shall gladly pass by the
polemic tracts by Claude Tillier, journalist and politician, I reserve an especial niche wherein are to be
found such things as the first American edition of
My Uncle Benjamin, in paper jacket, as issued by
Tucker in Boston, 1890 ; the second edition, pale
blue cloth, published by Merriam in New York, 1892 ;
the third, illustrated by Emil Preetorius and published
by Boni and Liveright in 1917 ; and a yet vacant waiting space for the 1843 edition printed at Nevers.

And I shall do likewise with Somerset Maugham.
Liza of Lambeth has power, pathos, humor, and its
last chapter is pretty nearly enough to persuade one

121

that it is a masterpiece, but not quite. The early chapters of *The Moon and Sixpence* are convincing, and inspire sympathy for Strickland and vast respect for Maugham : both have given way to irritation before the book is half done. Maugham's plays are extraordinarily clever, but uninspired. Among his short stories, *Miss Thompson* stands out in monumental relief. It is sincere, true, and full of both irony and pity. But the one book of Maugham's that I insist upon having in first state — and let me announce here my conviction as a collector that the advertisements after the text do not signify anything — is *Of Human Bondage,* which shares, with Butler's *Way of All Flesh,* the honor of being the finest of all autobiographic novels. Philip Carey lives, and in some ways is more vital than Ernest Pontifex. Nor is he alone in his livingness : old William Carey and his wife, fumbling pathetically in their efforts at parenthood ; Fanny Price, starving for art and love in Paris ; Cronshaw (Ernest Dowson), with his epigrams and absinthe ; Mildred, the waitress and strumpet, smashing Philip's dearest treasures ; Athelnys, pompous, dramatic ass that he is, with a genius for friendship and a rare understanding — they are all as alive as Picadilly Circus of a Saturday night. Brutality and pity jostle one another as they do on the streets. I do not care for another first of Maugham's, but *Of Human Bondage* grows on me with the passing years and I am quite assured that it is one of the most important books of this century.

Another writer who shall be represented by but one book is J. D. Beresford. He has done more than a score of books that I find unaccountably dull and mediocre. But into the making of his trilogy, *Jacob*

Stahl, went most of the elements of a masterpiece : a sympathetic imagination, sound psychology, solid construction, excellent characterization, shrewd observation and quiet humor.   This story bears a superficial resemblance to Mr. Maugham's *Of Human Bondage.* It is the life history of a young cripple who, after years of floundering, hampered by inferiority complexes, fear, weak will, self-pity and physical affliction, got acquainted with himself, overcame his difficulties, and found both love and a career.   Like Philip Carey, Jacob is orphaned, and brought up by an aunt — and a very notable lady she is.   But the resemblances are only in the outer crusts.   There is no touch of gall in Beresford ; there is more romance.   Writing of Carey's intellectual adventures Maugham is a master. One doubts him when he tries to write of love : Philip's masochistic weakness seems a trifle overdone. Beresford, lacking Maugham's wit and brilliance, has done a better job with Jacob's heart history.   Stahl's infatuation for Madeline, his absurd marriage with Lola Wilmot and his romantic escapade with Betty are made to seem natural, inevitable, foreordained. But while the two novels invite comparison, they likewise defy it.   It is enough to say that together they make a satisfying picture of an interesting phase of English intellectual and spiritual life : first editions of these rest side by side in my small library.

Since the three volumes were published under different titles, perhaps I should note here that the first volume appeared in 1911 — *The Early History of Jacob Stahl ;* the second — *The Candidate for Truth,* in 1912 ; the last — *The Invisible Event* — in 1915.

Ernest Bramah shall be represented by several vol-

umes, but only the ones in which the incomparable
Kai Lung, or the bewildered Kong Ho are his mouth-
pieces. His detective stories are silly and deserve the
oblivion to which they are surely doomed. Even
that scarce, early work of his on farming—*English
Farming and Why I Turned It Up*—tempts me but
little. Why should the joy which leads a man to collect *The Wallet of Kai Lung, The Mirror of Kong
Ho, Kai Lung's Golden Hours, Kai Lung Unrolls
His Mat,* and *The Moon of Much Gladness* be lessened by the sight of such clumsy yarns as *The Eyes
of Max Carados,* or an amateurish tale of drudgery?
I shall save both space and money : moreover, the
books I reject do not belong to that enchanted land
wherein Kai Lung relates his delicately ironic fables.
Indeed, these tales are in a class apart, and may be
compared to nothing whatever in our English-speaking
world. They are original in both matter and manner : they are perfect in that the manner of the telling is perfectly adjusted to the thing told.

Writing of *The Wallet of Kai Lung,* Mr. Belloc
once said that it was "a thing made deliberately, in
hard material and completely successful. It was
meant to produce a particular effect of humour by the
use of a foreign convention, the Chinese convention,
in the English tongue. It was meant to produce a
certain effect of philosophy and at the same time it
was meant to produce a certain completed interest of
fiction, of relation, of a short epic. It did all of these
things."

Concerning Ernest Bramah the man, there seems to
be no end of mystery. He is listed in no Who's Who,
and his name does not appear in English directories.
Catalogue informs us that his real name is Ernest

Bramah Smith ! It is incredible ! I believe that he dwells in the Temple of Mid-air, and that his name is Tong-King.

One's admiration for *The Wooings of Jezebel Pettyfer* may easily tempt one to the purchase of a first edition — the one with yellow covers, decorated by the author, and showing Jezebel seated upon the altar of sorcery — even a copy bearing the autograph of Haldane Macfall. In 1898, when Grant Richards first brought it to the attention of the British public, it was commonly held to be a plea for better morals in Barbadoes. People believe what they wish. It is sufficient to say that in our century this seems to be a highly amusing account of a people who are happily without morals of any kind whatever. Specifically it relates the adventures of one Jehu Sennacherib Dyle and Jezebel Pettyfer, both of whom knew tricks that might have astonished Casanova : a background of witchcraft lends color, and the unconscious knavery of the protagonists gives the tale that rich flavor seldom found in fiction since the 18th century.

My friend, Vincent Starrett, who introduced me to this picaresque narrative of West Indian life, has already said enough to convince a considerable number of collectors of its value : too much, in fact, for as a result of his enthusiasm the price of this one first edition would buy a shelf of ordinary moderns. I am deeply grateful to Starrett for many boisterous-happy hours spent in the company of Dyle and Pettyfer, Jamaica Huckleback and Boaz Bryan ; and I never look up at my own copy — once in the possession of Edwin Pugh — without a feeling of fat satisfaction. But apart from this one book, Haldane Macfall means but little to me. Jezebel led me to want *The Masterfolk*, *The Splendid Wayfaring*, and *The Three Students*, but, alas, I am not equal to them : they bring no spark of light to me nor I to them. I am content with this one first edition.

Richard Garnett's *The Twilight of the Gods* must stand alone also. Few books are worthy of a place by its side, and I have not even considered reading another book from the workshop of that quaint, humorous old scholar ; I lack the courage to face disillusion. I have said that the book stands alone. That is not quite true, for by the side of that pale blue octave of 1888 is the more sumptuous first illustrated edition of 1924 : and slipped within the first edition is a pleasant letter in which Dr. Garnett, making mention of Thomas Hardy and Austin Dobson, refers at some length to the second edition of his book. One must have both editions, for, in addition to its excellent illustrations, the later volume contains twelve new chapters, and no lover of beautiful prose or harmless-wicked philosophy should miss "A Page from the Book of Folly," or "New Readings in Biography."

Robert Blatchford is a writer, most of whose books I should never wish to collect. For they are tracts for the times, pamphlets of the propagandist,— his *Merrie England*, *Britain for the British*, and *Not Guilty*. But this fiery pamphleteer presents another face whenas he enters the door of his study. Like that other great labor leader, John Burns, he has builded for himself a retreat wherein, surrounded by tale-tellers, poets and philosophers, he gives himself to noble dreams and speaks with the tongue of men and angels.

And this labor leader, inspired by John Bunyan, Sir Thomas Browne and Gilbert White, has written two little books that should be known and will be loved by every book collector and reader in the world : *Among My Books*, and *My Favourite Books*. For he writes about books as a lover writes of his mistress, as a poet writes of his lady's eyes. He has earned his leisure and his books hardly, and he treasures them the more for the pains he has taken to obtain them. He luxuriates in books, rests in them, revels in them. Hear him, then, as he tells of the pleasure of reading abed, and judge whether his books are not worthy a place by Andrew Lang or Edward Newton. I choose a paragraph or two from *My Favourite Books* :

"If the reading of good books is ever sinful, it is at meal-time. He who reads at meal-times treats his meal and his digestion with discourtesy, and puts upon his author the affront of a divided allegiance. But to read in bed ! That is a good man's virtue, the innocent indulgence of the well-deserving. Therefore gossip about bed books will ever be acceptable to the just. And the wise man will show a nice discrimination in the choice of his literary nightcap. It is a case of means and ends. A man might write about bed books until he sent his readers to sleep, yet would get no "forrader" unless he followed some logical plan.

"Do you want to go to sleep or to keep awake ? That is the question. Are you a reader, or only one who reads ? Do you love books, or would you e'en be snoring ?

"A gentleman, look you, would fain go to sleep like a gentleman. That is leisurely, kindly, with a grateful smile to Goodman Day, his host that is, and a graceful greeting to Mistress Night, his hostess that is to be. None but a boor would turn his back upon the sun in churlish haste, and jump into the arms of Morpheus neck and crop, like a seal rolling off an ice-floe. Therefore, a gentleman reads before he goes to sleep."

That bit, I think, deserved a place in Part XII, section X, in the first volume of Mr. Holbrook Jackson's *The Anatomy of Bibliomania,* wherein he assembled the testimonies of so many luxurious night-readers.

Now that I have named it I see that I have but one first edition of Holbrook Jackson. Other books of his are here, but only as they were issued by the American publishers : *The Eighteen Nineties, Bernard Shaw, Great English Novelists.* For these books I entertain respect and liking : they have informed and amused. But *The Anatomy of Bibliomania* I love. I read it far into the night. I read it forwards, then backwards : I pick it up and open where I will, or when the leaves fall apart, and I fairly purr with content.

For Mr. Jackson, in this most catholic and inclusive work, has collected more interesting facts and fancies, gossip and anecdote concerning books and their lovers than have ever before been brought together. He covers the entire field of bibliomania : why men love books ; why they collect first editions ; why they yearn after bizarre bindings, and why they take pleasure in founding libraries. He discourses of book-worms and book thieves : the bookman's anxious problems, and his wife's angry jealousies : the cause of his mania, and its certain remedy. And by taking the Burtonian method, the quaint manner of an earlier and quieter age, he has succeeded in making not only the most encyclopedic, but also the most fascinating book about books that has ever been printed. I shall make no other apology for owning the limited, signed, first edition of so noble a masterpiece.

My eye passes from Jackson's elegant tomes to a rather shabby blue volume written by James Thomson —"B. V."—*Biographical and Critical Studies,* containing excellent critical essays on Rabelais, Ben Jonson, Heine, Browning and Shelley. It was posthumously published in 1896, and I believe it is a first edition : I do not greatly care, though it is a book I like to own and read, along with his *Satires and Profanities,* and his edition of Leopardi. But the only first of his that *demands* a place by reason of its original beauty and power is *The City of Dreadful Night,* published in 1880, six years after its serial appearance in Bradlaugh's *National Reformer.* This book is the young man's bible, wherein the cries wrung from his own tormented soul are perfectly echoed and set to the bitter-sweet music of despair. But the pessimism of this great poem was not born of a momentary mood : it is not a young man's hasty gesture of renunciation, nor the snarl of the jaded cynic. It is the product of studied maturity ; the fruitage of a life of pain. And it is beautiful poetry : a perfect realization of man's profoundest tragedies and pathetic fears. And though I am no longer young enough to feel its poignancy to the full, its sombre lines still have their power to please, and make me yield to a kind of infernal rapture.

Charles Reade is surely a one-book man, and few, I think, would now take pleasure in owning first editions of *Peg Woffington, Hard Cash,* or *Foul Play* —the very names suggest housemaids' delight. But *The Cloister and the Hearth* is one of England's great historical novels, and, unlike some great novels, it bears reading again and yet again. It is excellent history and rare entertainment; and it provides the best sort of introduction to the life of one of the world's most permanently interesting men, Desiderius Erasmus of Rotterdam.

The Cloister and the Hearth, in its first state, is a book I never expected to own — its price had put it far above my modest hopes. But accidents will happen, even in the best of bookshops, and so it fell out that one day I saw the four volumes bound in contemporary half-morocco and marked "Second issue." The date is 1861, and the chief "point" to remember is on page 372 of the second volume, where, owing to a printer's blunder, occurs this curious sentence : "Catherine threw her face over her apron and sobbed." Now in this pleasant shop a blank book is kept, wherein are neatly recorded, from time to time, just such memorable points ; but the unfortunate clerk who had copied this sentence had been a trifle careless, entering it as — "*She* threw her face over her apron and sobbed." And when this set came to the shop another clerk turned eager fingers to the book of points, and, misled by the "She" — as many another man has been — promptly marked the book "Second issue," and priced it accordingly.

If I strutted forth with my bundle of books in an orgulous fashion — and I more than suspect that I did — it is pleasing to remember that the shop had not lost — for the books had been acquired in lot — and that the owner is one of those delightful men who actually rejoice in a customer's good fortune.

It is better that Charles Montagu Doughty be represented by his one masterpiece, that most remarkable of all travel-books — *Arabia Deserta*. His *Adam*

Cast Forth and *Mansoul* convinced me that his prose-poetry has the sweep and power and majesty denied his verse. I keep *Mansoul* only because it bears the autograph of the man who wrote *Arabia Deserta,* but more than half of its heavy pages remain unopened.

Arabia Deserta is a vast book, to be read little by little, then laid aside for meditation. But, task that it is to follow that uncompromising old silver-bearded man through two years' pilgrimage over blinding desert sands, his book opens, as nothing else I know, whole kingdoms of wonder, wherein one loses all sense of brazen modernity and becomes a contemporary of the founders of Nineveh. "Hither lies no way from the city of the world, a thousand years pass as one day light; we are in the world and not in the world, where Nature brought forth man, an enigma to himself."

This book, published in 1888, companions well the vigorous travel volumes of the Elizabethans, and though there is a deliberate artificiality in its studied rhythms and archaic phrases, the manner is as well fitted to the matter as to the writer's own unique personality. Spenser, Chaucer and the English Bible were his models, and he conceived his own vivid experiences to be the very stuff of poetry. And yet, so accurate were his observations in that alien land that when, during the late war, the British government required a guide-book for its Eastern army, it could find none so reliable as this which had been made more than thirty-five years before.

Arabia Deserta should rest on that particularly intimate shelf with the world's choicest bed-books; books that provide one with some sense of human dignity and worth (when does one need this reassur-

ance more than at pyjama-time ?); rhythmic utter-
ances of profoundly quiet thoughts that best prepare a
man for surrendering consciousness to Night.

The average collector of books seems more intent
upon fiction, poetry and literary essays than upon history and works of scholarship. I confess that I do
not sympathize with this discrimination — certainly not
when these writings of the scholars give evidence of
true literary grace. All books that have yielded more
than passing pleasure or what I conceive to be profit
are my field, even some that are now dated and outgrown.

There is Thomas Buckle's *History of Civilization
in England* — a mere fragment of what was intended
to be a huge and comprehensive thing. One now
knows that this early attempt at creating a philosophy
of history neglected some most important factors of
man's social development. Food, soil, climate and
the general aspect of Nature are not sufficient to explain all social evolution or intellectual growth. We
require a knowledge of biological and economic forces,
and of that which we are pleased to call social psychology, before we may even attempt a philosophy of
history nowadays.

But what history is so readable as Buckle's fragment ? What book of history — unless it be Gib-
bon's — has exercised as much influence upon the
thought of the past seventy years ? You suggest the
popular work of H. G. Wells ? I grant both its
significance and interest, but compared with Buckle's
refreshing work it is a book of spare-parts — a thing
assembled and put together, lacking the vitality, originality and personality that made the older book a force
to be reckoned with. Buckle's book has the quality

that makes for survival, despite the mutations of time and theory. After more than threescore and ten years one may yet read it with pleasure and profit,— nay, it compels one, again and again, to lift it down from its shelf-solitude and restore it to human companionship, where it may unfold the life-histories of metaphysical Scotchmen, and their thoughts from the 14th to the 18th centuries, or explain the excessive superstitions of savages under the spell of a too luxuriant nature.

And, because of its great significance as a factor in shaping the modern mind, because of its stimulating power, it remains a prime collectors' item, soliciting a more than tender appreciation and care. Nor is it a book to frighten the impecunious. For a matter of three pounds or so the two volumes — 1857-1861 — may be transferred from the dusty isolation of the bookshop to the intimacy of the fireside. And a noble investment it is : a possession that yields both satisfaction and joy.

Winwood Reade's *Martyrdom of Man* suggests itself as a worthy fellow to Buckle, and a grateful prize to the purse-bound collector. Not as original in its ideas, a distinctly popular work, it is nevertheless a book that may be numbered among the classics of the 19th century, exerting as it did a revolutionary influence upon current thought. Shocking and irreligious as it must have been to Victorians, time has muted its thunders. But, though its author was overanxious concerning creeds that have lost their meaning, though its theme be that old one, the road to heaven leads by way of hell, it possesses a catholicity, a freshness and a vigor that have enabled it to more than hold its own among numerous outlines of history.

Neither of Reade's other books, both African sketches, is worth the collectors' or the readers' while, but in this one book, which has passed through more than twenty editions since 1872, he has earned himself an immortality of which his more famous uncle, Charles, might justly have been proud.

Darwin's *Origin of Species* has been so universally recognized as the turning-point of what we call modern thought that collectors' enthusiasm has put it well out of the average man's reach,—though chance will sometimes turn the book to a second-hand furniture shop where it may be had for much less than a song. Usually, however, the Darwin items run too high for the common man.

But, curiously enough, Herbert Spencer firsts one finds quite simply, and for absurdly low prices. Yet surely that spinsterish old man was one of the most important thinkers of his century—one of the most ambitious and daring philosophers of any time whatever. For all that, however, his works, many of them but skillful compilations, are outgrown, and fit only for the curious scientific historian. His sociology, his biology, his psychology are little better than relics. But the essence of the man's thought, his particular own contribution to philosophy, whatever it may mean to us now, is to be found in his *First Principles*, and I am convinced that this is the one of his works that should appeal to the collectors' instinct. It took more than the mere realization of its high place in modern thought to set me hunting for a first edition, I admit ; I was primarily driven to it by the memory of what it meant in my youth. That book made me an outcast in college. In my serious 'teens I suffered for it. Those days I was vain enough, foolish enough, to fancy that I understood its integrations of matter and dissipations of motion. It was one of my several bibles, and, I dare say, I understood it as well as men usually understand their bibles. As I grew older and less serious I deserted Spencer for Nietzsche, and Nietzsche for nothing, but I have never lost my affection for the cool logic of Spencer's pages, and when I saw the 1862 edition in its original cloth for no more than five dollars, I knew just what to do about it. And is not the first important philosophic statement of the implications of evolution worth our preserving ?

Near Spencer on my shelves are two other works that for years have been the delight of scholars, but have somehow failed to attract the collector's eye. They both have to do with that most permanently and universally interesting subject of the origin of religion : both are full of curious information and both are excellent companions against days of tedium.

One of them is sadly dated : both its method and its point of outlook are wrong. But Forlong's *Rivers of Life* (it was published in two quarto volumes by Quaritch in 1883, with a separately encased Chart of Religions), is a rich treasure-house of tribal lore, strange customs, ancient rituals and illustrations of symbology, difficult if not impossible to find, in their entirety, in any other single work. Encyclopedic and imposing, it is one of those books which, however dead its chief contentions — and its casual philological notions and startlingly facile comparisons are indeed outworn — never lose compellingness and will always serve to stimulate and satisfy human curiosity. The old army officer must have had a veritable encyclopedia of notes — odds and ends concerning tribal customs, folk-lore, images and festivals : personal observations made over all the Eastern hemisphere, supplemented by travellers' tales and rare brochures gathered from the remote corners of the earth. *Rivers of Life* remains a unique source-book for that very reason. Forlong's challenging personality and somewhat dogmatic manner at once take possession of the reader, whether to his amusement or edification, and before he is aware of it, hurry him along through a thousand pages. Finally, had I no other reason, I should cherish this work for the sake of its amazing chart of world religions. It is an unwieldy thing, nearly eight feet in length, and is, I believe, the first graphic representation of what may be called the evolution of religious beliefs. Many of the dates given on its margins are now known to be incorrect, some of its assumptions are wrong, but I know of nothing that presents so clearly and beautifully the notion that any one cult is but the outgrowth of others, and the parent of more to come. Books and chart together make this one of the most provocative and time-killing works that has ever been in my library, and I've had this book for pretty nearly a score of years.

Concerning the other work, Frazer's *The Golden Bough,* much has been written by modern scholars. Its third edition is a formidable thing, running into many volumes. Fortunately, the one I have is a first edition (two volumes, 1890), acquired in college years when I was a student rather than collector. It was a required text, and I had and have no more love for textbooks than any Grobian youth. But *The Golden Bough* was not written as a text book, a fact which I discovered on its first entrancing page : it is really a golden book, beautiful to read for its prose, and both revelatory and revolutionary in its wealth of thought and story. It has transformed an epoch of thought, revalued mythology, exposed the secrets of sympathetic magic, and provided us with a guide to many of the mysteries of religion. The priests of Nemi, guardians of the mistletoe in Diana's sacred grove, at long last have spoken, the rituals of corn and vine are explained ; sacrifice and resurrection are become intelligible, and the tales of the gods, of Osiris and Baldur, have lost their cold and meaningless austerity.

Some of Frazer's ideas have been modified and yet others supplemented by a more extensive accumulation of facts since 1890, and the scholar will need a long shelf for the expanded and revised edition ; but the average reader who but browses in these pastures will find Frazer's original version a freer and finer thing ; more pleasing to read and less encumbered by detail.

The Golden Bough is today the key book in any library of religious origins as well as a fine body of literature, and yet, in its first state one sees it begging in the book stalls. How long will the discriminating collector let it lie ?

I have already mentioned, with due modesty I hope, my copy of *Tristram Shandy,* but since it is the only first of Laurence Sterne's works I own, and the only one I ever really wanted, this will be an appropriate time to boast of how it came into my possession.

It was during the summer of 1920, and I had spent the better part of an afternoon looking through the main room of a shop in High Street, Oxford, when the salesman suggested that in another building across the passage (we'd call it an alley), was a yet larger stock of old books I might care to see. As I had scarcely spent a pound, and had wasted hours of the good man's time, I followed him, hoping that I might really encounter temptation. But as we stepped out into the cobbled way, a frocked youth was in the act of dumping a whole barrow of books on to the dirty stones of the pavement. In reply to my shocked inquiry at this vandal's act my companion assured me that the books were but old sermons and tracts destined for the "penny box." I dropped to my knees — an act prompted by curiosity and scepticism, not piety — and began to finger the grimiest lot of attic trash I had ever beheld, noting as I did the salesman's frown. The American had not been up to his expectations — he had turned out no millionaire — and now seemed bent on wasting the balance of his day.

"There's really nothing there of interest, Sir."

But my attention was held for several reasons : the books were nearly all of the 18th century, most of them were bound in sheep or calf, all of them were so black with coal dust that the titles were obscure, and some were done up in parcels held together by filthy twine. What is hidden is ever promising, so I persisted, and presently found nine black volumes, labels blotted out with dust, which proved to be a set of *Tristram Shandy*. I glanced at volumes 5, 7, and 9. In each was the authentic signature of L. Sterne. Five of the volumes were first editions ; the others were seconds, and a fourth. I looked up at the dignified and annoyed salesman. His face was a mask of boredom : he was not interested in my finds, being convinced that there was nothing to find.

"A shilling for the lot," was his answer as I held up the nine little duodecimos. His superior indifference did not permit him to so much as glance at my discovery, and so, under the circumstances, I promptly paid the shilling and had my parcel wrapped without enlightening him concerning his loss of approximately two hundred dollars !

Speaking of Sterne recalls the fact that while I neither have nor desire another of his rare firsts I do have two interesting association items that are pleasant to cherish. The gay parson made excellent use of good books, and turned them to ready account when fashioning his own. If one owned his copy of Rabelais, his Burton and the two little volumes of Beroalde de Verville's *Moyen de Parvenir*, one might congratulate one's self upon having cornered the main sources of *Tristram Shandy*. Well, I have made a slight beginning : I have the *Tome Premier* of *Le Moyen de Parvenir*, issued in two duodecimo volumes in 1738 : the flyleaf bears Sterne's signature, and somewhere I once read how he had these volumes especially bound for carrying about. I cannot find the reference, but my volume is bound in contemporary orange morocco with black inlays, and I fancy it looks much as it did when Yorick used to chuckle over its indecent pages, taking notes for the future.

The other item is questionable. It is a copy of Burton's *Anatomy* that once belonged to Sterne's leading parishioner and patron, Lord Bellayse, and bears his bookplate. Sterne was living in Yorkshire near to Newburgh Priory while *Tristram* was being written, and is said to have been a frequent visitor at his lordship's house : he may or may not have handled this volume. He had another edition (the sixth), in his own library, but I like to think that on occasion, 'twixt dining room and parlour, he took furtive peeps at these very pages.

One might thus multiply a list of odd favorites to

an interminable length. Many of my own catch my
eye as I write — *Drunken Barnnabee's Journall,* not
in a first, but an early edition, is the only one of perhaps
two score works by Richard Brathwaite that still has
power to amuse, and is the only one I care to own.
Near him is the first authorized author's edition
(16mo) of Butler's *Hudibras,* done in 1663-1678.
Of these three volumes there are two editions that the
real Butlerite should possess : the small octavo and the
one I have named, bearing the same dates ; and, out
of curiosity, one should include a copy of the spurious
Second Part, also printed in 1663,— for that part is
never reprinted. But the impecunious may be content
with the smaller author's edition, though, in that case,
the third part will not be uniform in size with the
other two. I have also, for my own reading, the two
volumes illustrated with colored plates by Clark in
1822 : but for the "Genuine Remains" and "Posthumous Works" I confess indifference. Butler is at
his superb best in *Hudibras,* our finest satire in verse,
and I am well content that it alone should represent
him here.

One should be thankful that some great writers
were sparing with their pens. Where they have been
profuse without either profundity or wit the collector
should give way to the critic and save only the worthy.
Southey, for example, may best be pruned down from,
say, fifty items to two, letting his disciple choose as
he will. In my case I select *The Doctor* (1834, 36,
37, 38, 47), and the *Common-Place Book* (1849-
51), for in these one discovers him in his most dis-
cursive moods, informative, genial, witty, whimsical,
unconventional and less inclined to show off. Excellent books to read abed, they may be picked up at will

and will seldom fail to yield a smile or a curious bit of information. The words were set down in the 19th century, but the spirit is that of the 17th.

Have you ever read the *Memoirs of William Hickey*? It is the personal record of a life, from 1749 up until 1809, spent in the British navy, seeing India, China, Jamaica, Cape Town, and all points east and west : a life of fighting, duelling, wenching, litigation and business,—a full life. And so well is it written that before I came to the last of the four stout volumes I was firmly convinced that I had fallen into the hands of the world's best historical novelist. It seemed too dramatic to be really true. But the last volume gives enough documentary particulars to allay suspicion : William Hickey was a real man, and, first and last, a resident of Twickenham. It is valuable as a record of eighteenth-century manners, British politics and world history : it enlists the reader's sympathy in the author's personal affairs so that its sixteen hundred pages are turned as eagerly as those of an adventure novel. I mention Hickey here for the reason that this one work is all that he left behind : own these *Memoirs*, and there is no more Hickey to collect : read the *Memoirs* and you will want the first edition of all the volumes as they were issued by Hurst & Blackett, London, 1913, '18, '20 and '25. There is something satisfying about a man who writes one good book and then stops short !

I know that there is another side to this business. I have been writing from the poor man's point of view, and illustrating a poor man's methods. I, personally, rejoice in the good book that has no blood-brother, and in the writer of one, or but few books : I have been forced to select from among my favorite writers, even where their output has been restricted. And I am well aware that there is both pleasure and profit in making a complete collection of a first-rate writer — all his books, and the books to which he has contributed chapters or an introduction. Such collections are valuable, and the preservation of them is of incalculable benefit to scholarship. Unfortunately, limited space and more limited means require us to select here and there from more famous firsts, or to seek out the unknown and uncollected. But even when one has chosen to work in a neglected field, where prices are moderate, there are difficulties and embarrassments that provide argument against the complete collector. Several examples come to mind from my own experience.

The late Charles Whibley has ever seemed to me one of the most engaging and accomplished essayists since the days of Walter Pater. He was first of all a scholar, a man of knowledge, method and taste. But he was not a pedant, and was never dull. His wide reading was lightened by a felicitous wit and a quiet humor. He knew thoroughly the social and political backgrounds of the 17th and 18th centuries, and brought to his facts shrewd insight and a kindly tolerance. His books are characterized by gusto and discrimination. His studies of Rabelais, Montaigne, Burton, Swift, Congreve, Saint-Simon, Petronius, Lucian and Sir Thomas Urquhart ; his brilliant and satisfying essays on the neglected Tudor translators ; his excellent introductions to many an English classic, and his racy accounts of rogues and vagabonds in *A Book of Scoundrels,* have made for Charles Whibley a unique place in the prose literature of this century. I like both to read and re-read his books, and, naturally enough, I proceeded to collect his first editions.

My first step in that direction was taken in Stratford-on-Avon, where, after a day of strolling convinced me that every house in Shakespeare's quaint old town had been converted into a tradesman's shop, I saw a copy of Whibley's *Literary Portraits*, with other volumes, on the window ledge of an attractive old house. I remember thinking that this was by far the nicest shop I had seen in Stratford, so, without hesitation I entered and asked to see the item I wanted. A gracious and smiling lady standing near the doorway bade me make myself at home, and a few minutes later sold me the book at a ridiculously low price. But when I began to inquire for other prices the lady seemed to grow a bit constrained, and finally was forced to confess that this was a private house, and that she was not in trade at all! She saw my confusion and hastened to add that many other Americans, bewildered by the profusion of curio shops in Stratford had made the same mistake. Her brother, she said, had made many delightful acquaintances in that manner : charming liar! It was the home of the late A. H. Bullen! Not only did she insist that I keep the book, but to further relieve my embarrassment she took me over the old house, which was once the residence of Julius Shaw, the man who witnessed Shakespeare's will. I never think of the experience without a blush, but I wouldn't have missed it for less than a first folio. But all this is beside the point.

There are only fourteen of what I would call legitimate Whibley items : *In Cap and Gown*, *A Book of Scoundrels*, *The Pageantry of Life*, *William Makepeace Thackeray*, *Literary Portraits*, *William Pitt*,

American Sketches, Studies in Frankness, The Letters of an Englishman (1st and 2nd series), *Essays in Biography, Jonathan Swift, Literary Studies, Political Portraits* (1st and 2nd series), *Lord John Manners and His Friends.* Of these the first is really not legitimate, as it is an anthology of Cambridge University wit, gathered together and introduced by the young Whibley : it is of little interest to any save a Cambridge man. It remains in my library because it is the first book to bear Whibley's name, and because it is a presentation copy from the author. The real collector swears that it is the corner-stone of the Whibley collection : the reader knows it for a space filler. But that is not all.

The collector compels one to add to one's shelves the books to which Whibley merely wrote an introduction, such as *The Collected Essays* of W. P. Ker, Methuen's edition of *Tristram Shandy, A Book of English Prose,* collected by W. E. Henley and Whibley, George Wyndham's *Essays in Romantic Literature,* Richard Graves' *The Spiritual Don Quixote,* the entire Second Series of *Tudor Translations,* and a whole roomful of *Blackwood's Magazines.* And I have named but a few of the real collector's demands respecting a complete Whibley collection. I have the fourteen volumes that are necessary to a sane collection and some of the volumes containing his suggestive introductions, but I call a halt at the journals and the Tudor classics. It would require a museum to collect in this fashion.

I did the insane thing in collecting Arthur Machen. The man who wrote *Hieroglyphics, The Hill of Dreams* and *The House of Souls* is a fine literary artist. The man who translated Casanova, *The*

Arthur Machen

A CHAPTER

FROM THE BOOK CALLED

THE INGENIOUS GENTLEMAN

DON QUIJOTE DE LA MANCHA

WHICH BY SOME MISCHANCE HAS NOT TILL NOW
BEEN PRINTED.

LONDON
GEORGE REDWAY
YORK STREET COVENT GARDEN

One of Arthur Machen's scarcest "items"

Heptameron and *Moyen de Parvenir*, is possessed
of uncanny skill and remarkable taste. I like his
work as well in 1934 as I did in 1918, and I do
not regret collecting him ; but, really, when I look
at the twelve-foot space he occupies in this room,
and at many of the absurd little items I have come
to possess through curiosity and collector's pride, I
am a little ashamed.

Let me illustrate. Mr. Henry Danielson, in his
Bibliography, published in 1923, listed twenty-four
items. Mr. Machen has written ten books since 1923,
and several volumes of collected essays and tales have
been gathered for publication ; but, including these,
I find that I now have thirty-one Machen items not in
Mr. Danielson's book, one of them published as far
back as 1898. Nor have I included in this count
more than a dozen magazine items, such as *Chapman's*
for December, 1895, which contains "The Red
Hand," and the sixteen bound volumes of *T. P.'s
Weekly*, from 1902 to 1912. To have a complete
Machen one must have at least two volumes of *The
Academy*, *Walford's Antiquarian Magazine*, Volume
2 of *The Whirlwind*, Volume 1 of *The Gypsy*, Volumes I and II of *Horlick's Magazine*, one stout
volume of *Lyon's Mail*, *The Neolith*, *Book Notes*,
Hesperian, and *Now and Then*. But the end is not
yet : there are theatre programs for which Machen has
written introductions, book catalogues for which he
has done a foreword, bakeries for which he has made
an advertising booklet. I have them, bound and unbound, in bundles, envelopes, slip-cases, all sizes and
shapes ; an ungainly, unlovely assortment of rarities,
representing the life work of one of England's most
fascinating writers.

And I have been led to do all this out of admiration and love of his books. But what books, I ask myself. Well, possibly a dozen, including his admirable translations. Yet, there on the shelves are such things as George Dewar's *The Pageant of English Landscape,* Thomas Moult's *Cenotaph,* Robert Hillyer's *The Halt in the Garden,* M. S. Buck's *Afterglow,* Gabriel Miro's *Our Father San Daniel,* Frederick Carter's *The Dragon of the Alchemists,* John Gawsworth's *Above the River,* and Robert Douglas's translation of *Les Cent Nouvelles Nouvelles,* dull tales with the ghastly illustrations of Clara Tice : and all of them are assembled here, slight things, stupid things, merely because a great man has been persuaded to write for them a word of introduction, or to contribute an essay. A mad business, collecting in this way. I shall not repeat it. Yet, notwithstanding all that I have said, I am rather proud of it !

Nor have I, even yet, confessed all my folly. A few years since Mr. Nathan Van Patten, who is one of America's most energetic and pious Machenites, published a provocative little brochure in which he suggested, with appropriate interrogations, that Machen is author, or editor, of a duodecimo called *Tobacco Talk and Smoker's Gossip,* published by George Redway in 1886. The book described by Mr. Van Patten is bound in red cloth, with appropriate decorations on the front cover. In spite of the fact that Mr. Machen denied the authorship, Mr. Van Patten's arguments were too good to be disregarded by a serious collector. I got the book as soon as I could, and, not to be outdone, found a still earlier edition, bound in decorated gray paper and issued in 1884 ! Thus, even after exhausting the bibliographies, buying all the

books done under the author's name (or anonymously), all the association items, introductions, post-
scripts, advertisements and handbills, the poor ass of a
collector, to be perfectly safe, must needs go on and
on, possessing himself of all that, by the remotest
chance, may be attributed to his author, either by
critics or by his fellow collectors.

Mr. Van Patten's ingenious arguments supporting
the Machenese authorship of *Tobacco Talk* recall
my own private conviction concerning an anonymous
little volume published by James Hogg and Sons at
London, some time in the late eighteen-eighties. A
London bookseller advertised it as Eden Phillpotts'
first book, and, as a Phillpotts collector I cabled for it
at once. In format and pagination *The Ghost in
the Bank of England* is pretty nearly a perfect twin
to Phillpotts' accredited first book, *My Adventure in
the Flying Scotsman*, also published by Hogg and Sons.
Its content reveals it to be of the stuff in which the
young Phillpotts then specialized. It is done in his
manner — the manner he adopts when telling of
ghosts, crime, or the detection of crime — and, as in
many of his early tales, there are familiar references
to Jamaica and the mysteries of Obi.

Mr. Phillpotts says he did not write *The Ghost*,
and his learned bibliographer, Mr. Percival Hinton,
joins in the denial ; but, on little more than internal
evidence and the external similarity of the volumes
I presume to doubt. 'Tis an ungracious thing to do ;
an impertinence, but there 'tis. Mr. Phillpotts is
author of more than one hundred and fifty books,
written over a period of more than fifty years. May
he not have forgotten at least one of his ill-favored
offspring ? We know that he failed to remember

The Prude's Progress, a play done in collaboration with Jerome K. Jerome back in 1895.

Not long ago an old lady whom I had not seen for over twenty years told me that she recalled my lecturing at her club on Ruskin. Aloud I mumbled some words about being flattered, but I was quite positive that she was mistaken. I know nothing about Ruskin, and only recall my sense of boredom at being compelled to read a few of his essays during my college days. I am not accustomed to lecture about writers who have bored me : moreover, twenty years ago I wrote out my lectures, and that act of writing usually fixes a thing in the mind. So I was quite sure that the lady was mistaken. And yet, a few weeks after this encounter, turning over some old papers, I came upon a printed announcement of the lecture ! Once upon a time I had been interested, had read and had presumed to talk about the man and his books.

Now I am a simple fellow, author of less than a dozen books, and yet in twenty-two years I had clean forgotten the writing of that lecture. May not Mr. Phillpotts, after fifty years of constant writing, have forgotten the existence of a sixty-three page story ?

As long as I have presumed so far, I may as well present some show of authority for my cocksureness. Very well, then, of Mr. Phillpotts' one hundred and fifty books I own more than ninety, and have read them — some of them thrice. Of those I do not own in my collection of first editions I have read more than a score. I believe I know somewhat of his manner ; to me it is unmistakable. So, then, when, in 1922, a bookman handed me a detective story called *Number 87*, by "Harrington Hext," saying that it

THE PRUDE'S PROGRESS:

A COMEDY

IN THREE ACTS.

BY

JEROME K. JEROME

AND

EDEN PHILLPOTTS.

LONDON:

CHATTO & WINDUS,

PICCADILLY, W.

MDCCCXCV.

A Book Mr. Phillpotts Forgot

was undoubtedly by an experienced writer, I was able, by the time I had read fifty pages, to identify Mr. Phillpotts as the author. And I have two reliable witnesses to support my story!

Well, I leave the matter there. May the idea of this anonymous book torment and delight some other collector as much as it does me! And for the further puzzlement of this collector let me suggest that he seek out such strays as *The County Counsellor* (1892),. and *The MacHaggis* (1897), both of which are plays said to have been done with Jerome, who, speaking of the last-named, on page 139 of *My Life and Time*, said,—"I wrote 'The MacHaggis' in collaboration with Eden Phillpotts." Let the collector look also for *The Counsellor's Wife*, another play attributed to Phillpotts on the title page of *A Pair of Knickerbockers*. According to Mr. Hinton's authorized bibliography these three items, though announced, were never published, and I am pretty sure that Mr. Hinton knows what he is saying. Still, strange things happen — stranger than even bibliographers dream. I name the books but to stimulate those who have sought in vain for copies of *A Breezy Morning* (1895) and *The Unlucky Number* (1906), to further effort, and a yet more ecstatic madness.

This that I have said may or may not deter the collector from going to the extremes I have indicated. I grant that there is pleasure to be found on either road. I am proud of my Burtons, Machens, Phillpottses and Erewhonian Butlers: but in attempting to complete these collections I have been forced to gather under my roof much that, while amusing to seek, is, at best, but curious to own. The collector to whom time is of importance, space limited, and money scarce, would better remain free of his author, and limit himself to only his most notable and lovable books. In the long run his library will yield him less shame and a far greater measure of satisfaction.

IV

FOOTNOTE FINDS AND FOLLIES

" 'I always read the footnotes,' said my uncle, 'for though the author may be both fool and liar in bold type, he is mindful to fortify his follies by a show of wisdom and accuracy in his footnotes ; moreover it was in a footnote that I once made a curious discovery.' "
— From *My Uncle Gregory*, by Gordon Ray Young

> "Grant I have mastered learning's crabbed text,
>   Still there's the comment.
> Let me know all ! Prate not of most or least,
>   Painful or easy !
> Even to the crumbs I'd fain eat up the feast,
>   Ay, nor feel queasy."

— From *A Grammarian's Funeral*, by Robert Browning

Robert Burton.
from the Portrait Brasenose College Oxford

Portrait of Robert Burton

IV

FOOTNOTE FINDS AND FOLLIES

I

THE collecting of books is apt to involve a man in an endless chain of desires and discontents. One book begets the wish if not the necessity for another, Virgil leads us to Homer, and, before we are properly aware of it, we are bounded in on every side by books. This is especially true of the man who collects for research. The investigation of one problem opens many more, until presently one is apt to be lost in a multiplicity of interests. I speak from happy if harassed experience.

Several years ago Mr. Floyd Dell and I decided to edit Burton's *Anatomy of Melancholy*, turn its Latin into English, remove its formidable framework of more or less unintelligible notes, and strive to convert it once more into a really popular book. But, after we had transformed the Latin tags into a fair imitation of Burtonese English, corrected a crop of misprints that had either stood unremedied or had somehow been augmented and multiplied for above three hundred years, after we had very nearly satisfied ourselves that our original intentions had been fulfilled, it suddenly occurred to Mr. Dell that the removal of the abbreviated footnotes in which the old Oxford scholar had indicated — in part — his sources, would necessitate the making of some kind of biographical and bibliographical index. I must confess that after four years' constant labor I looked with mixed feelings upon this new notion of arranging an index to Burton's vast catalogue of names. Still, the fact remained that without some such instrument Burton's references to Strozzius Cicogna, Rudolph Goclenius, Gualter Bruel, or his cryptic "Zanch. cap. 10. lib. 4" would forever remain as Greek to the average reader. Indeed, when we began to question one another concerning some of the more obscure scholars and books of the 14th and 15th centuries we were compelled to admit an appalling ignorance. Encyclopedias afforded scant assistance : even medical histories omit more names of these once illustrious scholars than they chronicle, and we saw directly that we had let ourselves in for many more months of steady research. At last, however, after toiling through a half dozen of America's greatest libraries, and sending repeated calls for help to the British Museum, the publishers' patience and our immediate resources came to an end and we were able to tell ourselves that even though we were not wholly satisfied with the results of our efforts, we had at least managed to put out a more useful and informative index to Burton than any done by our predecessors.

In due time the Burton was issued in two handsome volumes, and my colleague, sensible man that he is, put away his notes and turned to the making of more modern things. But I had become possessed : Burton had laid fast hold upon me and would not let me go.

In order to correct the text of the *Anatomy* I had bought most of the editions printed between the years 1621 and 1652, so that already I had begun to have a fair collection. In the attempt to gain information concerning upwards of a thousand forgotten celebrities back of the 17th century I had acquired several boxes of unused notes. There was nothing for it but to go on and complete what I had begun. There was, for example, Burton's untranslated and practically unknown Latin comedy, *Philosophaster,* and his fugitive verses — one book there, surely, and it cried aloud for some recognition. Then there was the question of Burton's sources. In the field of mental pathology alone Burton had brought together more authorities, quoted and classified more opinions concerning the causes and treatment of mental disease than any man prior to the 19th century. Moreover, many of these footnote men, important to any history of this subject, had remained unmentioned in modern histories, and their books have been wholly forgotten : a second book demanded attention.

Finally, being by instinct a collector, it seemed both necessary and desirable that I lay hands upon all the books I could find that related either to Burton's life or his theme. Meantime, those insistent footnotes had awakened my interest in more than a score of writers whose very obscurity was a challenge. I had, as many another before me, discovered that writers who have ceased to be remembered are not always those who most deserve being forgotten. The mere fact that a man is not immortalized in the encyclopedias need not lead one to the conclusion that the fellow's books were dull nor his life lacking in drama.

To collect Burton — for I must let this mad business follow its natural course — seems simple enough, seeing that he had but one book published during his life of 63 years. One soon discovers, however, that simplicity and book collecting are not on speaking terms. The book collector may be simple enough, God knows, but his feet must inevitably move amid entanglements. And in the case of Robert Burton, one finds readily enough that to each successive edition of the *Anatomy* the author made extensive additions to the text, so that to possess a complete first edition of that book requires the purchase of at least six great volumes : the fat quarto of 1621, and the five folios of 1624, '28, '32, '38 and '51. (There are more to come, but I must pause here.) The principal revisions ended with the 1638 folio. Burton died in 1640, but, according to Henry Cripps, his publisher, he left a few notes which were added to the folio of 1651 : to complete one's set of Burton, then, one must add at least one posthumous volume.

But, in my case, the ambition of the collector was complicated by the necessities of the editor. (Such complications serve to fortify one's conscience mightily, and are a vast comfort.) To prepare a sound text of the *Anatomy*, all the editions containing Burton's corrections must be compared, line by line, from beginning to end. For each edition had its especial crop of typographical blunders, and none of the editors, prior to 1927, had taken the trouble to correct the text in this manner. All had assumed the Sixth edition to be the final authority, and, as a result, every modern reprint from 1800 down to the 20th century had either perpetuated the accumulated misprints of the seventeenth-century printers, or added a new assortment of its own.

Neither the collector nor editor has the right to assume anything. Every edition must be examined with particular care. In the absence of a bibliography, one must be made. May I indicate the penalty of assumptions?

In 1660, Burton's Sixth edition was reprinted for Cripps at London. Its engraved title, save for the date and the words "Seventh Edition," is quite enough like to that of the Sixth to deceive the amateur. Still, the experienced collector would know enough to read the page and find for himself that he was looking at a Seventh edition. But, as is not infrequently the case, copies of these old books undergo strange vicissitudes, and it comes to pass that the frontispiece-engraving is torn out. What then? The dedication page, immediately following this leaf still bears the misleading *Jam sexto Revisam*, lying words that proclaim the sixth edition! In both sixth and seventh editions the text ends on the page numbered (erroneously in both cases) 723; in both, the table at the end contains five leaves, with Cripps' address to the reader on the last. Suppose, then, our copy to have lost both title and final leaf, what then? The collector must know more: he will glance at the first line of text on page "723," where, in the sixth edition the first words are "self to the advice," whereas in the seventh the first words on that page are "calls it, hear them speak": he will look at the first page of "Democritus Junior to the Reader" and note that the initial "G" in the sixth lies on a background of formal leaves and flowers, whereas in the seventh that letter serves as a chair for a sleeping child. The experienced bibliographer will examine the signatures of the volumes and he will observe that page 719 of the 1651 edition bears the signature Zzzz, while at the foot of the same page of the 1660 folio is Zzz3. There are many other differences in ornament, type and spacing, but these will suffice to enable the merest amateur to distinguish even badly damaged copies of these editions.

To give point to all these dry observations I name but two instances. In 1893 Professor A. R. Shilleto, a well-known English scholar, translator of Pausanius, Plutarch and Josephus, brought out an edition of Burton's *Anatomy*, enriched with new notes, translations and corrections, that was acclaimed on every hand the most scholarly edition ever done. It was. But unfortunately the scholar had paid no attention to Burton bibliography, and despised the trifling details in which collectors rejoice as "points." Prefixed to that edition was a publisher's note, wherein it was stated Dr. Shilleto had based his work on the Sixth edition. But on examining the text it becomes evident that this scholar had mistaken a Seventh for a Sixth. The facsimile of the engraved title page used in the Shilleto should have been a warning ; it was taken from the Seventh : and the publisher in his note stated that "The seventh and eighth editions were *literal* reprints of the Sixth" ! Thus upon the notoriously inaccurate Seventh edition Professor Shilleto wasted much of his time with great ado. He might have saved himself even then had he, instead of assuming that the last edition of a man's work is of necessity the most accurate, compared all the issues, section by section. For had he done so he would have been spared the futility of trying to trace Burton's "parats" to *apparitor*, when, in reality, it was but a printer's slip for "parasites."

The other incident concerns the Seventh edition more remotely. In the British Museum (Press mark 8408.1.10) there is a copy of the Third edition of this great book which has, before the engraved title,

the verses called *The Argument of the Frontispiece.*
Assuming the Museum copy to be perfect, the editors
of the Cambridge History of English Literature (Vol.
IV. P. 497) assure us that the *Argument* first appeared in 1628 (In the forthcoming new edition of
this work that error is corrected). I have seen two
other copies of the 1628 folio also dressed out with
the *Argument.* But the fact of the matter is that
the *Argument* did not appear until 1632, and a later
examination of the Museum copy showed Professor
Bensly that this leaf had been taken from a copy of
the Seventh edition. In the two copies I have seen,
one such leaf had been stolen from a Fifth edition and
the other from a Sixth. How, then, did these things
come about ? It is quite simple : some collector, finding that his copy seemed to lack a most interesting leaf,
secured one from another, and perhaps damaged copy
and had it bound or pasted in. He had assumed im-
perfection where none existed !

While I am about it — though I confess that this
preamble has already grown all out of proportion —
I may suggest a simple test for this preliminary leaf
that may be of interest to the collector : In the first
appearance, 1632, the last three words of the first line
of the poem are, "heere seene apart" ; in the 1638
folio these words are printed thus, "here seene apart" ;
in the Sixth edition (either date, 1651 or 1652), the
words are "here seen apart" ; in the Seventh edition
these lines remain as in the Sixth, but whereas in all
previous editions the second word of the fourth line
in stanza 4 is "dittie," it was changed in the Seventh
to "ditty."

I have dwelt at length upon these trifles to show
that the collector must keep his eyes well open to

detail, and fortify himself with all the bibliographic knowledge he can obtain before venturing far amongst books of the past.

The keystone of a Burton collection is, of course, the quarto of 1621, which, during the past decade, has risen in value so as to be rather beyond the reach of the average collector. Thank heaven I got mine before it became known to the American millionaires! One must be sure that the book collates perfectly, that the title is genuine and that the errata leaf is present. My own copy is sound, clean, genuine, but, while it has not been trimmed into the text, headings or signatures, it is not as tall as it should be (being $6\frac{7}{8}$ by $5\frac{1}{2}$ inches, whereas a fine copy will measure about $7\frac{1}{2}$ by $5\frac{5}{8}$). Neither is mine in its contemporary dress, Riviere having cased it in modern calf. There is tipped within, however, a fragment from a letter of Burton's, bearing the words, "Your lovinge brother, Robert Burton," so that I am very nearly content — or should be.

The 1624 *Anatomy* is the first in folio, and, as is the case with its fat little predecessor, is seldom found untrimmed; I have seen but one copy in original boards. That one measured $11\frac{7}{16}$ by $7\frac{1}{4}$, and while its binding and dimensions made it most desirable, its pages had been badly stained and the flyleaves and title had been defaced by some ignoramus who had fancied it for a copy book, and had thoroughly covered the pages with silly maxims done in ink. Under those circumstances I preferred a copy $\frac{4}{16}$ of an inch shorter, clean, sound and collated perfect, though in modern inlaid morocco, fresh from Douglas Cockerell's deft hands.

In collecting the later editions one must see to it

that the 1628 folio have a clear, clean and reasonably untrimmed impression of LeBlon's engraved title, (for that page is the principal point of this edition, in which it makes its first appearance); that the 1632 have both title and the preceding leaf of *Argument* in good state ; the 1638, important in that it was the last to receive the personal attention of its author, requires more attention. It would seem that Burton, ambitious (as what author is not?) to see his work set out more handsomely, made arrangements some time in 1634, for one Robert Young to print at Edinburgh an edition which, according to a letter he wrote to George, Lord Berkeley's secretary in August, 1635, was to have been issued during the following September. This publication was prevented, probably by Henry Cripps who owned half the copyright. For while it appears that Burton had a right to have his book printed in Scotland without consulting Cripps, Young, the Edinburgh printer, had been violating stationers' laws by sending Bibles across the line into England, so that Cripps was able to call down the wrath of the authorities upon the pirate and put a stop to the venture : the sheets already printed in Scotland were therefore surrendered to Cripps, who had the remainder of the sheets set up in London and Oxford, and issued for sale in 1638. Bibliographers have estimated that 151 leaves were printed at Edinburgh, 199 at Oxford, and 68 at London. Naturally there were some difficulties encountered when these sheets came to be assembled ; and these were further complicated by Burton's additional revisions, undertaken during this publishers' storm. In patching the sheets together, the L1 leaf (pp. 259-260), was seen to contain duplicated matter, and was deleted. Through

some happy oversight, however, a few of these dupli-
cate leaves were bound in, and the collector will
rejoice to own a copy bearing this evidence of old Burton's vanity. And, lest the reader suspect that the
ownership of such a copy be mere vanity also, I should
add that the marginal notes on the rare leaf differ
from those on the retained leaf, and that by observing
these changes I was enabled to add somewhat to the
scant sum of knowledge concerning Burton's life.

There is a yet rarer variant of this edition described
by Mr. Holbrook Jackson in a recent number of the
Book-Collector's Quarterly — a copy having, in addition to the engraved title, a typographical title page,
set in a frame of double rules, bearing the printer's
device and imprint : "Printed by Leonard Litchfield,
for Henry Cripps." This copy, however, is probably
unique.

I have already said too much about the Sixth and
Seventh editions, though I should add that only a collector's whim would lead a man to possess himself of
two copies of the Sixth — the Oxford imprint dated
1651 and the London of 1652, since they are, save as
to imprint and colophon, practically identical.

The Eighth edition is easily distinguished from its
fellows by reason of its having been printed in double
columns. Moreover, it is usually at least an inch
taller than any of the earlier folios.

None of the other editions is worthy of the collector unless it possess some association value : though
here I must confess to fondness for my shabby copy
of the 1845 Tegg imprint, bearing both the autograph
and bookplate of Henry Thomas Buckle. For edi-
torial purposes I have picked up a dozen different
modern imprints, dating from 1800 to the present

time. But most of them are quite unsatisfactory : poor type, bad paper and careless editing. The Nonesuch edition is handsome enough to satisfy a connoisseur of fine printing, but the true Burtonian despises its omissions (it leaves out some of the amusing front matter), its grotesque cuts, and its abominable burlesque of LeBlon's title page.

After completing the collection of Burton's *Anatomy*, one turns to his minor writings ; and here I must speak in a thin voice. In vain have I searched the bookshops here and abroad for a copy of his comedy, *Philosophaster* ; eight years I have looked for this scarce quarto. Sir William Osler succeeded in obtaining one at the end of fourteen years, so I take hope. This play was acted but unpublished during its author's lifetime, and it was not until 1862 that it became a printed book. That brings it well within modern times, and one may wonder at its scarcity until one learns that the Roxburghe Club issued but sixty-five copies to its members. I fear that I shall have to content myself with the photostatic facsimile on which I worked in turning this curious Latin comedy into English.

Then there are the poems : one needs to get eighteen thin quartos, published — with one exception — at Oxford between 1603 and 1638 : anthologies in praise of men or events, done by university scholars. They were issued unbound, and are more desirable in that state. Ten years ago it was possible to pick them up at a guinea apiece ; now they are apt to fetch five pounds. These little items are full of interest to the Burtonian, each of the eighteen containing one of his poems and others by his friends and students ; seven of them preceded the appearance of the *Anatomy*.

They celebrate such matters as the accession of James
I. ; the death of Prince Henry ; the marriage of
Frederick V.; Sir Thomas Bodley, and his great gift
to Oxford ; Queen Anne of Denmark ; Sir Henry
Saville ; William Camden ; Charles I., etc. Moreover, in many of these verses Burton anticipates his
own phrases, later used in the *Anatomy*. In addition
to these there is another poem — and likewise a
preface — by Burton in Francis Holyoake's revision
of John Rider's *Dictionarie*, which was printed by
J. Barnes at Oxford in 1612. This poem, addressed
to Holyoake, was reprinted in the edition of 1617 and
1633, but the signed preface only occurs in the 1612
and 1617 editions. Copies of these are exceedingly
scarce, however, three of the 1612 and two of the
1617 editions being known in England, and none in
this country. The Huntington Library has a copy of
the 1633 edition ; and I was once made happy by
finding another on a bargain table in an odd lot of
Latin dictionaries, priced at two dollars !

This business of being a crank carries one into ab-
surdities. In my own case I have fabricated brave
justifications for acquisitiveness by turning editor : thus
I excuse myself for permitting curiosity to beget
curiosity, and once unleashed, proceed from the books
Burton wrote to the books he once owned.

At his death Burton bequeathed more than a thousand of his books to the Oxford libraries, where they
remain snugly housed to this day. Aside from these
major bequests, many books from his library were
given to his friends and fellow students — his English
medical books, atlases, herbals and some histories.
And, from time to time he was wont to present books
he had read to his brother William, the antiquary and

PVRCHAS

HIS *Ex libris C. Burton*   *1645*

PILGRIMES.

IN FIVE BOOKES.

The fixth, Contayning Nauigations, Voyages, and Land-Difcoueries, with other Hiftoricall Relations of *AFRICA.*

The feuenth, *Nauigations, Voyages, and Difcoueries of the* Sea-Coafts and In-land Regions of *Africa*, which is generally called Æthiopia : *by* Englifh-men, *and others.*

The eighth, Peregrinations and Trauels by land in *Paleftina, Natolia, Syria, Arabia, Perfia,* and other parts of *ASIA.*

The ninth, *Peregrinations, and Difcoueries by Land, of* Affyria, Armenia, *Perfia, India, Arabia,* and other In-land Countries of *Afia*, by *Englifh-men,* and others ; *Moderne and Ancient.*

The tenth, *Praeteritorum,* or Difcoueries of the World, fpecially fuch as in the other Bookes are omitted.

The Second Part.

Unus Deus , Una Veritas.

Rob:  *Burton.*

LONDON

Printed by *William Stansby* for *Henrie Fetherstone*, and are to be fold at his fhop in *Pauls* Church-yard at the figne of the Rose.
1625.

Facsimile of the title page of Robert Burton's *Purchas*
which he seems to have acquired in 1626

historian. So it comes about that books bearing Robert Burton's well-known signature, private mark, and library hieroglyph, will occasionally turn up in English auction rooms. His copy of his brother William's *Description of Leicestershire* (1622), was offered for sale less than a decade since and finally went to the Library of Congress ; the title page of his Cardan's *De Subtilitate*, Basle 1602, is at present in possession of an English scholar ; this year (1932), his copy of John Gwillim's *Display of Heraldrie*, 1611, was sold in London ; his copy of Thuanus' *History of His Own Time*, Paris 1604, and his set of *Purchas His Pilgrimages*, in five folios, have dropped into my own hands — and only this devilish depression kept me from ordering the folio copy of Ptolemy's *Geographia* of 1597 which, besides the usual autograph and library marks, is said to be well margined with Burton's notes.

One buys these books out of an affection for the great author, but one ever hopes that on margin or flyleaf will occur a note that may explain, perhaps, the unusually long novitiate at Oxford, where he entered at 16 and only proceeded to Bachelor at the age of 25 ; explain his friendship for Lady Frances Smith-Cecil, dowager Countess of Exeter, and his sudden resignation from the living at Walesby. But whatever the motive, the handling of these old volumes of dear association affords a satisfaction that may only be understood by proper madmen of the Bibliophagi.

II

I SEE that I have required too many pages to introduce my footnotes, but having indicated how the pursuit of one book multiplies interest and depletes the pocketbook ; having indicated Burton's *Anatomy*

as my starting point, it will surprise no one who has
looked upon the marginal references in the *Anatomy*
that a man foolish enough to begin tracking down
Burton's authorities has launched himself upon an endless voyage to Nowhere. And while I own that the
destination of such a man must inevitably be Nowhere, I must insist that *en route* there are many
happy islands and notable experiences.

For example, there is the list of players who took
part in the production of *Philosophaster* in 1617.
Burton wrote down their names on the margin of
his manuscript, and there they remained hid until
1862, when W. E. Buckley published the play and
gave brief biographical accounts of such actors as were
known to the University historians. Since so little has
come down to us of Burton's life, it seemed wise to
learn whether these young men had left any written
records : had they done so it would seem likely enough
that they would have made some mention of the play
and some references to the dramatist, who was probably both their master and their friend. One name
struck my attention more than others,— that of William Strode, who acted the part of *Tarentilla*. The
other actors (there were twenty-seven in the cast) had
written some verse, and two or three had achieved a
certain fame, but Strode had gone on to write many
poems, and, following in his master's footsteps, had
produced a play, *The Floating Island*, which was acted
in Christ Church in 1636. Strode's work, therefore,
must be studied. But more was to follow. Running through the indices of *Notes and Queries* for
mention of the man I came across this highly interesting account, in the first volume of that great reference work :

FOOTNOTE FINDS AND FOLLIES

"Many of your readers will remember the beautiful song in Fletcher's play of *The Nice Valour*, act iii. scene 3, beginning —

> 'Hence, all you vain delights,
> As short as are the nights
>   Wherein you spend your folly !
> There's nought in this life sweet,
> If man were wise to see't,
>   But only melancholy,
>   Oh, sweetest melancholy !'

"Milton was indebted to it for the idea of his *Il Penseroso* ; and Hazlitt calls it 'the perfection of this kind of writing.'

"My object in now calling your attention to it, is to point out a copy, hitherto, I believe, unnoticed, among Malone's MSS. in the Bodleian Library. It is entitled, *A Song in ye praise of Melancholy*, and has appended to it, in the handwriting of Malone, the following note : —

> 'Dr. Strode, the author of this beautiful little piece, part of which has been ascribed unjustly to Fletcher, because it is sung in his *Nice Valour*, was born about the year 1600, and died canon of Christ-church in 1644. Milton evidently took the hint of his L'Allegro and Penseroso from it.'

"The same Ms. (marked no. 21 in the Malone Catalogue) contains *A Song against Melancholy*. . . It is also ascribed to Dr. Strode by Malone." This note, made by Dr. Edward F. Rimbault in 1850, gives rise to many interesting speculations. How did Strode's poem, if indeed it be his, get into the Beaumont and Fletcher folio of 1647 ? It was not attributed Fletcher before that date, and *The Nice Valour* was first printed in the folio ; did Milton get the hint for his great poems from Strode ? What is the relation between this melancholy song and Robert Burton's "Abstract of Melancholy," with its line,

FOR THE LOVE OF BOOKS

"All my joys to this are folly
Naught so sweet as Melancholy" ?

The "Abstract" was printed first in 1628 ; neither Malone nor Dr. Rimbault make mention of it in this connection, though James Wharton, back in 1785, was of the opinion that Milton was inspired by Burton's verses.

To me the note was exciting news, for I recalled at once Strode's association with Burton's comedy. Rimbault and the others could have had no means of knowing that fact, since Burton's manuscript was not uncovered until 1862. Burton and Strode were undoubtedly friends, and it would be interesting to know which of the poems was written first.

The poems of William Strode were collected from MSS. and printed by Mr. Bertram Dobell in 1907, and in the preface to that interesting volume we are informed that the verses on Melancholy were published anonymously in 1635, and that two MS. versions then in the editor's possession date from about 1632. If Mr. Dobell's evidence be taken as satisfactory it would seem that to Burton must be yielded the honor of having inspired both Strode and Milton !

But this is not the place for going into such vexatious problems. I have set down the tale to show how the collecting of Burton led of necessity to the collecting of William Strode, canon of Christ Church.

And speaking of Burton's influence upon poets recalls Floyd Dell's brilliant discovery of the source of Keats' "Ode on Melancholy." The indebtedness of Keats to Burton had been acknowledged by the poet himself at the conclusion of "Lamia," and various of his editors have suggested words or ideas of his that may have been taken from the *Anatomy*.

But until Mr. Dell's article on "Keats' Debt to Robert Burton" appeared in the *Bookman* of March, 1928, no one had been able to show the organic kinship existing between the central thought of the ode and any idea out of Burton. It was during the reading of the final proof sheets for the 1927 edition of the *Anatomy* that Burton's words (from Part I, Sec. 2, Mem. 3, Sub. 5) suggested to my colleague the actual origin of the ode. Burton had written :

—"in the Calends of January Angerona had her holy day, to whom, in the temple of Volupia, or Goddess of Pleasure, their Augurs and Bishops did yearly sacrifice."

Burton, drawing from Macrobius, had elsewhere described Angerona as the goddess of Melancholy, and Mr. Dell, who has an amazing familiarity with English poetry, from Chaucer to Masefield, was quick to see that the paradox of finding the goddess of Melancholy in the very temple of Pleasure provided the key to both the meaning and origin of Keats' ode, wherein he affirms —

"Ay, in the very temple of Delight
    Veil'd Melancholy has her sovran shrine."

A clever bit of detecting, that, and another proof that dabbling with old books is neither dull nor unprofitable.

A footnote is held by many to spoil an otherwise fair page. It is the bane of the indifferent freshman's so-called life, and, for that matter, many an enthusiastic reader has cursed the note that distracted his attention from a beautiful line. I have found myself at one with these carping ones full often, but I remember that frequently the note is more exciting than the text : for confirmation of this view let the reader turn to Bayle's *Historical Dictionary*, where entrancing footnotes dominate almost every page. Frequently the scholar who has been too nicely accurate in the body of his work will venture to suggest mad hypotheses in the notes : the sad facts (he seems to say), are probably thus and so ; but in the note, which he no doubt hopes may escape the eyes of envious colleagues, he lets himself out, eases himself of the burden of scholarship, gives fancy rein, repeats gossip, expands into speculation, soars into Utopia in a manner not quite becoming in a philosopher, and all with an air of — "Tut, tut, these are but trifles, and I set them down by the way."

Or, as was the case with my wayward author, who got me into all this complexity, he tucks down deep in his notes the abbreviated names of books that for two centuries have been amongst the forgotten, so that by the time one has made out the name of author and book, one's curiosity is aflame : the book cannot be found, therefore it must be read, it must be both important and interesting. But I must own that after running some of these ancients to earth I was less sorry they were unremembered than that I had taken the pains to dig them from a peaceful oblivion. But the exceptions ! That is another story, and the one I should have been at from the outset. For there are jewels in the dust bins around bookshops, and only foot-note mention would have ever led me to probe about for them. Having therefore discoursed at tedious length concerning the occasion, the method, the cause and the source of my curiosity, I shall now turn to the "finds" that have delighted me, and while, no doubt, some of these are yet well enough known to the learned, there remain others which, to some who may be as ignorant concerning these ancients as I, will offer pleasant prospects and open up new worlds for roving fancy.

I forget by what circuitous path I was led to John Swan. He is not in Burton, but a note in a late edition of some old medical writer, searched by the way, led me to the hope that here was a man somewhat after the pattern of Democritus Junior. And he is.

Swan's *Speculum Mundi* is the only one of his five publications which called for more than a single printing ; this was thrice reprinted, having first appeared at Cambridge in 1635. The whole title is needed to give one a taste of the book — "A glasse representing the face of the world ; shewing both that it did begin, and must also end : the manner how, and time when, being largely examined. Whereunto is joyned an Hexameron, or a serious discourse of the causes, continuance, and qualities of things in Nature ; occasioned as matter pertinent to the work done in the six dayes of the World's creation."

Concerning the man little is to be found save that he seems to have been born during the latter days of the 16th century and to have died near the middle of the next century ; that he was a student at Trinity College, Cambridge, and that he was vicar at Sawston about 1639. His book will have to stand in his stead.

Speculum Mundi derives from Pliny, Topsell, Gerarde, Gesner, Polydore Virgil, and the usual authorities that were then in high esteem, but Swan had the wit to mould his story of creation into an amusing creation of his own. For his book is no less than an account of the origin, nature and destiny of the whole world. Swan's chronology is based upon the current

opinions of theologians ; the order of his account is
scriptural, but once launched upon the tale he tells
with gusto of the origin of continents and islands,
of Atlantis and its wonderful culture, of earthquakes
and tides.   He is most interesting when describing the
magical qualities of precious stones, of the ruby "that
expelleth sad and fearfull dreams," of the amethyst
that "hath power to resist drunkenness," and of the
sardonyx which "preserveth chastitie and healeth
ulcers" ; or of animals, including, of course, dragons
and unicorns.   He tells us that "The squirrell is a
quick nimble creature which will skip from tree to
tree with great facilitie.   When she is out of her
nest, her tail serveth to secure her both from sunne
and rain.   Howbeit, it is sometimes a hurt to her :
for the hairs of it be so thick, that striving to swim
over a river, her tail is so laden with water, that
sinking she drowneth.   Wherefore nature hath taught
her this prettie piece of policie ; namely, to get upon
a little piece of wood, which swimming wafts her
securely over : and wanting a sail, her bushie tail set
up and spread abroad, supplies the room of that defect."   Of the cockatrice he informs us that it is the
King of Serpents,— "not for his magnitude or great-
nesse, but for his stately pace and magnanimous mind :
for the head and half part of his body he always
carries upright, and hath a kind of crest like a crown
upon his head.   This creature is in thickness as big as
a man's wrist, and of a length proportionable to that
thicknesse : his eyes are red in a kind of cloudy black-
nesse, as if fire were mixed with smoke.   His poyson
is a very hot and venimous poyson, drying up and
scorching the grass as if it were burned : in which he
is like to the Gorgon.   And amongst all living crea-

tures there is none that perisheth sooner by the poyson
of a Cockatrice than man ; for with his sight he
killeth him : which is because the beams of the Cocka-
trices eyes do corrupt the visible spirit of a man. . .
That they be bred out of an egge laid by an old
cock, is scarce credible : howbeit, some affirm with
great confidence, that when the cock waxeth old, and
ceaseth to tread his hens any longer, there groweth
in him, of his corrupted seed, a little egg with a thinne
filme in the stead of a shell, and this being hatched
by the Toad or some such like creature, bringeth forth
a venimous worm, although not this Basilisk, that King
of serpents."

We see that in some concerns Swan was not without
his share of scepticism, though he could never resist a
pretty tale of the marvelous.   Natural history becomes
as interesting as Arabian Nights under the guidance
of this strange parson, and while our scientists may
reasonably doubt his informative value, none can say
of him that he is dull.   His mermaids may not convince, but they will ever entertain.   Nor can I find
it in me to say that John Swan of Sawston is not as
rational in his interpretation of nature as, for example,
our own extremely learned but quite mystical Professor Eddington.

Speculum Mundi is seldom read in our century : its
virtues are not noised abroad, and I believe it is only
mentioned in the book catalogues because of a misquotation of some lines from Shakespeare's *Romeo and
Juliet,* which has given it a place in the literature
called Shakespeareana.   And, for the benefit of the
curious, perhaps I should here set down the quotation.
It occurs on page 299 of the first edition of *Speculum ;*
page 293 of the second edition (1643).   The lines

are from Act II. sc. 3, line 15 ; I italicize the variant
words :

> Oh mickle is the pow'rfull *good* that lies
> In *herds, trees,* stones, and their true qualities :
> For nought so vile that on the earth doth live,
> But to the earth some *secret* good doth give.
> *And nought* so *rich on either rock* or *shelf,*
> *But, if unknown, lies uselesse to itself.*
> *Therefore who thus doth make their secrets known,*
> *Doth profit others, and not hurt his own.*

It is not as a Shakespeare item, however, that I
commend Swan's old book, but as a proper source of
light amusement for those who delight in such things
as Gesner's *History of Four-footed Beasts,* Browne's
Vulgar Errors, or the works of Master Cornelius
Agrippa. (Curious things happen in a book's life : a
few years ago Cabell's early works were listed only
for their Pyle illustrations ; *Gulliver* declines into a
child's amusement ; *Pilgrim's Progress* ascends from
the shelf of religious tracts up to its proper place
among literary masterpieces ; and Swan's natural history of creation survives because of a misquotation !)
And let me say to the collector that he make sure of
getting a copy containing the quaint engraved frontispiece by Marshall, as otherwise his book will be of
but little value.

Many of Burton's notes point to Bishop Joseph
Hall, whose ideas are likewise echoed more than once
in *Philosophaster.* And Hall is eminently worth looking into. This great satirist was born in Leicestershire in 1574, was graduated from Cambridge in
1592, and, after a brilliant and somewhat contro-
versial career, was made bishop of Norwich in 1641.
Hall died in 1656, leaving behind him some fifty

books, most of which being polemics are of but slight interest. One now turns to him for the clever satires done in his youth, for his *Characters of Virtues and Vices,* and his *Mundus alter et idem* (Another World and the Same), in which last, under the pretext of flaying the hypothetical inhabitants of the then unknown land of Australia, Hall used his whip upon the backs of his countrymen in anticipation of Dean Swift. He belonged to that tribe of which Henry L. Mencken is a modern exemplar. In another mood he might have appealed to Ralph Waldo Emerson, particularly in that *Quo Vadis* of his wherein he set upon gentlemen who travel abroad for their cultural advancement.

But I must not fall into misleading ; I have no intention of commending the whole works of the old theologian to this generation ; but there is one pearl which I would wish more widely admired for its excellence — that youthful book of verses, the "toothlesse" and the "byting satyres," called *Virgidemiarum,* first published in 1597. The toothless satires were aimed at society and the conventions of society and letters ; the biting satires Hall used against his contemporaries, addressed under such pseudonyms as Labeo, Lollio, Scrobio, and Villio.

Bishop Hall was a modern, a "young intellectual" of the late 16th century, laughing at the outmoded poetry of the past : he poked fun at Spenser and those who sang the threadbare tales of old romance, with all the seriousness of a Montmartre bohemian ; ridiculed the lawyers and doctors who took their fees without regard to justice or health ; poured out his wrath upon emptiness and show, upon the ignorant rich and the self-indulgent, upon quacks and as-

trologers. There is no question but Burton must have
enjoyed these Juvenalian satires almost as much as
he did the profanity of the bargemen. And he took
a hint from Hall more than once in his play, for he
too sympathized with the poor clergy who were compelled to teach and play chaplain to tight-fisted gentry
for bed and board — "trencher-chaplaines" they called
them then. Hall wrote :

> A Gentle squire would gladly entertaine
> Into his house some trencher-chaplaine ;
> Some willing man that might instruct his sons,
> And that would stand to good conditions.
> First, that he lie upon the truckle-bed,
> Whiles his yong maister lieth o'er his head.
> Second, that he do, on no default,
> Ever presume to sit above the salt.
> Third, that he never change his trencher twise.
> Fourth, that he use all common courtesies ;
> Sit bare at meales, and one half rise and wait.
> Last that he never his yong maister beat,
> But he must aske his mother to define,
> How manie jerkes she would his breech should line.
> All these observ'd, he could contented bee,
> To give five markes and winter liverie.

Burton makes Pedanus advise the young teacher,
Theanus, "take care how thou goest about to thrash the
sone of a nobleman save first thou hast obtained permission from his mother."

I commend Bishop Hall's little volume of satires to
such as take pleasure in *Hudibras*, to antiquaries, ever
curious concerning the customs of earlier days, and
to all who love the flavor of nicely balanced clauses
and sharply turned phrases. Finally, I would remind
good Shandeans that their master borrowed many bits

from the old Bishop to brighten the pages of his masterpiece.

No man will condemn footnotes heartily once he has been led by that means to the discovery of such a writer as Giambattista della Porta. Notes in both Browne and Burton led me to the reading of this Neapolitan genius and to the happy discovery that his works are not hard to come by.

But first as to the man. Porta was born in Naples about 1536 ; travelled extensively throughout Europe ; was the founder and president of the first scientific society ever organized — the *Academia Secretorum Naturae* — in 1560 ; wrote at least eight successful comedies ; was one of the first to describe binocular lenses ; inventor of the camera obscura ; the first ecologist (1583) ; a student of magic ; precursor of Johannes Lavater as a physiognomist ; an opponent of witchcraft ; a noted cryptographer ; and one of the first to explain the queer doctrine of signatures (that plants indicate by their appearances the human diseases they are fitted to cure). Thus we see that Porta was, like so many of his contemporaries, a versatile gentleman.

I here commend but one of his numerous works, that of *Natural Magic* — *Magiae Naturalis* — first published at Naples in 1558, and translated into English one hundred years later. This small folio — and the collector must see to it that his copy have the engraved title by Gaywood — is nothing less than an encyclopedia of curiosities. Therein you will learn secrets of beauty, of cookery, fishing, hunting, invisible writing ; the manufacture of precious stones, of lenses ; of the production of new plants, of vari-colored animals, and the methods by which one may

materially increase one's household stuff, and whereby
one may be rid of an unwelcome guest. It is not the
book for continuous reading, but few volumes I know
possess its eclectic virtues. For while it was conceived a book of science (and to this day it remains
of interest to the student of scientific history), it is
become a repository of quaint conceits and amusing
experiments. One may learn how to fashion an egg
the size of a man's head by very simple means ; how
to terrify fierce dogs without raising one's hand or
voice ; of how to charm and captivate beautiful
women to whom one would otherwise be repellent.
In a word, it is compact of useless information,
amusingly conveyed, and has now a definite place
among the great, soul-solacing bed books, by means
of which one is enabled with gentle touch to close
the door upon a busy day and open the gates to pleasant
dreams.

No man should be permitted to pass through college without at least some introduction to that great
anonymous German satire, the *Epistolae Obscurorum
Virorum* which, from the time of its issuance in 1514
and 1517, played such an important part in revolt
against scholasticism. No doubt it had been mentioned in my presence in the classroom many times,
but I was far away from the university campus when
a note in a late edition of Erasmus sent me flying to
this amazing collection of letters.

This book, as every scholar knows, belongs on the
shelf with *The Ship of Fools, The Praise of Folly,
Don Quixote,* and the five books of *Gargantua and
Pantagruel.*

The Letters of Obscure Men (to use the English
title), had its origin in the controversy between Johan

Reuchlin, the great German humanist and scholar, and one Joseph (afterward Johann) Pfefferkorn, a Jewish butcher, who, after a brief career as burglar, being ostracized by his own people, turned Christian zealot and joined the persecutors of Israel. Pfefferkorn, under the spell of his new faith, proposed to destroy or suppress all books of Hebrew literature save only the books of the Old Testament, and his ambition was to become the leading agent in this righteous inquisition.

Hatred dominated his actions, though it was hinted that Pfefferkorn knew the wealthier Jews would come forward to redeem their precious manuscripts, and that, profiting by their love of letters, he might thereby greatly enrich himself.

As one might expect, this renegade was shrewd but not scholarly. He won to his following, however, a number of unsuspecting and sincere Christian sympathizers, some of whom, after a fashion, were able to remedy this defect, and, in the effort to arouse popular indignation, a number of books bearing Pfefferkorn's name were circulated throughout Germany. It was held that Ortwin Gratius, head of the Dominican Brotherhood at Cologne, was the editor if not the actual writer of Pfefferkorn's books.

Reuchlin, being a scholar and one of the foremost Orientalists of his age, saw at once that this vulgar uprising might lead to consequences disastrous to European culture, made brave efforts to promote sweet reasonableness, and thus drew down upon his head the rage of the anti-Hebraists. He became the center of the storm and, naturally enough, was suspected of rank heresies. To defend himself from some of the charges brought by his enemies, he published a volume of testimonial letters from notable European scholars and theologians — *Clarorum Virorum Epistolae*. Even so, the rabble were out for blood by now : they deemed Reuchlin the friend of Jewish heresy and possibly Anti-Christ himself. The testimony of scholars was suspect.

Then it was that, seeing his predicament, Reuchlin's friends came to the rescue.

Johan Jäger (known in his published writings as Crotus Rubianus), and Ulrich von Hutten, bold reformers and illustrious scholars, saw an opportunity to laugh these ignorant fanatics out of countenance, and put a stop to the whole mad business. To this end they prepared an elaborate hoax — a series of letters, done in the very doggy Latin characteristic of the Pfefferkorn tracts, and purporting to have been written by that agitator's admirers to Master Ortwin Gratius of the Dominican College. The first volume of these letters appeared in 1515, and they met with such instant success that within two years they were followed by a second.

The letters were scandalous and frank confessions of ignorance, gluttony, drunkenness, fornication, greed, cruelty, prejudice and fanaticism. Not infrequently they embodied either actual quotations from or parodies on the Pfefferkorn books, and always they took pains to overstate the theses of those who were out to throttle the ideas of the Reformation. Ignorance was glorified with reckless abandon : every sensible idea, every good book, was vilified in a shameful fashion. The backsides of vulgar enthusiasts were never more nakedly exposed nor flayed : learned Europe rocked with laughter, and even the unlettered, though they might not understand to the full the implications of these brilliant pasquinades, were quite able to enjoy their Rabelaisian (and the word is here correctly employed) humor, and appreciate the discomfiture of the ill-starred anti-humanists.

That the modern reader may understand at once the cruelty and jocundity of these letters I would direct his attention in particular to those signed by Master Conrad of Zwickau, who tells quaint tales of unholy love, and that of Anton N., wherein he boasts of his proficiency in medicine and poetry, and likewise of his meeting with and attack upon Erasmus. A fragment of the latter will not be amiss.

According to this letter, Anton met Erasmus at a dinner in Strassburg, and after some theological discussion the conversation was turned to poetry. "Our host, therefore, who is a humanist of parts, fell to some discourse on Poetry, and greatly belauded *Julius Caesar*, as touching both his writings and his valorous deeds. So soon as I heard this, I perceived my opportunity, for I had studied much, and learned much under you in the matter of Poetry, when I was at Cologne, and I said, 'Forasmuch as you have begun to speak concerning Poetry, I can therefore no longer hide my light under a bushel, and I roundly aver that I believe not that *Caesar* wrote those *Commentaries*, and I will prove my position with argument following, which runneth thus: Whosoever hath business with arms and is occupied in labour unceasing cannot learn Latin; but *Caesar* was ever at war and in labours manifold; therefore he could not become lettered and get Latin. In truth, therefore, I believe that it was none other than Suetonius who wrote those *Commentaries*, for I have met with none who hath a style liken to *Caesar's* than Suetonius'. Erasmus laughed, but said nothing, for I had overthrown him by the subtilty of my argument."

The editions for collectors to own are those bearing the imprint of Aldus (Venice, 1515), and Von Neuss (Cologne, 1517); both quartos. The first edition to contain both parts, a small duodecimo, was issued at Rome in 1556. But most moderns will rejoice to know of the excellent English translation made by Mr. Francis G. Stokes in 1909, and reprinted in 1925.

The Letters of Obscure Men no longer has the power to evoke angry passions, but the point of its humor has not been lost through the tumbling centuries. And it suggests, painfully perhaps, the notion that a similar book might be a wholesome tonic for this gang-ridden, parasite-infected country of ours. One can easily imagine a series of such letters written by our mayors, congressmen, governors, gangsters, bootleggers, ward heelers, popular parsons, Kukluxers, and others of the ignorant rabble now dominating what Mencken calls the American scene. These would be addressed to some nationally known super-ass, and would embody hysteric confessions of stupidity, ignorance, criminality and incompetence, faithfully characteristic of such swine. I suggest that the subjects of these epistles be dictated by Theodore Dreiser and James Truslow Adams, and that they be written by James Branch Cabell, Henry L. Mencken and Sinclair Lewis. If the task were done with the gusto and thoroughness I conceive possible, these excellent gentlemen might require temporary shelter on more hospitable shores until after the shooting. On their return I believe they would find a country restored of its mental and spiritual costiveness, purged of its evil humors, and ready again to take up the business of joyous living.*

Another book of delectation I was led to purchase from the reading of a marginal note is that best of all guides to fashion, John Bulwer's *Artificial Changeling*, which appeared first in 1650, under the imposing title of *Anthropometamorphosis : Man Transform'd : or, The Artificial Changling Historically presented, in the Mad and cruell Gallantry, foolish Bravery, ridiculous Beauty, filthy finenesse, and loathsome Lovliness of most NATIONS . . . With Figures of those Transfigurations.* To which *artificial and affected Deformations are added, all the Native and Nationall Monstrosities that have appeared to disfigure the Humane Fabrick,* etc.

From its engraved frontispiece (important to collectors), down to the last of its five hundred and fiftysix pages this book is a joy. Its illustrations alone will provide entertainment sufficient for the dullest week-end party, and the text, as Mr. Holbrook Jackson has indicated by placing it at the head of his list of "Bed-books," makes a happy introduction to dreamland. Bulwer wrote it in an age when travel books were eagerly read and when men were as curious as they were credulous, so that fable is freely mixed with fact and men are displayed as they never were, on sea or land.

As I noted above, one should have the edition with engraved frontispiece and illustrations ; I should add

---

* In this connection I cannot refrain from commending the tonic quality of the Kaufman-Ryskind-Gershwin uproarious musical comedy — *Of Thee I Sing.* Every collector should hasten to lay hands on a first edition of this priceless satire.

that the best edition is not the first, but that of 1653, which contains all the additions and frills necessary to the book's full enjoyment.

Then there's Richard Whitlock's *Zootomia, or Observations on the Present Manners of the English.* Whitlock (1616-73) was an Oxford man, a London physician, and author of this one book of essays, published in 1654. *Zootomia* may not be a great book, its style is difficult in spots, the paragraphs interminable, parentheses too numerous, and many of the themes are now without appeal. But there are many delightful passages scattered throughout this tiny book. There is a chapter on women —"Who's the Magnetick Lady?"—that is amusing enough; one on publishers that will bring a smile to any author, even though it does contain an evil judgment upon Rabelais, calling the life of Gargantua an "Ingenious Nothing"; a noble essay on scholars—"Learning's Apology"—and one on books—"The Best Furniture"—that should be included in every bookman's prose anthology. May I say in passing that this little volume in modern times found two valiant champions in Sir William Osler and Mr. Holbrook Jackson, both of whom have obeyed Whitlock's injunction: "Count thy books in the Inventory Jewells, wherein a variety is the most excusable Prodigality, and right use the best Husbandry."

Boswell's *Johnson* has, no doubt, sent many a man to the bookshops, looking for Johann Cohausen's *Hermippus Redivivus,* for therein the great Cham expresses the opinion that this book is "very extraordinary as an account of the Hermetick philosophy, and as furnishing a curious history of the extravagancies of the human mind." Dr. Johnson's advice concerning books is not to be lightly dismissed, and when we find it supplemented by his modern counterpart, Arthur Machen, who, in his *Chapter from Don Quijote*, describes it as "a merry, witty treatise," the matter is settled : the book must be read.

But neither of these sent me to Cohausen. It was this way : a note in Burton turned me to Johann Cornarius, and his book on longevity ; and whilst seeking information about Cornarius I stumbled on the reference to Cohausen. And I have found my copy of this singular old book a choice companion for many otherwise dull hours.

This German physician based his work upon little more than an old Roman epitaph, unearthed sometime during the 17th century, which read, in translation—"Dedicated to Aesculapius and to Health, Clodius Hermippus, who lived 115 years and five days on the breath of little girls, which even after his death astounds physicians no little. Prolong your lives in like fashion, all ye who follow after."

Dr. Cohausen enlarged upon this theme, enriching it with scriptural references to David's experiments with young maids and to prophets who, by their breath, were able to restore the dead ; fortifying it with comments of learned physicians and alchemists, from Galen down to his own century ; and enlivening it by creating a fanciful life for Clodius Hermippus, whom he described as head of an orphanage for little girls.

The sub-title of *Hermippus* sets it forth as "The Sage's triumph over Old Age and the Grave," a happy suggestion that must have stimulated many a middle-aged man to buy. In fact, with no more than the Latin epitaph and his imagination Cohausen made a book so ingenious and diverting that it was eagerly read by thousands, all over Europe, during the 18th century. Drinking breath became a fad, and one physician is said to have left his home and moved into a boarding school to receive benefit from the exhalations of the young!

The idea, briefly, is this : air, breathed into the lungs, partakes of the body humors and salts, and the exhalations of the strong are life-giving : the breath of the healthy young human affords a most potent tonic. Best of all is the breath of young women, especially when they are virgin. If a man would prolong his life to the utmost let him dwell in a chamber beneath which are a company of gay young virgins whose tonic vapors will ascend to him through a vent in the floor. Let him see to it that they play, sing, and dance in that room below, so that they may thus give off of their abundant strength. As a further precaution let him distil their breath and perspirings into a liquid draught : he may then sit at ease and laugh at both age and death.

'Tis a pretty notion, and few men would find it repugnant. But our first enthusiasm is somewhat lessened when we learn that Dr. Cohausen, with full knowledge of this subtle elixir, was able to live but eighty-five years!

Notwithstanding this last melancholy fact, however, *Hermippus* is rare treasure to those who seek amusement, and will prove a source of delight to cynics who hold but little faith in the fads of medicine.

The editions desired by collectors are the octavo published at Frankfurt in 1742 (the first edition), and the first English edition which was translated, edited and enlarged by John Campbell, the Scotch historian, in 1743. I suggest, however, that the second English edition, an octavo published in London, 1749, is the best for reading.

But I might thus run on interminably telling of finds in footnotes, shouting my enthusiasms over Sir John Harrington's *Metamorphosis of Ajax*, in which he preceded Aldous Huxley in some notions of privy proprieties ; and over that other Harrington, James, whose *Oceana* belongs so worthily in the long line of utopian literature reaching from More down to the late Samuel Butler ; or over John Reynolds' masterpiece of compilation, *The Triumph of God's Revenge against the Crying and execrable sin of Murther*, which, written to edify and warn, has now become a book of giggles, able to brighten the dreariest day (and do be sure to lay hold of the 1679 edition, which contains also Reynolds' ten histories of adultery : the illustrations are better than any modern comic strip). And I should commend to American collectors the pleasure of gathering the works of Julius Caesar Scaliger and Joseph Scaliger, two men who, next to Erasmus and Rabelais, were most important light bearers in a most interesting age. These books are not expensive, and they are laden with wit, learning and wisdom.

These that I have named, and more, have come to me by way of obscure references, and have proved their worth. I have not gone into obscurity for its own sake, and the mere fact of rarity has meant little or nothing in my library. But there are collectors who scorn to seek any but the abidingly famous books of the ancient days. Now a fifteenth century book is an incunable — magic word to most — they argue ; an item from a famous press is a mile-stone in the art of printing; and for the rest one should collect famous names, meaning by that, names undimmed by time. Well, to all that I have but little to reply. I collect books for their inherent interest, for comfort, companionship, joy. Only a few of the incunables possess that interest — a first Aldine Homer, or the *Hypnerotomachia* of Francesco Colonna; most are but respectable monuments of dead theologies, worthy of preservation in museums, but thoroughly uncomfortable intruders in one's private library. Even though one's object in collecting be but to preserve great treasures for the future, it would seem that human interest and history might outweigh mere scarcity. For my part, give me the works of the fighters, the wits, the scholars, who, though their names may have been clouded over with the centuries, are yet charged with their original gusto, and bear with them the rare flavors of a bygone but doughty age.

This brings me to the most exciting of all my footnote treasures — the works of Jerome Cardan, the sixteenth-century scholar-physician. Cardan opens a wide and entrancing field to the collector, with books on mathematics, medicine, music, astrology, gaming, ethics, natural history, physics and inventions. The books, dating from 1536 down to 1663, are numerous, but not especially difficult to obtain, if one be willing to spend a little time reading German and Swiss catalogues : they are not expensive.

It is just as well to admit, concerning these books, that their chief present merit lies in what they reveal of Cardan's life and the manners of his time. This requires elaboration : Cardan's life is of such exceptional interest that a separate chapter is demanded.

V

JEROME CARDAN AND *THE "GOLDEN COMPLEX"*

"Of all those curious volumes that I have patiently collected, let me but keep the works of that old Milanese physician, Jerome Cardan, whose droll comments on books and life will forever fortify me against attacks of boredom."

— *J. A. Plaudron*

V

JEROME CARDAN, and THE "GOLDEN COMPLEX"

WHAT malapert imp of perversity and affectation inspires a man to write about Jerome Cardan in this 20th century? It seems to me that I overhear the reader muttering something like that : or is it merely a vexed, "Who was the fellow?" Well, I shall plunge at once into a catalogue of his accomplishments,— for the life of this forgotten scholar is well-nigh as strange as that of Benvenuto Cellini.

One of the most famous and fashionable physicians of sixteenth-century Europe ; friend of Alciati, the jurist, and Vesalius, the first scientific anatomist ; patronized by archbishops, cardinals, popes, princes and kings ; writer, according to his own reckoning, of more than a hundred printed books, read all over Europe, and passing into as many pirated as authorized editions during his lifetime ; a celebrated mathematician, remembered in history as the first man to expound cubic equations ; widely known and often consulted as astrologer — an astrologer bold enough to have drawn the horoscope of Jesus Christ, and so prejudiced that he changed the date of Luther's birth, in a published nativity, to make the reading justify his own ill opinion ; a poet ; philosopher of sorts, whose book on *Consolation* was read to advantage by Shakespeare ; inventor of a machine for sifting flour, and of engines to raise sunken ships ; one of the first, if not the first, to suggest teaching sign-language to the deaf, and possibly the first to point out the practicability of using rocket power for aviation ; musician and writer on music ; a physicist of no mean ability ; a naturalist who had a prevision of the theory of evolution ; a man who gave profound advice and behaved with reckless folly ; a neurotic who dreamed curious dreams and saw strange visions ; professor at three great European universities ; a loving and loved husband ; a kind father, who failed miserably in the rearing of his sons, and did not hesitate to lop off an ear to emphasize his displeasure ; a man who made fortunes, and then turned about and gambled them away ; generous to a fault, loyal to his friends, dignified in the treatment of his enemies, heralded by the scholars of the world, Jerome Cardan should have died a happy man. Instead he died demented and miserable. For he was a bastard.

I repeat the disagreeable sentence : he was a bastard. But why should one thus underscore so unfortunate a circumstance ? Have not scores of the most noble and notable men of all time been products of a so-called illegitimate union ? Have not even the gods been open to suspicion in this particular ? Would not the word "love-child" be more appropriate, seeing that many "illegitimates" of the year 1500 grew up in high favor, and rose to positions of honor ? But stay a moment. There is a reason for all this pother. "Love-child," both sloppy and misleading, definitely indicates, law or no law, church or not, one conceived and born of love. Cardan was not so fortunate. And the word bastard — a pack-saddle child — used as an epithet in our tongue since the

13th century, suggests one unwelcome to his parents and an object of ridicule among his fellows.

The principal reason for emphasizing this ugly circumstance is that one Gabriel Naude (1600-1653) once wrote a biographical introduction to the collected works of Cardan, which, ever since its publication, has been a source of misunderstanding and misinformation. He did not understand the reason why Jerome Cardan was bitter, suspicious, aggressive, so ambitious that he neglected those he loved, and so, given to self-castigation. He had not the understanding of what we now call "compensation," or of the much misused "inferiority complex." And no man can understand the life of Cardan without keeping in mind the fact that he was a bastard.

Jerome Cardan was born at Pavia on the 24th of September, 1501. His mother, Chiara Micheria, was a short, fat, hot-tempered widow in the middle thirties, hysterical and given to tantrums. She came of an intelligent family, however, and Jerome relates that his maternal grandfather was an excellent mathematician. His father, Fazio, a doctor of both law and medicine, was an attorney with a considerable if not very remunerative practice. At the time of Jerome's birth he was 56 years of age, already old, and, like his mistress, possessed of a violent temper. On his bald head he was accustomed to wear a cap, less for warmth than as protection for a tender spot left by a surgeon's saw. Despite his unattractive appearance (or perhaps because of it), he was a man of superior intelligence, a mathematician of standing, and, many years before the birth of his son, he had edited, greatly to his renown, Archbishop John Peckham's *Perspectiva Communis,* a work on optics highly

prized by scholars of that period. From both father
and mother Jerome inherited a tough constitution and
a predisposition to long life.

How long the widow Micheria (her maiden name :
her husband's name was Antonio Alberio) and her ancient lover had been meeting is unknown, but when she
found herself pregnant it is recorded that she made
use of all the herbal lore known to gossips and mid-
wives to rid herself of the embarrassment. But drugs
were powerless : Jerome was determined to be born,
and, in the final effort, belabored his mother for three
agonizing days to the end that he might see the light
of day.

Undesired, the infant came into a world stricken
with plague : his nurse, during the first month of his
life, fell victim and died within a day. His mother
would not be burdened with the unlucky child, but
one of his father's friends, Isidore di Resta of Ticino,
standing godfather, assumed the responsibility, and,
under his direction, it was placed in the keeping of
another nurse. By the time Cardan was four he had
been put out to three foster-mothers in as many different places, and, owing no doubt to unsanitary surroundings, had all the known ailments to which children of
the 16th century fell heir.

When Cardan had passed his fourth birthday, his
parents were living together in Milan, and the child
was taken "home" to meet his father, hear quarrels,
receive cuffs and to be tormented by the scornful gibes
of his playmates.

His father being a lawyer who had to spend, in the
round of his duties, a good part of his days in walking
about the city, a use was found for Jerome, and at
seven he was given the task of carrying his father's

bag, or, as we would say, brief case, stuffed with books and papers. The following year he fell ill with dysentery, and, as he seemed on the verge of dying, his father, in addition to calling a physician, dedicated his son to the blessed Saint Jerome, on the strict understanding that, granting his recovery, he should be named in honor of the friendly saint. Thus, at the age of eight, the boy received a Christian name. He was not, however, strong enough to resume his duties as the lawyer's lackey for two years.

Jerome's parents were given to shifting. They moved from one shabby dwelling to another, and Chiara's sister, Margaret, accompanied them. Sometimes old Fazio lived with them ; frequently he betook himself to other quarters. Neither of the parents seem to have cared for the boy until his eighth year. Margaret scolded and slapped him when he was indoors : when he went abroad boys informed him, amid jeers, that his mother was a "whore."

Here, then, is the background for a subjective life. Reality is hell : dreams provide escape. The physical is a burden : imagination affords relief. Outwardly thwarted by man and nature, without any token of affection, the world within offers a haven and a home. Mankind wars against him : he seeks a world at peace. In later life he wrote (in his autobiography — *De Vita Propria*, chapter 37): "By command of my father I used to lie abed until nine o'clock, and if perchance I lay awake any time before the wonted hour of rising, it was my habit to spend the same by conjuring up to sight all sorts of pleasant visions, nor can I remember that I ever summoned these in vain. . . I beheld the shapes of castles and houses, of horses and riders, of plants, trees, musical instruments, theatres. . . In all this I took no small delight, and with straining eyes I would gaze upon all these marvels."

But as he grew older other means of escape were provided. Seeing that his child had an active mind, Fazio taught him to read and write, introduced him to arithmetic, geometry and astrology, and, perforce, enabled him to speak Latin. Latin was then the universal language. In it the Europe of scholars was a single state, and with it all the secrets of mankind could be discovered. With mathematics he held a key to another kind of speculation, and, while yet in his teens, he wrote a book called *The True Distances of Objects*, teaching a method of calculating the distances of the stars. Nor was this his only essay in authorship at this early period. Already, shocked by the death of a young kinsman, he had written a little tract on *The Earning of Immortality*. These creations of his boyhood were never published, but another book, written about that time, was later revised, and has been preserved among his collected works. It is a volume devoted to games of chance. Despised and neglected, it is not surprising that the youth of eighteen was uncontent with abstract dreams, and what with his mathematical bent and his need of money it was only natural that he speculate on the laws of probability, and put his theory to practice at the gaming table. The book was published under the title *Liber de Ludo Aleæ*, and gave evidence that Cardan was a youth of more than usual mathematical ability.

Even his mother began to be interested in the precocious youngster. She was shrewd enough to realize that if Jerome should live to manhood he would never be able to wrest a living from the earth with his hands. He must have a profession or become a burden.   Fazio had already passed his threescore and ten, and poverty was something to guard against. Observing the boy's fondness for music, she had him take lessons in secret, and she insisted that he receive a formal education.   At last his father agreed, and, at the age of nineteen he left Milan for the University of Pavia.

Away from home, and in an atmosphere of books and speculation, he knew happiness for the first time. He was free to do as he liked, and was beyond the hearing of domestic brawls.   At Pavia he attended his classes, walked about the countryside, fished, kept up his music, and divided his evenings between books and dice.   That he was an exceptional student is shown by the fact that during his second year he was made instructor in geometry, gave some lectures in dialectics, and, during the absence of one of his professors for a short time, took over a class in philosophy.

In those days of quarrels between Charles V. and Francis I., scholastic life was liable to interruptions, and, at the end of his second year, the doors were closed to study, and Jerome returned to Milan.   It was now time for him to choose a profession, and Fazio, who had a lectureship in law at Milan, thought it best for his son to succeed him.   Jerome did not agree.   His father seemed to him no outstanding success, and days spent in carrying a bag of books about Milan had not given him a love of law.   Medicine was fitter for a philosopher.   His father fumed and made great speeches, but the son was adamant, and Fazio at last surrendered.   Pavia remaining closed, the young man now took up his studies at Padua, where, nearly a hundred years later, Galileo announced his great discoveries.

In 1524 the University of Padua was in almost as sorry a plight as that at Pavia. It was in sad need of funds. However, its doors were kept open, and though the times were trying, Cardan was enabled to receive as sound instruction there as could have been had at any institution in Italy. The professor of medicine, Matthew Curtius, took a keen interest in Jerome and even debated with him in public, an event which was considered an especial honor. And Jerome made friends. Gaspardo Gallearto, Ambrose Vardeus and Ottaviano Scoto were the most intimate of his companions, the last-named afterwards becoming his first publisher.

In the year 1525 old Fazio breathed his last. He had been too careless with his money, lending freely to his friends and never exacting interest, and thus his estate, while enabling the widow to live in comparative comfort, left little room for luxury. Moreover, his accounts were in such a state as to provoke years of litigation before his heirs could recover what was due them. Fazio had been more thoughtful of his son during his latter days, and had endeavored to atone for his years of negligence, winning thereby, for the first time, Jerome's affection. Jerome had insisted on remaining with the old man during his last illness, but Fazio would not hear of it : the business of education was of supreme importance, and the young man must get back to the university at once.

After his father's death, Jerome succumbed to a great temptation. Padua was without a Rector. The office had been vacant for nine or ten years on account of poverty. The occupant of that office was supposed to overlook the government of the university and to settle disputes Actually, his duties were performed by a pro-rector, and he merely strutted about in finery, presided at ceremonials, and gave costly dinners. Under the circumstances no one could be found who would accept the office. Here was an opportunity. Cardan now had a little money. He had never had position. The office was elective, and, from all accounts, any man who would provide dinners for the hungry officials, though they might despise the donor, would be assured of their votes. Cardan, ill-fitted for the post though he was, sought and received the costly honor, and his mother, now looking to this ugly duckling for future support, was willing to make every sacrifice for his advancement. Thus, within a few months after his father's death, Jerome Cardan became Rector of the University of Padua, though it seems that he never received the honors that usually accompanied that office. He had, however, a position of which he might well boast to his scornful neighbors at Milan, and with such sums of money as were sent by Chiara, supplemented by his winnings at the card table, he lived what he afterwards termed a "Sarda-napalan life." At the university it was certainly deemed an empty honor, and his occupance of office was not held to his credit when he came to receive his doctor's degree in 1526. He was rejected twice before obtaining the degree. The ghost of the past rose against him. Elected to the degree by ballot, the officers forgot his dinners and remembered the disgrace of his birth, his disagreeable manners and his persistency. The last-named, however, proved too much for the faculty, and at length, at the age of twenty-five, he was given his diploma.

It is now time to consider the appearance of this young man.

In his autobiography (*De Vita Propria*) and in a work on horoscopes (*Geniturarum Exemplar*) he has left self-portraits that are sufficiently unflattering. He declares that he was small of stature, narrow-chested, lean and gouty. His complexion was fair, hair yellow, head bald, and temples massive ; a yellow beard fringed his chin. There was a scar on his forehead, his eyes were small, blue-grey, and short-sighted (his left eye watered), his lower lip was pendulous, and his teeth were large. His voice was harsh and loud, his speech difficult to make out, and he was rude in manner. He wore his clothes badly, walked awkwardly, and his skin was covered with irruptions. He tells us that he suffered with "two attacks of the plague, agues, tertian and quotidian, malignant ulcers, haemorrhoids, varicose veins, palpitation of the heart, gout, indigestion, itch, and foulness of skin." To this self-portrait he adds many other details of a disgusting nature.

It is not an attractive picture, and, judging by contemporary portraits that have come down to us, it is only true in parts. Throughout his works he never loses an opportunity to confess contempt for both his personal appearance and his habits. One of these habits, attested by contemporaries, seems to have been that of beating himself with a stick whenas he felt undeservedly comfortable. And that should afford us a clue. The one virtue to which he lays claim is his love of truth. Again and again we find him expressing his hatred of lies, and declaring that he had never told a lie. Naude, his early biographer, accepts Cardan's abusive self-portrait, and feigns belief in all the ugly self-accusations : but when Cardan makes the claim that he was truthful, Naude says that he lies ! Naude was quick to believe confessions of guilt, but reluctant to credit innocence, even in the face of evidence.

Is it not clear that Cardan's unhappy childhood had driven him to an unhealthy introspection and self-interest? He is not handsome and that fact torments him more than it would a youth with a normal background. Therefore he anticipates criticism, and takes malicious satisfaction in exaggerating his own defects : he makes himself a very monster! "In the whole *corpus* of autobiographic literature," says Mr. W. G. Waters, "there does not exist a volume in which the work of self-dissection has been so ruthlessly and completely undertaken and executed as in Cardan's memoirs."

He is rejected and despised, therefore the young man will call himself names a thousandfold worse than any that his enemies have invented! However, allowing for this, it is well to remember that Jerome was not prepossessing in appearance, and was thereby greatly dissatisfied with himself.

But let us record another unhappy fact : from 1521 until 1531, that is to say, from his twentieth until his thirtieth year, he was impotent.

This physical incapacity seems to have had its origin in mental rather than physical causes. There is no evidence to show that he had acquired any venereal infection. His own love of cataloguing his ailments, his penchant for vilifying himself, his interest in medicine, would have made him confess or even boast of any such malady. The suddenness with which the misfortune passed away makes one sure that its occasion was fear (*De Utilitate ex adversis Capienda, & de Libriis Propriis*).

Speaking of it in another place he said : "I hold

that this misfortune was to me the worst of evils. Compared with it neither the harsh servitude under my father, nor unkindness, nor the sorrows of litigation, nor the wrongs done me by my fellow-citizens, nor the scorn of my fellow-physicians, nor the ill things falsely spoken against me, nor all the infinite mass of possible evil, could have brought me to such despair, and hatred of life, and distaste of all pleasure, and such lasting grief. I bitterly wept . . . that I must needs be a laughing-stock, that marriage must be denied me, and that I must ever live in solitude. You ask for the cause of this misfortune, a matter which I am quite unable to explain. For the reasons just mentioned, and because I dreaded that men should know how grave was the ill afflicting me, I shunned the society of women ; and on account of this habit, the same miserable public scandal which I desired so earnestly to avoid, arose concerning me, and brought upon me the suspicion of still more nefarious practices." (*De Utilitate* ; Frankfort, 1648 : p. 235.)

One may consider Cardan's misfortune as an effect of a miserable childhood in which his sense of confidence was undermined, or as a contributing cause, in its turn, of his subsequent rudeness and brooding suspicion against the world.

Whatever may have been its cause, the disability departed in an instant, and in 1531, having obtained his degree and found an opportunity for practising medicine at the village of Sacco, he met and married Lucia Bandarini, daughter of a captain of the Venetian levies in that district.

The residence at Sacco was not altogether fortunate. He would have preferred to return to Milan, but that city was besieged by plague, and starvation, as well as threatened by wars, and was out of the question. There was an opening at Sacco (about ten miles from Padua and twenty-five from Venice), and through the good offices of Francisco Buonafede, professor of the theory of medicine at Padua, the post was secured, and there he began his residence on September 24, 1526. The practice was small, and Cardan supplemented his slender income by his gambling. There too he continued his extravagance, indulging himself in rare books, fine pens and expensive paper, music, dinners, fishing, and, in the stead of practice, writing books.

As a result of his gambling habits he had abundant opportunity to become thoroughly acquainted with the hazardous side of life more than once, and in his *Vita Propria* he relates that on one of his excursions to Venice, playing at the home of a certain nobleman, he observed that the gentleman was using marked cards. Cardan had been losing to this man for two days, and when he detected the fraud practised upon him he drew his dagger and struck the man in the face, held up his two servants, and took back his money and other properties of which he had been defrauded, and left the house. The wounded gentleman either felt himself in the wrong, or was possessed of an amiable Christian spirit, for Cardan relates that on the same day, in the evening, walking about the streets, he fell into a canal, and that the man he had injured (probably Thomas Lezun, a patrician), rescued him from his plight, took him to his home, and gave him dry clothing.

Well-nigh every event in Cardan's life was preceded, he tells us, by an omen or a dream. He would have been a joy to a psychoanalyst. Was there a wasp in the room, a cow on the street, a bird on the roof, a dream in the night, or did a tile fall into the street, then Cardan read a prophecy. Shortly after the miraculous restoration of his manhood, he dreamed of a pretty woman dressed in white. He thought she was standing in the forecourt of a garden. He embraced her tenderly ; then came a gardener who closed the gate and shut them out. A little while afterward he met the double of this dream-girl in Lucia Bandarini. Just prior to the wedding a dog howled and a raven croaked upon the roof ! That, thought he in later years, was a warning, telling him of the fate of his sons.

In his *De Varietate* he informs us that he had four gifts : the power to pass at will into a sort of ecstasy, in which state he could hear but faintly the sound of voices, and in which his soul seemed to leave his body ; the second gift was the power to conjure up any image that he liked before his eyes ; third, that he never failed to be warned in dreams of that which was about to happen to him ; the fourth, that coming events were portended by spots on his nails, black spots of the middle finger being signs of evil, white spots portending good.

Despite the ravens and the howling of the dog, his marriage with Lucia seems to have been reasonably happy, though their married life coincided with Cardan's period of greatest poverty. There was but little practice at Sacco, and household bills were either met by his wife's parents or paid by money from the gambler's table. It must not be thought, however, that Cardan was wholly idle during these years. He was always writing, and usually on a number of books at once. Two of the works done at Sacco were later enlarged and published : one was his treatise on *Cheiromancy* and the other was a book on *Differences Amongst the Doctors.* The first represents to us his superstition ; the second was concerned with the history of his profession, telling of Hippocrates, and Galen, Avicenna, Ætius and Oribasius, their contradictions and their widely differing methods. Mr. Morley, commenting on this work, is inclined to think that Cardan liked to compare his life and work with that of Galen, and that he may have shaped his own career after the pattern Galenic. From the point of view of moderns the work is worthless, but it is interesting to note that in that day of authority, Cardan proposed, in balancing the judgments of great physicians, to be guided by reason rather than by authority. One may call to mind that the reasoned theories of that day were oftentimes little better than the authorities. Scientific anatomy and experimental medicine were yet unborn : it required Harvey to set medicine on the right path, and Andrew Vesalius, while he was later to become Cardan's friend, had not yet shown the physicians the right way to study the human body.

Sacco had provided Cardan with a wife, but it did not yield a living : and Jerome was ambitious. Milan was a great city. True, it was the city of his unhappy childhood. There his father had lived and was buried ; there his mother still had her dwelling ; and there, because of his early humiliations, he wished to make himself into a famous man. In 1529, three years after his settlement at Sacco, he had been summoned to his mother, and while at home had endeavored to obtain an opening. To do that, however, it was necessary to be admitted to the Milanese College of Physicians. A physician, without the sanction of this body, was not permitted to take fees within Milanese territory, nor allowed to teach in the university. And this body of respectable men, recalling the fact that Cardan was a bastard, refused him admission. Following immediately upon the heels of this rejection, Cardan fell ill and for seven months lay at his mother's home, unable to do aught. Back again at Sacco, conditions remained the same. There was not room in Sacco for so great a man, and there was no means of living in comfort. Surely the college at Milan could not persist forever in its cruel attitude ; and in 1532 Cardan once more returned to Milan, and once again the Milanese turned their faces against him. Lack of food, torn nerves, uncertainty, brought both husband and wife to desperate straits. Cardan was on the verge of prostration, and his wife suffered two miscarriages.

Milan being out of the question, the harassed couple cast about to find another location. A cousin, Giacomo Cardan, advised them to move to the town of Gallarate, little more than a score of miles to the northwest. This town had a certain attraction for Cardan, for the reason that the home of the noble Castillione family was near by, and the Cardans claimed relationship to them. Jerome later discovered that his family had erred in this assumption, and made public acknowledgement of the error ; but at that time he believed what his people had told him. At Gallarate, then, he might claim noble blood, and be held in honor for his connections. There were other considerations : the health-giving air needed by convalescents ; the possibility of a good practice, and the low cost of living. These were the inducements that brought about the change.

CARDAN, AND THE "GOLDEN COMPLEX"

The facts of Cardan's life at Gallarate are : that during the nineteen months of his residence there were scarcely any patients, and there was no money with which to take advantage of the cheaper living rate. He made, in fact, but twenty-five crowns during his entire stay, and the better part of that was received from Filippo Archinto, a young nobleman (later Archbishop of Milan), who had aspirations to be considered an astronomer. For him Cardan did some hack work that kept the wolf away, and, what was more important, gained a friend who shortly after became a valuable patron. To add to this sorry state of things, his first child, Gianbatista, was born, and Jerome's efforts to meet the added burden at the gaming board were so disastrous that he was compelled to pawn his wife's jewels. It was fitting that at this time Cardan began his treatise on *Fate*.

Once more the unhappy man, now with three mouths to feed, returned to Milan. Perhaps he felt his mother would come to his rescue. But the estate was not yet settled, and neither son nor mother could have what old Fazio had left for their comfort. And Chiara did not welcome her son : the three unfortunates had no recourse but the workhouse. He had now reached the depths. There was no room to fall. Therefore he began to rise.

Archinto was his friend, and through his efforts Cardan was given an occasional lectureship in mathematics. A little later, through the same Archinto, Cardan received the appointment as physician to a body of Augustin Friars. The two positions together yielded about fifty crowns a year, and by the rigid economies practised by his brave wife, he was enabled to live and write. Cardan had no right to solicit patients in Milan, but being a graduate of a great university, his appointment to a private post could not easily be prevented. Now the Prior of this Order, one Francesco Gaddi, belonged to a famous and powerful family : and he had long been ill of a disease that had baffled the best physicians of the city. Here, then, was Cardan's opportunity. The holy man despaired of his life, but was willing to let the young physician make trial of his skill. And Cardan met with his first success of note. Within six months, Gaddi was well and proclaiming the physician's ability. The praises of the Prior, however, were set at naught by the criticisms of the fashionable doctors of the College ; for, said they, how can this man be a good physician who spends his time on a poor lectureship in mathematics, astronomy, geography and architecture ? He is but a trifler.

Thereupon Cardan took up the cudgels. Shutting himself within his study for a fortnight, he wrote, more inspired by heat than light, a little book called *Mal Practice Current Amongst Physicians in Milan.* And at this juncture he bethought him of his old friend Ottaviano Scoto, now a printer at Venice, and to him he sent his manuscript. Scoto thought the book would probably be a financial failure, but in the hope that it might lend aid to his friend's cause, issued the work in 1536, and such was the eagerness of the author, that the printer was its sole proof-reader. As a result of so much haste, Cardan tells us that the volume contained over three hundred blunders, aside from misprints. And this from the ambitious young man who had hoped to point out no less than seventy-two errors in current medical practice ! The book, contrary to the expectations of author and printer, was a financial success, and was widely read ; but it brought its author little practice and much mortification. "Where I sought for honor, I found but shame," was Cardan's comment in later years. The medical men were infuriated.

One possible reason for the rage of the physicians might be found in the author's insistence that no drugs at all was a better rule than too many drugs. When, therefore, Cardan next applied for admission to the Milanese College, in 1537, that respectable body took great satisfaction in rejecting his application.

In the midst of misfortune there were some reassurances. The University of Pavia invited her former student to take the chair of medicine, and while the salary accompanying the position was so slight that Cardan was compelled to refuse the honor, the consideration must have given him no small satisfaction. At this time also there came to him for guidance, a very clever student, Lodovici Ferrari, with whom he was to accomplish his best work in mathematics, and who was to become his devoted disciple.

Cardan was keenly sensitive to the fact that he had blundered in his first published work, that he was pointed out as a mere tyro. He wanted to become famous ; to dazzle his enemies, and compel respect. Most, if not all, his literary efforts had been to this end. His enemies had admitted that he was a mathematician : very well, he would show them that he was a great mathematician by publishing the world's best treatise on arithmetic ; more than that, he would, when he got the opportunity, exercise such caution and wisdom with his patients that he would become known as a reliable doctor of medicine. And then came the opportunities.

First there was a druggist, Donato Lanza, who for many years had been spitting blood. Physicians had treated him in vain. He turned to Cardan. Cardan pronounced it a case of what was roughly called "consumption," and so treated his patient that he gained in weight and was so improved in appearance that all believed him cured. This "cure" caused much talk in Milan, and other consumptives were brought to the physician with similar results. Lanza was grateful and sang his doctor's praises in the ear of Francesco Sfondrato, a nobleman, senator, and member of the Emperor's privy council. This gentleman's eldest son was seized with convulsions, and appeared to be in a hopeless condition. Acting upon Lanza's suggestion, Sfondrato summoned Cardan, whose treatment resulted in a complete cure. A little while afterward, the senator's infant son was similarly afflicted and was being treated by the famous Milanese physician Luca della Croce, the procurator of the College of Physicians. As the child was in a serious condition, Croce insisted on consulting with another physician, Ambrogio Cavenago. Sfondrato agreed, but demanded that Cardan also be called.

Here, indeed, was a dramatic situation : the unrecognized and despised physician in competition with two of his leading critics. After Doctor Croce had uttered some prefatory remarks about the solemnity of death, Cardan made a diagnosis : "Do you not see that the child is suffering from Opisthotonos ?", he demanded, and, seeing their astonishment, he pointed out the evident symptoms, making learned quotations from Hippocrates. His colleagues were compelled to agree, distasteful as it was, but they stubbornly withheld congratulations, maintaining that they could speak no word in favor of a man whom the College looked upon with disfavor. Cardan applied his remedies, spoke tactfully about his fellow physicians, and when, two weeks later, the child had fully recovered, Senator Sfondrato, convinced that Cardan was a victim of spite, used his powerful position to force the College to admit him to membership. In this effort other distinguished men now joined, and in 1539, twelve years after his graduation in medicine, Cardan was grudgingly admitted to the learned body and permitted to engage in regular practice.

The clouds were lifting, and Cardan, anxious to profit by the improved status, now hastened the completion of his work on *The Practice of Arithmetic*, which was published at Milan shortly following his triumph. He was now thirty-eight years of age, poor, a failure in his profession, and yet he had found the time to write thirty-four unpublished books. To attain the fame he required he must bring these to the attention of the learned world. On the title page of his new *Arithmetic* he placed a likeness of himself, with the motto : "No man is a prophet in his own country" : at the end he caused to be printed a proclamation of Charles the Fifth, giving out that Cardan had applied for and received protection for all his unpublished books, covering a period of ten years. This was accompanied by a list of Cardan's works. An excellent stroke of publicity it proved to be.

The Practice of Arithmetic was read all over Europe, and Cardan was justly praised for having written the best work of its kind then extant. Learned men were eager to hear more of the new luminary. Andreas Osiander, the scholar, and Joannes Petreius the printer, both of Nuremberg, were the first to apply for permission to edit and publish the neglected genius. Cardan's fame was assured. From the year 1539 until the end of his days, though he was often impoverished, sometimes in disgrace, sometimes suspected of heresies, and sometimes bowed down in bitter grief, the physician was in demand by royalty and the Holy See, and the scholar was read and welcomed from Rome to the Low Countries, and from Austria to Scotland. The bastard had begun to take his revenge.

If I have dwelt at length upon the details of Cardan's early life it has been done in the hope of pointing out the principal sources of his bitterness, the distrust he showed toward his colleagues, his avidity for public recognition, and his notorious ill manners. Reading his life it seems clear that some of his outstanding virtues and most of his vices were but the outgrowth of a miserable childhood and of an extreme social hostility.

We come now to the principal charge against his integrity.

In the 16th century public mathematical bouts were as common in Italy as were the theological debates of our New England forefathers. Itinerant professors of the art passed from town to town challenging all comers to solve what problems they might propound, and offering to untangle any knotty puzzles that the local pretenders could devise. To stimulate an interest already keen, prizes were awarded the victor.

It should be noted that algebraic study in 1536 was little more advanced than in the days of its inventor, Mahommed-ben-Musa, in the 9th century. The first algebra to be printed was that of Fra Luca de

Burgo in 1494, and it was but a slight elaboration of what the Arab had evolved seven hundred years before. Then, in 1505, Scipio Ferreo, a professor at Bologna, stumbled upon a rule for the solution of a compound cubic equation. New fields were now opened, and every mathematician was an excited explorer. In November, 1536, there came to Milan one Giovanni Colla, a Brescian, skilled in the art and filled with new news. It seemed that the great Ferreo had a pupil, Antonio Maria Fiore, well acquainted with his master's secret and qualified to demonstrate his skill before the public. This Fiore was to hold dispute with Niccolo Tartaglia, a self-taught, boasting, rough fellow, whose manners made him a match for Cardan.

Colla's story moved Cardan tremendously, and he was eager to hear the outcome of the contest. He was writing his *Arithmetic*, but that did not preclude a lively interest in the more advanced art, the elements of which were treated in his own book. So that when word came that Tartaglia had not only triumphed over Ferreo's pupil, but had discovered a method of solving two additional cases of cubic equations — all in the space of two hours —, the Milanese physician knew that he could never rest until he too understood Tartaglia's art. Quite naturally he hoped that Tartaglia would publish his discovery to the world.

But Tartaglia knew no Latin, could use only one of the Italian dialects, and was busied in writing a book on artillery. It was not likely that he would soon reveal his methods to the world. Cardan waited four years, and then, through Juan Antonia, a bookseller, he applied to the Brescian for the rules whereby he had defeated Fiore. Cardan assured Tartaglia that if he would but let him know his method, that he in turn would publish it to the world, giving full credit to the inventor. Tartaglia replied that he would publish himself when he was ready to do so.

This reply threw Cardan into a rage, and he wrote an abusive letter, little calculated to soften Tartaglia's heart.

This is not the place to enter into the details of a long correspondence, during the course of which Cardan turned from rudeness to diplomacy in order to ferret out the inventor's secret. Suffice it to say that Cardan at last hit upon a way of taming the Brescian lion.

The Governor of Milan, in those days, the Marchese d'Avalos, was a soldier and patron of learning, and to him Cardan presented a copy of Tartaglia's book on Artillery, together with plans for certain instruments to be used in the control of these new engines of war, all to the end that the Marchese might assist the inventor in his ambitions. Should this succeed, Tartaglia would be under obligation to Cardan, and gratitude might prompt him to share the results of his discovery. As matters fell out, d'Avalos was interested in Tartaglia, and, through Cardan, sent word to him that he should be pleased to meet him in Milan. Cardan added a clause to this invitation, insisting that Tartaglia accept the hospitality of his home while about his errand.

Tartaglia was uneasy. Greatly did he desire the patronage of the Governor : but he disliked being under any obligation to the insistent Cardan. Hope, however, conquered fear, and in March, 1539, he was for three days a guest at Cardan's home : before he left he had parted with his secret, and Cardan with his honor.

During those days in Milan, Tartaglia explained his reluctance about this matter on the ground that Cardan was preparing a book on Arithmetic, and he feared that his rules might therein be published. Cardan swore that if Tartaglia so desired he would not publish them at all. Tartaglia answered that he did not believe him. Thereupon Cardan looked him in the eye and solemnly declared : "I swear to you by the sacred Evangel, and by myself as a gentleman, that I will not only abstain from publishing your discoveries — if you will make them known to me — but that I will promise and pledge my faith of a true Christian to set them down for my own use in cypher, so that after my death no one may be able to understand them."

Despite the fact that Tartaglia must have known that the oaths of Christian gentlemen were not always as binding as they ought to be, he now felt obliged to lay bare the secret which he had embodied in twenty-five lines of mnemonic verse. These he wrote down and handed to Cardan just before his departure. From that moment he knew no peace : he began to be tormented with regrets, and shortly afterward began a long and abusive correspondence with the man who now shared his precious secret. He accused Cardan of putting his rules in the *Arithmetic* : Cardan sent him a copy as soon as it was off the press to show that he had kept the faith. Tartaglia, refusing to be placated (perhaps enraged by finding his suspicion unfounded), declared that the *Arithmetic* was full of errors. In fact his letters were of such a nature that one marvels at Cardan's patience.

Cardan refrained from publishing the Tartaglian rules for six years, working upon them the while with his pupil Ferrari and advancing the knowledge of cubic equations far beyond the point achieved by his rival. In 1540 Giovanni Colla returned to Milan and propounded to the algebraists of that city some equations which baffled all save Cardan's brilliant pupil Ferrari, who, in solving one of the problems, discovered a general rule for the solution of all bi-quadratics by means of a cubic equation, and for five years following, pupil and master were ceaselessly engaged upon what was to be known over all the civilized world as the *Book of the Great Art*. It was published in Nuremberg in 1545, and was received with great acclaim.

Tartaglia's rules, greatly amplified and perfected, were there, but he was given full credit. Of course he was furious. He had, no doubt, a right to his indignation. Still, if he had occupied the six years between 1539 and 1545 in expounding his precious secret instead of writing insulting letters to the industrious Cardan, it might have worked to his greater glory. Ethically, neither of the gentlemen is deserving of great praise for noble conduct. Tartaglia behaved as an ill-bred, selfish child : Cardan as an impertinent, modern journalist. It may be held that Cardan, in thus violating his oath, did no more than the prelates and princes of his generation were doing daily. That is quite true. His conduct was no exception to the rule then prevalent among "Christian gentlemen." It may be further urged that since Cardan's book "raised the study of algebra to a point it had never reached before," that the end justified the means. It is possible that if Tartaglia had been reasonable at the outset ; if he had offered to work with Cardan — seeing that he wrote with difficulty, and under severe limitations, such a collaboration would have been to his advantage — Cardan, in turn, would have acted more honorably.

Cardan seems to have reasoned that it was far more important that the world have information than that he should quibble over a point of honor. The fact is that Cardan was determined to be famous. Nothing must stand in the way of his rise. Always he had been opposed, spit upon, cast out. The intellectual was the only world that offered hospitality and comfort. That world he would enjoy and exploit, and, seeing that both gentlemen and scholars had shown him scant courtesy, he felt little need of a gentleman's code or a scholar's conscience.

Whatever his moral standing, Cardan was by now known and praised over all Europe as a mathematician of the first rank.

Nor was this his only bid for fame. In 1542 one of the Scoto brothers had published his book on *Consolation*, which has been compared, not happily, it would seem, to Boëthius' *Consolation of Philosophy*. It was a book of moral maxims, done in a terse, epigrammatic style, and intended, he says, for the comfort of the unfortunate, beset by the ills of life. It was, according to the custom of the time, richly stuffed with classic maxims, and owes much to the moralizings of Cicero. In 1573 this book was translated into English by Thomas Bedingfield, and, if we credit such good Shakespeareans as Joseph Hunter and Francis Douce, was read to profit by the author of *Hamlet*. In his *Illustrations of Shakespeare*, Hunter quotes from Cardan several passages that show considerable resemblance to Hamlet's soliloquies. Cardan speaks of death and sleep : "Seeing therefore with such ease men die, what should an account of death to be resembled to anything better than sleep ... most assured it is that such sleeps are most sweet as be more sound, for these are the best wherein, like unto dead men we dream nothing." Whether it was or was not "the book that Shakespeare placed in the hands of Hamlet," as Mr. Hunter suggested in 1845, it was highly esteemed among Elizabethans and may well have been read by one who so esteemed translations into the vulgar tongue.

Cardan, as I have already indicated, was a prolific writer, and catholic in his range of interests. A book on *Wisdom*, one on *Immortality*, a number of almanacs, books on astrology, on dreams, pamphlets on syphilis, diet, mental disorder, quinine, urine ; poems, aphorisms, a book on his own books, and one on his life : all these were poured out, during a busy life of seventy-five years, to the number of more than a hundred separate volumes, and were brought together, in 1663, in ten great folio volumes.

With the single exception noted above, none of these books have been turned into English,* and but for the fact that men like Robert Burton quoted from them with eagerness, most of them would have been utterly forgotten. Cardan's mathematical works have been preserved in footnotes, and in every history of Algebra his life is sketched, his abilities praised, and his morals condemned on the authority of one biographer. His medical books contain little that would be of more than antiquarian value. His commentaries, wise

---

* Since this was written, *De Vita Propria* has been translated into English by Jean Stover, New York ; Dutton, 1930.

HIERONYMI CARDA-
NI MEDIOLANENSIS MEDICI
DE RERVM VARIETATE
LIBRI XVII.

Adiectus est capitum, rerum & sententiarum
notatu dignissimarum Index.

Cum Cæsareæ Maiestatis gratia & priuilegio.

Neq; deest illud Christianissimi Galliæ-
rum regis, ut uersa pagina indicat.

BASILEÆ, ANNO M.D.LVII.

enough for his age, did little to advance the science of medicine. It seems that he was usually careful and conscientious in diagnosis ; his remedies were orthodox ; his practice was better than his precept : diet, fresh air, and good cheer, helped his patients to health.

He shares the fate of all popularizers, best-sellers : the bulk of his writings was significant only for his own age. His claim upon our interest lies rather in his career, his misfortunes, his contacts, and those books of his in which he recorded the incidents of his stressful and varied life — his *De Vita Propria, De Libris Propriis,* and *Genituarum Exemplar* — are precisely the ones to which the modern turns with eagerness.

Two exceptions to what has just been said: there are two books, often quoted by Robert Burton, that deserve a kindlier fate. They may provoke a mere antiquarian interest ; nevertheless, they address themselves to so many phases of human curiosity that they afford a goodly bridge over the centuries. I refer to his *De Subtilitate* and *De Varietate.* The first was published at Nuremberg in 1550, and the second, in effect a sequel, appeared at Basle in 1553. (There is some doubt concerning the date of this book, some cataloguers claiming that the 1557 [Basle] folio is the first edition.)

These curious books may be compared to the *Margarita Philosophica* of Gregorius Reisch, the *De proprietatibus rerum* of Batholomew the Englishman, or Polydore Virgil's book of *Inventions :* in a word, to the encyclopedists. Or, they might be compared to those books of our own grandfathers, *The Reason Why,* and *One Thousand Questions Asked and Answered.* The sum of human knowledge was Cardan's goal. The work on *Subtilty* opens with a generous

definition : "By subtlety I mean a certain faculty of
the mind by which certain phenomena, discernible by
the senses and comprehensible by the intellect, may be
understood." The subtlety of Cardan possesses a
threefold character : substance, accident, and mani-
festation. After a brief discussion of the senses, he
considers the properties of matter. Following this preliminary survey, he plunges at once into a digressive
and catholic survey of nature, and man's intuitions :
the knowledge of all that may be known to the intellect and the senses !

In these books he tells the reader how writing ink
is made, pumps, siphons, scales ; how to cure smoking
chimneys, to raise sunken ships, to forecast the weather,
to make a furnace, to construct a cipher ; he explains
the laws of optics and the properties of precious stones
— in this connection Cardan gives a drawing of an
effigy, carved in agate, that will produce sleep.

He writes of monsters in nature, and spins wild
theories to account for them. Then he turns practical
and informs the housewife how to mark linen, how to
kill mice, how to recognize good mushrooms, how to
make vinegar ; to the maiden he gives a receipt that
will make her hands lily-white. Those desiring to
peer into the future are advised concerning the meaning of dreams, of how to read the stars, or how to
foretell events by lines in the hand or on the forehead. What is more significant to the modern, he
suggests that creation is progressive, that the inorganic
is animate, and thus, in a crude way, anticipates
Haeckel and the evolutionists. The vertebrates have
grown from worms. Treating of the soul, he grows
epigrammatic, and tells us that *envy is a thin hate ; suspicion a little fear ; audacity a vast hope.*

CARDAN, AND THE "GOLDEN COMPLEX"

There was something for the farmer, for the mechanic, the housewife, the merchant, the scholar ; for the curious of every class. It is not surprising that these works were so hospitably received throughout the literate world.

One of the greatest physicians and scholars of the 16th century was Julius Caesar Scaliger. He wrote learned commentaries on the Classics, made an important contribution to Latin grammar, and was a critic of notable ability and exceptional meanness. In manners he made Cardan seem a very courtier. Cardan reserved his discourtesies for the drawing-room and street ; in his writings he was generous and dignified. Scaliger was as rude on paper as elsewhere. He had attacked Rabelais and Erasmus in outrageous terms, and his criticisms were not infrequently characterized by a total disregard of truth. He had been a soldier, used to rough tactics. When he turned to letters, said his contemporaries, he used the manners of a soldier. As a soldier and as a physician he had won some distinction : as a writer he was as determined to attract attention.

So it was that when Cardan's *Subtilty* came to receive the acclaim of all Europe, Scaliger saw an opportunity to borrow some of his fame. He was no match for Cardan in medicine, mathematics or philosophy. Nevertheless he found some basis for his attack. The first edition of *Subtilty* (1550) contained certain errors which Cardan carefully corrected in the second (1554). Paying no attention to these later corrections, Scaliger chose, among other things, to attack Cardan for his carelessness. His book, *Exercitations*, was published in 1557 at Paris. Nearly a thousand quarto pages were filled with

Scaliger's criticisms, and even Gabriel Naude, Cardan's unfriendly biographer, admits that "the errors in these *Exercitations* were more in number than those he so wantonly laid to Cardan's charge." And the spirit of the book was such that even Cardan's enemies were able to perceive the petty animus that moved the critic. It bristled with personal abuse.

Having thus called fresh attention unto himself, Scaliger now awaited Cardan's reply with eagerness. But the nature of that reply, when it came, was so dignified, so quiet, so assured, that, had Scaliger seen it, it must have grieved him mightily. Cardan did not use an entire book in answering the attack; he incorporated it in the brief appendix to his second revision of *Subtilty,* but so concisely did he word his rebuttals that he succeeded in completely demolishing Scaliger's every point. Moreover, from beginning to end, not once did Cardan mention the name of his assailant.

It seems that Scaliger did not see this later work of Cardan's. Had he done so he might have been saved his ultimate folly. Some local wag informed Scaliger that Cardan was so overcome by the terrible attack that he had died of mortification and a broken heart. And Scaliger, conceited man that he was, believed it!

One is compelled to believe that what followed was prompted by genuine feeling. Scaliger was grieved over the calamitous result of his attack. He therefore tried to make amends by writing a most laudatory funeral oration.

"Now," said Scaliger, "the republic (of letters) is bereft of a great and incomparable scholar, and must needs suffer a loss which, peradventure, none of the centuries to come will repair. What though I am a person of small account, I counted upon him as a supporter, a judge, and even a laudator of my lucubrations ; for he was so greatly impressed by their weighty merits, that he deemed he would best defend himself by avoiding all comment on the same, despairing of his own strength, and knowing not how great his powers really were . . . I, when I addressed my *Exercitations* to him during his life — to him whom I knew by common report to be the most ingenious and learned of mortal men — was in good hope that I might issue from this conflict a conqueror ; and is there a living man blind enough not to perceive that what I looked for was hard-earned credit, which I should certainly have won by finding my views confirmed by Cardan living, and not for inglorious peace brought about by his death?

"He was a man of kingly courtesy, of sympathetic loftiness of mind, one fitted for all places, for all occasions, for all men and for all fortunes. . . A great man indeed ! and forsooth, when we come to consider the surprising swiftness of his wit, his fiery energy in all he undertook, I affirm that he may be called shameless who would venture to compare with him."

Thus Scaliger to Cardan, who survived his ill-timed eulogizer by nearly eighteen years !

Cardan was never rich, for all his fame. Even his books were affected by his poverty. His chief defect of style was diffuseness. His publishers reckoned his royalties by the number of his pages, and his need of money increased the thickness of his books. He did not set out to write for money, but he thought it no sin to "pad" for an extra penny.

In truth, the only occupation to which Cardan devoted himself for gain was gambling, and had it not been for cards and dice, his family must have starved. In the years 1540-42, a generous Milanese patrician, Antonio Vimercati, risked his fortunes with him daily, and what he lost enabled Cardan to live. When, in August, 1542, Vimercati signified that he had lost enough, and left off his gambling, Cardan was reduced to the pittance he gained from his occasional lectureship in mathematics. In May, 1543, his third and last child, Aldo, was born, and had not the University of Pavia, for the second time, offered him the chair of medicine, the condition of the family must indeed have been wretched. At that, he would have refused the offer on the ground that his writing could be done to better advantage in the city, had not the exigences of war now driven the University to take temporary quarters in Milan. Not having to move, Cardan accepted the post, but when, a year later, the University was enabled to return to its own campus, Cardan was on the point of resigning, when, luckily, his house tumbled down about his head. He tells us that this beneficent calamity occurred during the night, and without warning. All his family were asleep, when suddenly the old building, probably a miserable and rat-ridden shack, collapsed. None was harmed, and Cardan, regarding the occurrence as a signal from the gods, decided to go with the University as a member of the regular faculty.

By some sad irony, Cardan's actual poverty came to an end the year of his wife's death. Together, they had known fifteen years of hardship. The history that Cardan has left us shows that she had been a faithful and uncomplaining companion. She had witnessed some of his triumphs, but had enjoyed little physical comfort as a result of his successes. The year of her death, 1546, the University lacked the funds to pay her professors, and thus the Cardans were deprived of two hundred and forty crowns. During this time of want, when failure again seemed imminent, the only woman that Cardan seems to have loved was taken away, and he was left to his grief with three motherless children.

And now the gods began to smile upon the child of misfortune. The law-suits which began at the death of old Fazio Cardan, twenty-two years before, came to an end with a settlement in Jerome's favor, so that now, for the first time, he had a home that he might call his own. Moreover, through the good offices of his friends, the Cardinals Sfondrato and Giovanni Morone, Pope Paul III. offered Cardan a handsome pension to enter his services. This he declined, saying that the Pope was tottering and weak. The probability is that he feared being involved in some political intrigue ; furthermore, now that comfort and fame had come to him, he liked well enough to remain in Milan, where he had suffered so many rebuffs.

At Pavia, Cardan had become acquainted with Andreas Vesalius, the first real anatomist. Cardan was teaching medicine ; Vesalius anatomy. Both were, in a fashion, heretics ; both were famous. And now, when honors were raining, Vesalius commended his friend Cardan to King Christian III. of Denmark, who offered him 800 crowns a year if he would but act as his physician ; to this he added a commodious house and the use of three horses. Here again Cardan declined to accept his offer. His son, Gianbatista, was to be educated, and Jerome desired that he have the advantages offered by Pavia.

Absorbed as he was in promoting his claims for intellectual superiority, he had a genuine affection for his children, and seems, with a single exception, to be noted later, to have cared for them with tenderness and even indulgence. He wanted them to be happy, to be educated, and to bear themselves with honor: and now that his wife was gone, the problem of their care proved too much for him.

Cardan's days, as I have noted, were given to the writing of books and the delivery of his lectures. When night came, he sought to refresh his soul with music, and to fill his pocket by means of cards and dice. Not desiring to wander abroad for his amusements, he invited to his home such strolling minstrels as cared to come. These people were, more often than not, vagabonds and drunkards, and turned the house into a sty. When Lucia was alive the children were protected in a measure : at least they were put to bed. But the father, interested as he was in their welfare, never seems to have reflected upon the danger to which he was daily subjecting his youngsters. He liked children ; he brought books to them and encouraged study. He even adopted children of his poorer relatives and brought them to his home that he might help with their education. In his own childhood he had been cuffed about : he would treat his children with kindness and leniency ; surely that would be enough. More than that, it occurred to him that they might be in need of moral teaching to prepare them for the traps of life. Having little time to spare for their personal supervision, Cardan hit upon an idea that would solve this problem once for all. He compiled and wrote a little anthology of moral teachings called the *Book of Precepts*, which he gravely placed in their hands with the full belief that from that moment all would be well with them !

The action shows a pathetic ignorance of human nature. The book has admirable qualities. It opens with this preface : "Many, my sons, think that the chief part of happiness depends on fortune ; know that they are deceived : for although fortune does contribute something to it, yet the chief part of it lies within ourselves." The chapters that follow are on the duties to God, Princes, parents, society ; prudence, fortitude, journeys, diet, personal habits, and at the last, a list of good books. A young man, following the advice here given, would surely grow up to be a pious, courteous, generous, honest gentleman. Of the three children, his daughter Clara married well, was a good wife and a comfort to her father ; Aldo, the youngest, was frequently in jail, and was finally banished from the country. Gianbatista managed to get his degree from Pavia and to embark upon the practice of medicine. Cardan expected great things of him, but his end, as we shall presently see, was so humiliating and terrible that it brought utter ruin upon his father's head.

But there was one event in Jerome's life that must be chronicled before we can consider that final chapter.

John Hamilton, Archbishop of St. Andrews, and natural brother to the regent of Scotland, was afflicted with asthma. In 1551 he was suffering so greatly that his physician, William Cassanate, was prevailed upon to make an appeal to Jerome Cardan. Cassanate had read Cardan's *Subtilty*, his *Comfort*, and the book on *Wisdom*. In the last-named he had been impressed by Cardan's supposed cure of consumption. Therefore it came about that Cassanate, in September, 1551, wrote a long letter to Cardan describing the symptoms of the Archbishop, and praying that he would take the case. He forwarded two hundred crowns for his expenses, and asked that he meet John Hamilton at Paris, or, should that prove inconvenient, at Lyons.

At the time of the receipt of this letter, Cardan was in a mood for travel. Pavia was again in the grip of the military, and Cardan had resigned. His son, Gianbatista, was graduated, and his children were looked to by a housekeeper. One of the temptations held out in the letter from Cassanate was the opportunity of meeting with the great and famous throughout Europe. Cardan's life had revolved about Milan : here, now, he might not only see the cities of the world, but meet and receive homage from the learned men along the way.

In February, 1552, then, Cardan set out for Lyons with five retainers, and there he remained for more than a month. The Archbishop had been unable to leave Scotland ; political intrigue, the strained relations existing with England, the situation of Queen Mary, and the weakness of his brother, the regent, made it impossible to leave. But Cardan was not idle. Generals, marshals, noblemen of every sort, came to him for treatment, or offered him pensions if he would but enter their service. The delay was annoying but remunerative. At last the physician Cassanate arrived. He bore a message from Hamilton, explaining the situation, containing more gold, and requesting that Cardan hasten to Scotland.

The Italian physician was a bit afraid of the north-

ern island.   He had heard that it was frightfully cold,
and he suspected that the Archbishop had all along
intended that he should make the long journey.   However, the additional three hundred crowns, and the
prospect of further triumphs at Paris and London,
moved him to accept the offer.   He was to have all
his expenses and ten crowns a day while attending his
patient.

At Paris he met Johan Fernelius, the friend and
physician to Catherine de' Medici, and Jacob Sylvius,
a famous teacher of anatomy, who is chiefly remembered for having been the teacher of Vesalius, whose
genius he had not the wit to appreciate.   Cardan tells
us that he was hospitably received in the great city,
that he became warmly attached to Aimar de Ran-
conet, one of the Parliament of Paris, and that he
was given a dinner by the King's physicians : the thing
that stands out most prominently in his account of the
visit was the Church of Saint Denis, where he saw
"the horn of a Unicorn, whole and uninjured."   He
made accurate measurements of this curious object,
and refers to it repeatedly.   To account for his interest one must recall that in the 16th century it was
believed that this horn was potent in the cure of
disease, and that by its aid one might either detect
the presence of poison in wine, or, finding it there,
remove the venom by touching it with the tip of the
horn.

On the 29th of June, 1552, the physician met his
patient, John Hamilton, in the city of Edinburgh,
where he remained in attendance until the following
September.

The Archbishop was in a sorry state.   Even under
the eye of his physician his attacks of asthma came

once a fortnight and gave him twenty-four or more hours of agony. His habits of life did not favor improvement : he over-ate, drank to excess, worked too long, worried much, neglected sleep, was too gallant, and took but little exercise. In consequence, his body grew thin and weak, while his disease thrived upon wasting tissues.

Cassanate's treatments had proved of no benefit, and he had asked for Cardan's assistance. But while Cassanate was in Paris he had discussed the case with Fernelius and the King's physicians, and they had prescribed a certain course of treatment which he was now anxious to try. Cardan stood aside with becoming modesty, held his tongue, and watched the result. This conduct, professionally ethical, no doubt, and perhaps wise, viewed from the angle of the diagnostician, irritated the failing Archbishop. He was paying out his moneys and pinning his faith to the great Cardan, and he wanted treatment. It was Cardan's hour, and he was thoroughly prepared to make the most of it. He has left behind him full reports of the case, its diagnosis, the treatment and the results. These, with the letters of John Hamilton, give us a pretty accurate notion of the relation of Cardan to his patients, and, if we but pass over the jargon of the time, reveal to us a man who was governed by that common sense that has characterized the successful physician in all times and places.

Passing over the theory of the disease, all the talk of humours, vapours that heat the brain, fluids that soak through tissues, we find the treatment quite interesting. In the first place, the Archbishop was put upon a light, regular diet, concerning which Cardan, who was something of a cook, gave explicit directions.

He was to take regular exercise, walking in the morning, and riding horseback for an hour in the afternoon. To insure regularity he was advised to purchase a clock! Ten hours of sleep were to be followed by a shower bath (the first shower bath in Scotland, says Dr. Charles L. Dana), and a massage, combing his head with an ivory comb. He was to avoid purgatives, and in the stead thereof, take a compound of peaches and sugar of violets. One of the most important directions given to the asthmatic was that he should no longer sleep on feathers, but on a mattress of raw silk, with a linen pillow stuffed with dry straw or sea-weed.

Commenting on this prescription, Dr. Dana, writing in the *Annals of Medical History* (Vol. III, page 122) said : "All this, it seems to me today, was very good and modern treatment,— no bleeding, no purgations, no polypharmacy . . . personal hygiene, diet, exercise, cold baths, rest, sleep — what more could Sir James Mackenzie of London and St. Andrews have done for an Archbishop today ?"

The treatment was followed by a rapid improvement of the patient. John Hamilton began to regain his flesh ; his suffering ceased. In the days that followed a multitude came, begging to be treated, so that, in a single day, Cardan declares that he made as much as nineteen golden crowns. The people were pleased ; the Archbishop was delighted and wanted Cardan to remain as his private physician. But Cardan was lonesome for his home and children. Moreover, he feared the approaching winter. Nothing could tempt him to remain so far from Italy.

When at last it became evident that the physician would remain no longer, Hamilton gave him a parting dinner to which many of his new-found friends were invited. He was paid far more than he had been promised, and gifts were showered upon him in token of their gratitude. Scotland dealt more generously than Italy.

While he was in Edinburgh Cardan had received letters from the English Court, requesting that, en route to Italy on his return, he spend some time in London, and give his opinion concerning the health of King Edward VI., who was just then recovering from a long illness. In October he presented himself at Court.

In this case he was not so successful as he had been at Edinburgh. Apparently his treatment was not desired : the noblemen who gathered about the royal presence wanted to know how long the young king would live, or, rather, how soon he might die. Cardan the astrologer was now in demand. As a reader of the stars, Cardan does not seem more notable than most prophets. Moreover, he sensed an atmosphere of intrigue : and he was in a foreign country. He liked Edward, and marveled at his versatility. "He was an amazing boy," he writes. "I was told that he had already mastered seven languages. In his own language, in French, and Latin, he was perfect."

Cardan was afraid to commit himself : he was more afraid not to comply with the request. He made the horoscope, praising the boy king, and prophesying for him a life of more than fifty-six years. Now, as Mr. W. G. Waters has pointed out, Cardan was a skilled physician, and Edward was a sickly boy, fast sinking into a decline. Surely he could not have failed to see the fast approaching end. Edward, at the age of sixteen, died within six months of Cardan's visit!

Fortunately it was the fame of the physician rather than that of the astrologer that preceded him on his return journey through Europe. At Paris forty of the most distinguished scientists of France had met to hear him lecture on medicine. Cardan, being in a hurry to get home, and hearing rumors to the effect that there were warlike disturbances about that great city, refused the invitation. Henry II, King of France, offered him a handsome sum to secure his attendance : Charles V was eager for his services. Dukes and prelates bid against one another : Cardan refused them all. His children needed him at home. His journey was a triumphal procession ; he was heralded by men of learning at Brussels, Cologne and Basle. He was the guest of Gemma Frisius the mathematician, at Louvain : at Zurich he visited with Conrad Gesner, one of the ablest naturalists and scholars of his century. When he re-entered Milan, January 1553, the Duke of Mantua offered him thirty thousand crowns if he would serve as his physician. Cardan looked upon the offer as a temptation to slavery. He could afford to dictate his terms to the world.

In his *Model Nativities* (*Genituarum Exemplar*, Basle, 1554), written shortly after his return to Milan, he says of himself : "I, who was born poor, with a weakly body, in an age vexed almost incessantly by wars and tumults, helped on by no family influence, but forced to contend against the bitter opposition of the College at Milan, contrived to overcome all the plots woven against me, and open violence as well. All the honor which a physician can possess I either enjoy, or have refused when they were offered to me . . . I am well known to all men of worship, and

233

to the whole of Europe. What I have written has been lauded ; in sooth, I have written of so many things and at length, that a man could scarcely read my works if he spent his life therewith. I have taken good care of my domestic affairs, and by common consent I have come off victor in every contest I have tried. I have always refused to flatter the great ; and, over and beyond this, I have often set myself in active opposition to them. . . I have been most fortunate as the discoverer of many and important contributions to knowledge, as well as in the practice of my art and in the results attained ; so much so that if my fame in the first instance has raised up envy against me, it has prevailed finally, and extinguished all ill-feeling."

Cardan's self-satisfaction was sustained for perhaps seven years after his journeys across the Continent. He had a large and wealthy practice ; his books were in great demand and he wrote steadily, gaining the admiration and friendship of scholars. Milan *seemed* to have capitulated.

But now let us look to Cardan's children, for love of whom he had hastened home on such eager feet.

The seeker for fame had lavished upon them much affection, but had given them little of his time. For them he had written counsels and moral fables, and letters of sage advice. He had taken a wise man's interest in their reading. Their social life he had utterly neglected : more than neglected, he had brought into their lives the worst profligates and wasters of the city.

Fortunately, his daughter Clara was unaffected by these men. In 1556 she was married to Bartolomeo Sacco, a Milanese patrician, and all we hear of her is the commonplace story of a good, capable wife and daughter. Aldo, the younger son, was ever a profligate : from the time that he could walk the streets he was involved in questionable exploits, getting into jail, being subjected to fines, and, finally, was banished in disgrace. It is recorded that his father, exasperated by his misconduct on a certain occasion, leapt from his dinner-table and chopped off the profligate's ear. The act did little to reform the son and reflects but little credit on the father.

But it was Gianbatista, his favorite child, who turned all the father's triumphs into tears. Jerome's hopes were centered upon this boy, who had taken his degrees from Pavia, entered upon the practice of medicine, and had written one or two pamphlets, which, to his father, seemed full of promise. This boy, thought Cardan, would take up his work when he laid it down : he would bring added honors to the family name : he would edit and perfect his works. Actually, the boy was but an ordinary student, a not too capable physician, and a moral weakling.

In December, 1557, Gianbatista had been secretly married to a notoriously worthless wench, one Brandonia Seroni. This woman belonged to a poor and degraded family. Her mother was little better than a procuress, her brothers were ignorant soldiers.

Gianbatista was a simple-minded youth, physically unattractive. His father had urged him to marry a practical woman of a good family. But the boy had not been looked upon with favor by women of the better sort. He was a frail hunchback ; now silent, again, moved by some passion, he poured forth torrents of words. Perhaps it was not unnatural that, finding

235

himself unable to pick a woman of his class, he allowed himself to be picked by one who had something to gain.

The Seronis, ignorant people, were impressed by Jerome Cardan's fame, and supposed that he had unlimited means. Mother and daughter united to capture the boy.

Alas for their well-laid plans, Jerome, when the secret marriage was at last made known, refused to give the couple a place under his roof. He did, however, give them an allowance sufficient to keep them in food and clothes, and, to the end that he might be the more able to bear this expense, returned to the professorship at Pavia, which he had resigned in 1552. This, however, was not the luxury which the girl's family had anticipated, and mother and daughter once more united to torment the unfortunate youth. At last they hit upon a way to make him fairly cringe. In 1560 Gianbatista's wife had just given birth to her second child, and the mother and daughter, with a great display of evidence, declared to the young physician that he was the father of neither of the children. They laughed at him for a fool. Gianbatista was unable to stand more. He bought arsenic, had it put into a cake, and attempted to destroy his wife and her somewhat distasteful parents. The parents recovered; his wife, still weak from her recent confinement, succumbed. Her brothers, suspecting Gianbatista's guilt, had him arrested, charged with murder.

Jerome was at Pavia, busy with his lectures, surrounded by private pupils, and writing yet more books. He was living in honor and applauded by friends. But when the news of his son's crime came to his ears, he dropped everything and hastened at once to his side.

Cardan spent his money freely on his son's behalf. He must have the best defence possible. To that end he devoted his days interviewing the authorities, beseeching men of influence, writing letters. He left no stone unturned. Not only did he spend his money and pray for the assistance of the great in his son's behalf : defying disgrace and even infamy, he appeared before the Senate in person and made a touching plea for the boy's life. The arguments he used were unfortunate. He pled that poisoning was not a brutal way to commit murder ; the knife was barbarous and cruel. Gianbatista was simple-minded and unfitted for deliberate murder : he had been moved by passion. After all his mother-in-law and wife had taunted him with being a cuckold : they had proclaimed the two children bastards, and had named their real fathers. Would that not enrage any man to the point of committing murder? Moreover, young Cardan had a name to be proud of : his murdered wife had not. He was educated for a useful profession ; she was ignorant and worthless. Her death did not matter so much as that of a young physician with prospects of usefulness and fame.

These were among the arguments advanced by the grief-stricken father.

But all his labors were in vain. The young man broke down and confessed the deed. The Senate was, even then, willing to spare the young man's life if the prosecutors (the girl's family) would withdraw the complaint. To this the family replied that they would drop the suit provided that Cardan would in turn give

them a sum of money sufficient to compensate for the
loss of so dear a daughter! The sum named by
them, however, was so great that Cardan, who had
already expended his all, could not meet the demand.
On the 7th of April, 1650, the young man was
executed.

Jerome Cardan, from that moment, was an old,
heart-broken man. Bowed down by the weight of
shame, filled with bitterness and heart-ache, lonely,
suspicious, he shunned his friends and lived in solitude.
He was not so self-centred as he had seemed.

Many who had applauded him during his years of
success and fame, now betrayed the envy and hatred
that had all along been in their hearts. Ambitious
men wanted his position at Pavia. They recalled his
bastardy and spread evil stories concerning the young
musicians who frequented his house.

People were now as ready to hiss as they had been
to applaud. After all, a physician who defends a
poisoner, even though the criminal be his own son,
cannot hope to have the full confidence of the average
patient. His practice fell away to nothing. To forget his troubles he would flay his body with scourges ;
then, eased somewhat in mind, he would turn to his
desk. It was at this time that he wrote his *Commentary on the Anatomy of Mundinus*, the *Theonos-
ton*, a heavy miscellany, dealing with such varied themes
as "Tranquillity," "Immortality," "Contemplation,"
and including a medical treatise on the "Prolongation
of Life." But even in his writings he poured out
his private sorrows.

In 1562, unable to endure the slights and personal
affronts of his enemies, he resigned his position at
Pavia, and, through the influence of Cardinal Bor-

romeo, obtained a professorship at the University of Bologna.

Though now in new surroundings, ill-repute dogged his heels. Some of the faculty had opposed his coming to the University and they did not hesitate to make things unpleasant. Cardan, on his part, did not take trouble lying down : when he found his colleagues in error he exposed them with venomous satisfaction, and what was more disconcerting, with deadly accuracy. His standing was not improved by these encounters. If they could, these hostile colleagues saw to it that Cardan's hours were inconvenient : all the little tricks to which the small academic mind is ever inclined, were employed to fret the newcomer. In 1563 they succeeded in getting an order to prevent the publication of his books. He was charged with heterodoxy and impiety. They had searched diligently throughout his work for evidence of his wickedness, and in one edition of his *De Varietate* found some disparaging remarks about the Dominican brotherhood ; the fact that Cardan disclaimed authorship for the passage, introduced by the printer, Petrus of Basle, was disregarded. Moreover, in his *Commentary on Ptolemy's Books of Astrological Judgments* (1554) they found a horoscope of Jesus Christ ! Cardan was not the first man to cast a horoscope of Christ : Albumazar, Albertus Magnus, the Cardinal of Cambrai, and Tiberius Russilanus had preceded him in this act of impiety, but Cardan was at hand to punish. For the period of one year his books were forbidden. Then Cardinal Alciat came forward and removed the ban.

For a time it looked as though fortune were going to bestow her favors on the old man's declining years.

He was given the freedom of the city ; his classrooms were crowded ; brilliant pupils came to study with him. With renewed hope he began to plan for the future.

He had adopted the illegitimate son of Gianbatista, named for his own father Fazio, and clung to it with pathetic devotion. His son Aldo was likewise with him at Bologna, but proved of small comfort, contriving to get himself into public disfavor by unlawful escapades, and spending part of his time in jail.

Seven troubled years Cardan lived at Bologna : productive years, but lonely and harassed. At length his enemies triumphed. On the 6th of October, 1570, the charge of impiety was renewed, and Cardan was thrown into prison ; once more his books were banned. It seems that Cardan believed that wise men of all times and creeds were informed by a divine spirit : that this inspiration was not confined to Christendom. Furthermore, he followed Hippocrates in rejecting the supernatural origin of disease. Such beliefs were dangerous. He remained in prison for three months.

Still there were good friends who remembered his virtues — his ability as a physician, his standing as a scholar. Cardinals Morone and Borromeo intervened in his behalf, advised him to offer his resignation to the University of Bologna, and secured for him a pension from Pope Pius V.

Thus it came about that, in March 1571, Jerome Cardan, weary of the world, battered, rent by many sorrows, but still driven by an unconquerable energy, arrived, bearing his infant grandchild, at the city of Rome.

Concerning the life of this strange man there is

little left to say. Five years more were allotted to him : five years of writing, and waiting for the end. His mind had turned to the past. He wrote of his books and his life ; of his wife and son. He tried to adjust himself to fate. He was not compelled to practise his art for money now : he gave his services to the poor. Now and again his old pupils, some of them now famous, visited him. As he wandered about the streets, shabby and unkempt, curious people whispered of his impieties. They even called him an atheist. An atheist patronized by the Pope !

Sometime in the autumn of 1576 the old man breathed his last. It was said that he had predicted the day of his death, calculating by the stars. His enemies claimed that he starved himself to fulfill the prediction. The exact date of his death no one knows. He was buried in the Church of Saint An-drea : subsequently, by his grandson Fazio, perhaps, the body was transferred to Saint Mark's at Milan, where it lies beneath the stone which he himself had caused to be erected for his father.

Cardan was a child of his age : he was no fore-runner of an age to come. Superstitious, but hungry for knowledge, he desired to know everything. Anxious to justify himself, humiliated by his youthful experiences, he pursued fame with feverish eagerness, and sought to win a name by spreading abroad such knowledge as he gained. Made bitter by the taunts of others, and sensitive over his own physical blemishes, he eased himself both by physical castigations and the exaggeration of his own faults. This tendency to self-blame increased after the death of Gianbatista. Out of remorse he builded the heap of his faults into a veritable tower. Those acquainted with the sub-

terfuges of them that suffer are able to penetrate behind the mask of falsehood to the truth.

As a physician he was but a successful practitioner,
helped on to success by a vast reading, coupled with
keen powers of observation ; as a philosopher he was
but an echo ; as an astrologer he was no outstanding
success ; his science shared the faults of his age ; his
inventive ability was prodigious in the realm of me-
chanics and devices for household use, though it has
been hinted that some of his most brilliant contrivances
were taken from Leonardo da Vinci ; as a father he
was an admitted failure ; as a mathematician he commands a lasting place in history ; as a man he moves
us to pity and to admiration.

Loving to his family, loyal to his friends, magnanimous to his enemies, a dynamo of energy, his baser
qualities, his sins of omission and his repeated misfortunes, were more the results of unkind circumstance
than the outcome of an evil nature. Let Gabriel
Naude, the biographer, who, more than any other, has
been responsible for the ill-repute that has gathered
about his name, pronounce his epitaph :

"Where shall we find any one who had mastered so
many sciences by himself, who had plumbed so deeply the
abysses of learning, and had written such ample commentaries on the subject he had studied ?   Assuredly in Philosophy, in Metaphysics, in History, in Politics, in Morals,
as well as in the more abstruse fields of learning, nothing
that was worth consideration escaped his notice."

VI

ON COLLECTING NORMAN DAVEY

"There were few bookshops in London with the dark corners of which he was unfamiliar : his knowledge of Paris was particular, and he could have found his way from the Quai d'Orsay to the Odéon by a score of different routes with his eyes bandaged."

The Pilgrim of a Smile

VI

ON COLLECTING NORMAN DAVEY

CATULLUS in a modern drawing-room, Juvenal at a London club, Laurence Sterne flinging aside his slightly spotted vestments to masquerade as a very quiet man-of-the-world. That composite, a little exaggerated, to be sure, may be taken as a fair picture of Norman Davey the novelist. As for Norman Davey the poet, that is quite another story.

I came to collect him through the reading of his *The Pilgrim of a Smile,* an astonishingly clever yarn. Indeed, it is so amusing, so engagingly wise and wicked that had he not written another line he would remain for me one of the ablest of modern writers. I bracket this book with *Penguin Island, My Uncle Benjamin,* and *Jurgen.*

Mr. Davey is author of six novels, a few short stories — already collected by the anthologists —, two volumes of verse, two authoritative technical works, one on *The Gas Turbine,* the other, *Studies in Tidal Power,* and a most appetizing manual of gastronomy, *The Hungry Traveller in France.* For light amusement he devotes himself to the study of aesthetics. Epicure, philosopher, engineer, poet and satiric novelist, his is the versatility that is characteristic of the first rate.

Satire, irony, humor, relieved by a sympathetic understanding of human nature, are ever at play

245

over his pages. His characters are lifted out of London clubs and drawing-rooms, and the resorts along the Riviera. Back of his backgrounds one gets a glimpse of Petty Cury, the Granta, a village in Surrey, models of gas engines, trigonometric hieroglyphs, vellum-clad editions of Latin poets, and the interminable trenches in war-time France, where for four years he did graduate work, studying the results of human stupidity.

His prose is lucid, flexible, precise and full of flavor. Seldom does he venture elaborate descriptions, but when he does, as in *Guinea Girl*, his habitual economies of phrase are comfortably tossed aside to make way for a Latin sensuousness not common to English writers of this age. I take, for example, four paragraphs from *Guinea Girl*:

"Once upon a time the Ile de l'Escope, this place of the Watch Tower, this guardian island, had been a Greek colony. Before the good St. Louis had set out on his crusades from the port of Aigues-Morte, away to the West: before the mob in Jerusalem had shouted for the release of Barabbas and the Colonial Governor had washed his hands in public: before Cæsar's legions had overrun the mainland: before Theban Pindar sang or Alexander set his face to conquest, before the Stagyrite had thought or written, or Socrates had drained the hemlock: the Ile de l'Escope was a home of piety and of the worship of the gods.

"Little now remains of these many temples: the sea and the rain and the wind have worn away the lasting stone. The worshippers of a Newer God have thrown down the old altars and upon the foundations of the Temple of Apollo rises the fortified church of St. Appollinaire. Grass has split the marble and weeds have overgrown the ruins that remained, until now there is left

246

but a few feet of a mosaic pavement to show where once stood the Temple of Aphrodite.

"High up, upon the tallest cliff, whose face is sheer, so that a stone upon its edge, stubbed with the toe, will fall cleanly into the water seven hundred feet below, lie these few fragments, buried in flowers. Here, once, had risen the temple of the Goddess. Slender pillars of the finest marble had upheld the roof : upon the graven altar had forever flickered the undying flame : here the mosaic of the forecourt had been pressed beneath the soft feet of virgins, dedicate to Her worship ; and inland, with the slope of the hill, the gardens had fallen away, terrace by terrace, in which the devout might wander, and where, on certain feast days, the passer-by, even if he were no more than a shepherd from the grazing lands below or a sailor off a ship in port, might, in the shadow of the myrtles, claim, in the name of the Goddess, her largesse.

"But long ages since, the gardens had grown over with weeds and the myrtle had withered : the courts no longer echoed with song : wine-spilth no longer stained to purple the white flowers among the grass. The sunset no longer flushed the milk-white marble to rose and the altar stone was no more reddened with the blood of the slain kid. Here and now, the green lizards, the painted butterflies, beetles, fireflies and the moths of night courted one another in this broken and deserted fane."

The organization of Mr. Davey's novels is not always in accord with Aristotelian canons, though a modern critic has little enough to do with such strict academic prescriptions. But in *The Pilgrim of a Smile* as in *Good Hunting,* to name but two, the conventional unities are perilously near the rocks. In both these tales the treatment is episodic, the narratives being built about a single character shifted in both time and space at the whim of the author. *The Pilgrim* chronicles the adventures of one Matthew

Sumner, a quiet, philosophic gentleman who, in the company of three jolly fellows from his club in the Adelphi, questions the Sphinx at the foot of Cleopatra's Needle. The others, slightly intoxicated, ask for money, beauty and love, each according to his need. Mr. Sumner asks but to know why the Sphinx smiles : in the episodes that follow it is related how each man got his wish. A very simple device, and dangerous, since it carries Mr. Sumner over a goodly part of the globe and introduces new and strange folk at every turn. In the final chapter one meets again, briefly, with the original group, who give account of the rewards they have received.

In *Good Hunting* the device is even simpler. The hero, Julian Carr, is the victim of seven intrigues, and at the end of the sixth amusing episode he escapes designing woman in a thoroughly ungallant fashion, and is about ready to congratulate himself on being a most clever fellow ; but at the seventh attempt, having by now spent the better portion of his life in sprinting, he succumbs and falls victim to a mercenary wench who bids fair to reap a revenge quite in proportion to the years of Carr's exemption. Hare and Hounds is an old game, and Mr. Davey contrives to make it amusing, but as a whole the book is less a novel than a collection of clever short stories.

Judgement Day, in its structure, recalls *The Pilgrim of a Smile*. Herein during the darkness of the night, eighteen of the inhabitants of a west country town are brought to Judgement. Not anticipating so august an event these unfortunate are not all of them as fittingly employed as a good churchman could wish at the moment of Divine summons. And, in or out of bed, they have now to give account of their deeds and listen to words that are not uniformly pleasing. Mr. Davey has handled his episodes skillfully, with Peter Young serving here as Sumner did in the *Pilgrim*, and has thereby given the effect of unity.

Well, what of it? If the lack of what is called a plot makes the story labor and puff and the reader yawn, much might then be argued : but Mr. Davey's books are never dull, and one need only remember that the cleverest of Anatole France's tales were bare of anything resembling a plot. The episodic, for all of Aristotle, is not necessarily ineffective. It remains that these three novels are compounded of wit and wisdom : that they are written neatly and with grace. Clever men who have somewhat to say need not be overmindful of technique. Mr. Davey is not writing for scullery maids.

In his first novel, *Perhaps*, in *Guinea Girl*, and again in *Babylon and Candelight* one finds that this author knows quite well how to manage his plots.

The plot of the first novel in the hands of a writer less restrained might easily have swept into a popular melodrama. Briefly, here is the story : Captain Ransome, young army officer commanding a fortress on the Isle of Wight, is so befuddled by the love of a stubborn maid, and goaded so sharply by an unconscionable journalist that he abducts the girl, locks her in the fortress and declares — only to his men in the fort — a state of siege. But the smart journalist, without informing Ransome, announces to an astonished British public that the Isle of Wight demands home rule and is in a state of revolt. Owing to a secretarial blunder in the war office, the English officials come to believe that Captain Ransome is in charge of some extremely powerful guns, and fear that international complications may follow on the heels of any drastic action. The entire government is paralysed by fear, and, to top it all, the suffragists take advantage of the situation and abduct the Prime Minister. The untangling of these political and amorous affairs is cleverly done, and the incidental satire on the home rule policy has a rich Shavian flavor.

Upon his verse Mr. Davey bestows the meticulous skill one might expect from the reading of his prose. His lines are neatly polished and effective ; his themes original, his manner fanciful, richly allusive and frequently reminiscent of Byron.

Desiderium was written in the trenches, somewhere in France, but one would never suspect it were it not for the introductory *Ad Lectores,* and the epistolary *Bibliophiloi.* He sings, rather, of the "Naiäd-guarded streams," of lonely shrines and dancing feet. He contrives with Gallic gaiety to mask melancholy with laughter and to convert the scholar into a pixy-led and playful child. But for all his seeming lightness he cannot always forget that when his fantastic play-acting is over man is —

"Once more a tiny part of God's Great Joke,
   Which He, on the world's stage has caused to be
   Acted, a Joke that only He can see !"

It should not be difficult to collect a man who, according to publishers' catalogues, has done but twelve volumes, and none further back than 1914 : but it is not so simple as it might seem. I found it rather hard going in the London of 1923.

Take the case of his first novel, *Perhaps* (1914). England was entering the war that summer, and the madly driven authorities, having quite enough trouble already, and in need of every available soldier, were

PERHAPS

A TALE OF TO-MORROW

BY

NORMAN DAVEY

METHUEN & CO. LTD.
36 ESSEX STREET W.C.
LONDON

Norman Davey's First Novel

fearful of anything that might, ever so remotely, suggest offense to the truculent Irish. Mr. Davey's
satire, they reasoned oddly enough, might be misin-
terpreted : the Isle of Wight might be taken for Ireland ! The book was, therefore, ordered pulped on
the day of its publication, and, so far as could be
learned from the publishing house of Methuen, only
the six author's copies escaped destruction. That, according to publishers, seemed to end the matter. The
insistent American is not so easily daunted. Knowing
somewhat of the ways of publishers he felt sure that
at least one copy had been put aside for record, and
hoped that some careful proof-reader had taken another to his home. This hope he confided to a very
obliging bookseller just off the Haymarket, who was
somewhat shocked by the notion that he should be expected to demand record copies from the publisher.
Such precipitate action, such vulgar insistence, is foreign to England. But a clerk at the shop did know
a man who knew one of the proof-readers at
Methuen's and he was willing to make cautious in-
quiries. And so it turned out that one of the proof-
readers had taken a copy of *Perhaps* home for
checking, and, on being informed of the book's sup-
pression, he had been curious enough to keep it among
his own books : he was willing to part with it for a
modest sum, and the American sailed to the west
bearing with him one of possibly a dozen copies of a
rare first edition.

*The Pilgrim of a Smile, Guinea Girl, Good Hunt-
ing, Babylon and Candlelight,* and *Yesterday* (*Perhaps*
was reissued under this title in 1924), are not difficult
to find, though the first named is by no means common in the shops. The same may be said of *Studies*

in Tidal Power : but *The Gas Turbine* took me well over two years to get, and that I did get it was entirely owing to the courtesy of an eagle-eyed friend in France.

Then there is a wicked little book called *The Penultimate Adventure,* being one of the original episodes of Matthew Sumner's life which, for some curious reason, was omitted at the time of publication. It is not too easy to come by, as but three hundred copies were issued in 1924. It was rapidly bought up by those who had already come to love *The Pilgrim,* and when it does turn up in the shops seems to have a way of vanishing overnight.

To make the Davey collection complete it is necessary to have Mr. Edward O'Brien's *Best Short Stories* (English) of 1923, and Volume 3 of *The New Decameron,* which appeared at Oxford in 1922 : in both of these will be found stories by Norman Davey. Stories, verse and reviews by Mr. Davey will also be found in *The Granta* (1909-13), a Cambridge journal, and in *Punch* from 1913 on ; articles and stories may be found in *The Golden Hind* and *John O'London's Weekly.* Some of the *Granta* verses were reprinted in a volume called *The Granta and its Contributors,* 1924. Of these *The Golden Hind* is most difficult to obtain.

Scarcest of all is a volume of verse published in 1914, *Poems.* There is, I am told, but one copy in existence. It was privately printed, and a very beautiful volume. I had it in my hands once for a moment, and read enough to see that Mr. Davey's lyric gifts are more apparent there than in his later verse. There is more tenderness, more spontaneity

and a clearer vision of beauty : the later poems have
gained in idea content but lost in music. I wish I
could remember one of the poems I read during the
half hour I held the volume — I think it was the last
poem in the book — but I cannot. I do, however,
recall a part of the Dedication : "To the apple-blossom
that is over : the lily that has withered : and the rose
whose petals have fallen away." And I hope that
some day the poet will see fit to make public the thin
quarto that contains some of his choicest work, but
for the present that is one "first" his collectors will
seek in vain. But if I may not quote from his earlier
volume I may choose some lines from *Desiderium*
that hold an especial appeal for book collectors.
As I have already pointed out, this poem was
written in the trenches, sometime between 1914 and
1918 :

> O Christie, christened Biblióphilos,
> How runs the road to-day by Charing Cross ?
> Are shelves still ranged under your murky sky
> Where poor men may discover books to buy ?
> Are there still men of so humane a mind
> As to keep shops from floor to ceiling lined
> With books — old books — in vellum, paper, cloth,
> Drilled by the worm or ravaged by the moth,
> Where one may while the lettered hours away,
> Unheeded, nor be ever dunned to pay ?
> Are there yet shelves within the common reach
> Weighted with volumes priced at sixpence each ?
> Vellum 8vo's black with London's grime
> By printers who were famous in their time : —
> Dodsley's Miscellany : some prints from Cuyp :
> An Æschylus in boards and Caslon type :
> Froeben's Euripides : a Plantin Persius :
> "On the Sublime" by Burke : Elzevir's Mersius :

FOR THE LOVE OF BOOKS

And is there still that lively paradox,
The treasure-chamber of the penny-box?
To tempt caprice of fate men travel far:
They strive to sound the seas or reach a star:
They strange adventure seek by sea and land;
In western woods or on the Orient sand.
But throughout all the alley-ways of Chance,
Or near or far, I know of no Romance:
No wealth of wonder: no ecstatic glee,
Such as the penny-box can give to me.
Once on a rainy day (you were not there)
I lost myself behind Red Lion Square,
Where, in a grimy shop, I found a woman,
A tousled, unwashed creature, scarcely human,
Who rummaged in the window midst the litter
Of faked brass-ware and common lustre glitter,
To reach some tattered volumes, brown with stain,
I had caught sight of through the window-pane.
She wrapped the book up in "The Evening News":
I paid threepence for it: I shall not lose
In buying at that price (unbacked, 'tis true)
A Pico (Proctor 10052).
And once, when you and I were walking up
Shaftesbury Avenue, we chanced to stop
Before a small and unpretending place
Some dozen doors from Rimell's; such a case
Of books as stood in view beside the door
Never in book-shops had we seen before . . .
Vellum 8vo's by the Flemish men;
Plantin and Elzevir and Etienne:
Giunta and Jenson and their nearest cousins
And Aldine duodecimos by dozens:
But thus I might forever catalogue,
So rare those volumes gleamed through London fog,
All ticked in shillings: five, six, seven —
We asked each other — was this earth or heaven?

ON COLLECTING NORMAN DAVEY

Which we would take we two together planned,
But found, alas ! we had no cash in hand,
Save just enough to pay our homeward fare,
And not a solitary sou to spare.
We noted well the shop, and on the morrow,
Returned with all the money we could borrow ;
But though a dozen times we passed the place
Where the shop had been, we found no sign nor trace
Of any bookshop there —'twas very odd ;
Yet I've a theory that it is God
Who keeps that shop, that there poor scholars may
Find a brief gleam illumine their dull day,
And stir their hearts, deadened by damned routine
In seeing what no scholars yet have seen :
That just for once beneath their starless sky
Some shadow of their dream might fructify.
I like to think of this — that God is kind
To folk of empty purse and eager mind.
(And yet I find the joke a little grim ;
Surely His humor ran away with Him,
Thus to present His books upon the shelf
For us to purchase when we had no pelf,
And afterward, spirit them all away !)
How pleasant is the sober, sombre grey,
Yet bravely gallant road from Charing Cross.
And now, today, your gain becomes my loss :
No more, before the shelves, do I decoy
Your errant gaze on to some worthless toy,
Leaving me free to search the shelf's dark end.
But now, alone, in our old haunts, dear friend,
You have no more my eager search to foil,
Lest I should win on you and seize the spoil.
Now all the books are yours ; and yet I know
You will not always feel the lover's glow
In seeing some rare prize, and I not there,
Your lack to envy and your joy to share.

FOR THE LOVE OF BOOKS

So dreamful here, I like to think it true,
That, sometimes, when some jewel gleams for you,
You do not, all-forgetful, seize the prize,
But passing by with humble, lowered eyes,
Say : "Had he been here too perhaps his eye
Would first have seen this book in passing by,
Therefore in friendship's courtesy I ought
This once to leave the book I love unbought !"
I like to think that sometimes this is so.
And here in this satiric puppet show,
The dupe of cruel gods and sports of chance,
Weary in these beleaguered fields of France
I dream of days that were and days to be
Happy to think you still have thought of me.

But this is all a dream ; and now my books
Are lonely in their shelves, and no one looks
To see what company are gathered there.
Old friend, I pray you, let it be your care
To go into my library and pay
That duty that I owe to friends who stay
So patient in their shelves for my return.
Take them and study them ; I know they yearn
For human friendship in the silent hours ;
Take them and talk to them — true friend of ours —
And tell them that when this calamity
Has passed away, if happily I see
My own place once again ; no force shall tear
Me from their fellowship ; and that I swear,
By all the gods, never again to brook
Aught that shall part the scholar from his book."

I have quoted at length from two of Mr. Davey's
least interesting books : I find it impossible to select an
single passage from *The Pilgrim* that would not mis-
represent the book as a whole. The very listing of
these fantastic episodes, however, may be sufficient to

tempt the sceptical. I call to mind four in particular :
"The Facetiae of Professor Phipps"—a warning to
inhibited scholars who let their minds run at large
through the minor classics, with incidental admonitions
to certain book-collectors of advanced age ; "The
Joyous adventure of the Lady and the Large Sponge"
— a study of domestic loyalty and the sad effects of
absence ; "The Diverting experiences of the prudent
Lover," which proves that caution is not always a
virtue ; "The Entertaining stories of the Things that
talked," wherein it is shown that a conversational
bed and a gossiping dresser may prove damnably inconvenient and more annoying than a radio ; "The
Young man who was afraid," provides a warning to
those who put their trust in reputation, and shows
how, once gained, a reputation pursues one like a
dragon. Each adventure of Matthew Sumner, complete in itself, is a footnote to some phase of man's
ironic tragi-comedy ; each affords a clue to the mystery of the sardonic Sphinx, and explains, in its own
measure, the laughter of the gods.

Norman Davey is among the disillusioned, but he is
not bitter. If he is a satirist, it must be noted that he
is a romantic satirist. More than that, he is one of
those who realize that in art there is, if not salvation,
healing. And for a generation as bewildered and
hurt as our own there is nothing more salutary than
the ministration of an art that serves to lighten pain
with laughter and challenge fear with a smile.

VII

CARADOC EVANS

"Some books are capable of giving such tempestuous shocks to the intelligence, the emotions, or to both, that they disturb the bloodstream and thus induce an action which breaks up obnoxious or obstructive matter. . . They galvanize atrophied or awaken dormant energies, and thus release new and generous life-forces, which have been known to restore sight to the blind and to make the mute vocal."

— Holbrook Jackson, in *The Anatomy of Bibliomania*

VII

CARADOC EVANS

CARADOC EVANS is not greatly loved by his countrymen. I call to mind two incidents that illustrate this melancholy fact. The day of St. David (Dydd Dewi Sant, as they say in Tenby), is dear to every Welshman, and those dwelling in London town are wont to foregather and hold a feast on the first of every March. A few years ago it is related that Mr. Evans purchased two tickets for this holy festival, and that *after* his money had been securely pocketed and the tickets delivered, the treasurer of the tribe solemnly but firmly informed Mr. Evans that he would be well advised to remain away altogether. A perfect illustration, that, of the morals and manners of Capel Sion : Welsh nature imitating the art of Caradoc Evans.

And I recall a day at Tenby, that quaint, walled town in southern Wales, when, after purchasing a number of volumes from the proprietor of a little bookshop, I was so unfortunate as to ask for a copy of *My People*. The tradesman drew himself up with stiff dignity and replied : "Sir, you cannot be well acquainted with the books of Caradoc Evans !" Somewhat ill at ease I murmured that I had heard fine things of Evans' work. "I'm sorry, sir," he said, "but we regard his books as libels upon our people, and I'm quite sure, sir, that if you'd read them you'd agree with me. In fact," he added, "we never carry them, sir."

But how very like that was to the treatment Thomas Hardy received from his neighbors in Dorchester not more than twenty years ago. Indeed, as late as 1920 I remember well a bonneted and basqued old lady who, when I asked to be shown the short path that leads from Dorchester to Max Gate, shook her head and warned me : "There's no light there, 'tis not a good place to go."

The author of *My People, Capel Sion, My Neighbours, Taffy,* and *Nothing to Pay* must indeed seem a very devil to those who dwell in Carmarthen and Cardiganshire ; a blasphemer and anti-Christ. Their canting pieties, their petty cruelties, their pet superstitions, their cunning, and their greed are brutally exposed for all men to see. He laughs at the chapel-folk and their parsons, who have reduced religion to a travesty, and use it as a cloak for knavery.

He pictures his men and women in a phrase, and punctures them with an epigram. Merciless in his savage onslaught, he is sparing of his adjectives. His style is trenchant, bleak and unadorned.

He is as ruthless in the castigation of his people as were the ancient Hebrew prophets, calling the wrath of Heaven upon the unrighteous. Their wrath is his, and his words are as aflame with ecstasy. For behind this fire and fury is a thwarted love. To an outsider it is quite plain that Caradoc Evans loves his land and its people with a tense ferocity. He hates their ignorance, their savagery and their greed.

The themes that engage this curious young writer are not pretty : he confines himself, for the most, to the scatologic and the mean. He holds his reader by his vividness, his vitality, his humor, his pungent phrases, his obvious sincerity : he refreshes him, at rare, rare intervals, by an almost lyric compassion and pity.

In Cardiganshire it would seem that God is known as the "Big Man," and is placated by the sacrifice of cats and pigs. Deacons of the Chapel lie, cheat, steal and throw pebbles of lecherous invitation at the windows of lusty-pious women whose bedroom chairs provide a ready welcome for strange trousers. But the people of that county resent it that Mr. Evans has reported their folkways to the world outside. One is not surprised.

Whether the real folk of Cardiganshire disport themselves as do the creatures of *Capel Sion* I know not.* If they do they are not unlike many of the pious fanatics of Georgia or Texas. Indeed, these simple sinners are not unlike those immortalized in certain pages of the Scriptures, nor are they less amusing. For that matter Mr. Evans has chosen to chronicle their naïve iniquities in the swift, laconic style of the Hexateuch. He wastes no words.

But all this is beside the point, which is that, for all his bitterness, Caradoc Evans has invented a method and devised for himself a manner, both of which are unique. He has written some of the most original short stories of our time. Chekhov is the only modern with whom he may justly be compared.

Mr. Evans has done but one novel — *Nothing to Pay* (1930). This is the chronicle of Amos Morgan,

---

*Certainly Mr. Rhys Davies, in *The Withered Root, Count Your Blessings,* and in many of his decameronian tales, contrives to make these Welshmen seem more amusing, though his pictures are very nearly as unflattering as those of Mr. Evans.

who — even as his creator — left the rude hut of his
fathers to become an assistant in a draper's shop.

The male ancestors of Amos Morgan were a jolly
lot of pious thieves, liars and monsters of cruelty.
Not the least interesting of their quaint customs was
that — when whispers of bastardy were afloat — of
calling in public chapel-meeting, upon the "Big Man"
of the sky to give His testimony concerning the sexual
purity of accused males. Any incipient bastard was
thus successfully disclaimed — so be the tone were
holy — and the unfortunate mother, usually the ac-
cuser, was lucky to escape a Sabbath stoning.

Amos got well away from this rustic simplicity, not
because he was a sensitive soul, but out of a desire to
make more money and to see the great world of towns
and cities.

In the shops life was just as mean, just as cruel,
though its brutality was less obvious. The drapers,
given also to gospelling, were not above letting a back
room for honest assignations, and the life of the
clerks was not spoiled by sweetness and light.

Amos Morgan is as thoroughly despicable as any
hero of a Ben Hecht novel, but he is more convincing. Also he is nearer to the impossible. His
courtships, his marriage, his business relations, are fun-
damentally dishonest. He reaches the depths of depravity : but perfect knavery, out of such depths, may
well reach to heights of sublimity ! Amos stealing
his father's hoarded gold ; Amos tricking his neighbors ; Amos trying to hide his money that his widow
may starve : one never comes to love Amos ! But
he is a diverting rascal, and one thanks God that one
has never met — not yet — his equal.

Common villainy is sordid. Caradoc Evans creates

living, breathing scoundrels and sluttish wenches so
vile that they lift one to a sort of rapture.

Eden Phillpotts makes us love the little farms of
Devon ; John Trevena and J. Mills Whitham paint
pictures that make the city captives sigh for the scent
of new-mown hay. Caradoc Evans recalls to us the
scents of the pig-sty and points to the dung-heap.
Mary Webb gives us glimpses of pity, her yokels know
compassion : but *My People* and *My Neighbours* are
cursed with an unrelenting cruelty.

Caradoc Evans will never be popular, save amongst
those who are able to rejoice in his exceptional vividness and craftsmanship. He is tonic, sharp, bitter :
and, by God, I like a man who hates heartily in
words of one syllable !

VIII

COLLECTOR'S TRIFLES

"It is a poor book-barrow that does not boast a presentation copy or two."
— From *Penny Wise and Book Foolish*,
by Vincent Starrett

VIII

COLLECTOR'S TRIFLES

THE MERE discovery of a book, thrilling as
it is, by no means exhausts the hoarded
pleasures awaiting those who browse in the
stalls. That, to be sure, is the primary object of the
scholar, and of such as confine their seeking to those
varnished shops where smart late-comers stand at stiff
attention upon the shelves. But the mellower book-
men, who begrime their fingers in shabby stacks and
poke their noses into crackling black folios of another
century, are ever on the heels of romance, and just
around the corner from mystery. For, picking up a
yellowed volume of the 16th century one touches
more than a book. Wisdom may no doubt dwell
within, but Love may show her face on any flyleaf.
What hands, long laid beneath the nestling sod, may
not have caressed these crumbling boards, or inscribed
herein a long-forgotten name? In a hillside cell
on the shores of the Ionian Sea some lonely monk may
here have savored joys of a world outside. Parson
Hall may have hugged this book to his bosom as he
walked the narrow, wind-swept lanes of Dartmoor.
Deserted by his friends, his family gone, an aged
solicitor of the Middle Temple may here have found
his comfort. Or, surrounded by ɔlished calf and
morocco, trimmed with gold, it maɟ have looked down
from the heavy-laden shelves of Marlborough's library
at Ditton Park.

No, while the book itself is, so to say, the veritable *logos*, it by no means exhausts the sum of the bookman's pleasures. I call to mind a fortunate collector who, whilst browsing at a little, out-of-the-way shop not long ago, happened to find, on the bargain table, a battered set of Dodsley's *Old Plays*. It was not a "first," and being thoroughly annotated in pen and pencil, was deemed but a poor and homely thing. No name of importance met the eye : its binding was inelegant, and it was therefore quite properly priced at a sum that must insure immediate sale. The bibliophile in question was delighted to get his Dodsley for so modest a figure, and bore it away for what it seemed to be. But once in his own snug library, reading Davenport's *City Nightcap* and Marston's *Malcontent*, the penciled notes along the margins recalled a later library edition which he had before consulted. Turning to this he found there, in print, many of the notes that were here in penciled manuscripts : they were the notes of W. C. Hazlitt. Further search resulted in uncovering a facsimile of Carew Hazlitt's handwriting which settled the matter once for all. My friend had, in all innocence, possessed himself of the very Dodsley that Hazlitt once owned and used in editing the splendid issue of 1874-76 !

It was at that same shop that I was lucky enough to pick up William Stewart Rose's own copy of his translation of *Orlando Furioso*, interleaved and revised in his own autograph. It happens to be a first edition which, according to Lowndes, appeared in 1825. In this set, however, the first of the eight volumes bears the date 1823. It was to have been thoroughly revised : even the dedicatory poem to Sir Walter Scott has here undergone drastic changes, and fully half of the first twelve cantos have been marked out and rewritten by the translator's pen. New notes have been added, and, throughout, one finds the man dissatisfied with lines that had been highly praised by his contemporaries. Scott thought Rose's the finest English rendering of this famous Italian poem, and the critics who followed have thus far agreed, so that it remains the standard English version. I have looked at the latest editions published by Bohn, and find that the corrections buried in these tattered volumes have never appeared in print. Perhaps they show no marked improvement. For example, the second stanza of the first Canto, which, in the printed editions reads :

> In the same strain of Roland will I tell
> Things unattempted yet in prose or rhyme,
> On whom strange madness and rank fury fell,
> A man esteemed so wise in former time ;
> If she, who to like pass has well
> Nigh brought my feeble wit which fain would climb
> And hourly wastes my senses, concede me skill
> And strength my daring promise to fulfill.

— has been changed to read : —

> With this of Sir Orlando will I tell
> Things unattempted yet in prose or rhyme ;
> He that through love into strange madness fell,
> Of judgment heretofore esteemed so prime ;
> If she, that wellnigh with as cruel spell
> So wastes my little wit from time to time,
> And hath nigh made me such as Brava's knight,
> Lets me fulfill the promise which I plight.

I grant that neither of these stanzas is great poetry, and that the revision shows little if any gain in quality

FOR THE LOVE OF BOOKS

(how much more faithful it is to the Italian original
I am unable to judge) ; but I'd rather have these
shattered, tattered volumes, upon each page of which
lies scrawled the testimony of its maker's care and
pains, than the most sumptuous set of Ariosto in the
world — unless, of course, it should chance to be the
one that Casanova owned and marked !

But there are yet more intimate secrets that may
be uncovered on the shelves of the old bookshop —
secrets that were thought to be forever hid from curious, foreign eyes. One fine day it was my good
fortune to uncover, from its chaotic hiding place, some
miscellaneous paper in the autograph of Sir William
Gell,— a leather portfolio and a thick bundle of notes.
Sir William Gell (1777-1830), it may be remembered, was a noted antiquary, whose works on the
typography of Troy and Pompeii were eagerly read
in the early part of the 19th century, and whose
drawings are prized among the curious to this day.
This bundle of old papers contained the opening chapters of a projected novel which was to have been
called "The History of the Tregannocks" ; a short
treatise on the history of houses ; on the Saracens ;
on Ammonian terms ; on the Perugian Stone ; on
epitaphs ; sketches of Greek vases, heraldic devices,
etc. Many an interesting note, done in the cramped
hand of that old antiquary, have I unearthed from
this queer assortment, many a scrap of paper that is
now, and to me, but a meaningless bit of symbology.
Meaningless ? That is not the word : not so long as
imagination can lend significance to the slightest gesture of the human hand. For ghosts are here : faces
rise, and in touching these fragile bits, set down when
Charles Dickens was but a school boy, another world

lifts itself into visibility. That same magic has been wrought by many a writer of uncanny genius, but his reader was there quite conscious that he was being deliberately deceived : here there is no contrivance. For now the reader finds his author in his lounging-robe, catches him unawares, and, while he may not be at his literary best, he is exhibiting, all unconsciously, his foibles ; perhaps even unmasking his soul.

I recall having acquired another manuscript at an obscure West-coast shop. Johannes Watson, in 1742, had copied Addison's translation of *Anacreon*, notes and all. Printed thus by hand, it is a lovely thing, finer, I think, than any typesetter could have done. It was a labor of love, and as rare a testimony to his skill as translator as John Addison could have wished. I take it that Watson was a poor curate who loved but could ill afford to purchase his favorite authors, and that, borrowing the printed volume (issued in 1735), from one of his more affluent parishioners, he made it thus his own, afterward taking it to a humbler member of his parish, the local binder — who, no doubt, owed him full many a favor — for a stout calf jacket. Or, who knows but this John Watson may have been that rector of Stockport in Cheshire who wrote a history of the Earls of Warrington, and contributed some verses of his own to the journals of his time — 1724-83 ? By all accounts the latter was a gentleman of lean purse who might well have followed some such course.

On the day I found this *Anacreon*, I dug up also a beautiful letter written by Samuel Taylor Coleridge (March 20, 1828), which illustrates what I have just said of the author in his dressing gown. Conscious that he is to appear before a jury of his critics in solemn print, the fellow is apt to strut about, strike attitudes, and think carefully before committing himself to rash judgments concerning the craft of letters. Privately, more often than not, he will be swept away by a momentary burst of feeling. Coleridge is here writing to Thomas Pringle (1789-1834), a much afflicted minor poet, now quite forgotten, of his "Afar in the Desert," a composition which opens as follows:

"Afar in the desert I love to ride,
  With the silent bush-boy alone at my side ;
  When the sorrows of life the soul o'ercast,
  And sick of the present, I turn to the past," &c. *ad nauseam.*

In his letter the poet was kind, which is a beautiful thing ; he was full of pity for the cripple, which is noble : but surely it was only in a dressing-gown mood that the great critic could say of this doggerel, "I do not hesitate to declare it among the two or three most perfect lyric poems in our language. I was taken so completely possession of, that for some days I did little else but read and recite your poem . . . *Preceptandus est liber spiritus,* says Petronius : and you have thoroughly filled the prescript."

In contrast to that is a note of Walter Pater's, found between the leaves of a rather ordinary English textbook in an unpromising second-hand store. The author of a stodgy work on "literary style" had presented a copy of his book to the gentle critic in the pathetic hope of receiving an encouraging word. Pater, with characteristic courtesy responded at once : "I have read your ingenious 'Art of Authorship' with great interest. I feel that it will interest and be useful

274

27 Tanza Road
Hampstead.
Dec. 21. 1904.
My dear Lane,

I have had numerous complimentary letters respecting the play, from Thomas Hardy, Austin Dobson, Gosse, Dowden, and other persons of note. Letters from America are now beginning to come in, and I have had one in particular Furness, the editor of Shakespeare, and to whom the Twilight of the Gods is dedicated, which has pleased me

Facsimile of Richard Garnett's letter to John Lane, mentioning his *Twilight of the Gods* so much that I cannot forbear sending it to you. Please to return it.

There do not seem to have been many reviews as yet: but I see by your advertisements that there have been notices in the Daily Express and the Telegraph. And I suppose that you will see the short but generally satisfactory one in this evening's Westminster. In blaming the quotations, the reviewer condemns the very point which Dr. Furnivall particularly admires, so seldom are critics unanimous.

Have you taken any especial measures to bring the book to the knowledge of the Stratford booksellers? There should be more demand for it there than elsewhere.

Yours most sincerely,

R. Garnett.

to a large number of readers." That was all! Pater may have worn a lounging-robe in the seclusion of his study, but it never betrayed his critical conscience.

It will be noted that the treasures I seek are not always of the sort that demand a great outlay of money. One of my choicest possessions was picked up from the "Shilling box" of a London shop. It is not a rare book, being, indeed, but a facsimile of *Religio Medici*. But on opening this dingy little volume I perceived at once that it had "points": it was one of but a few copies bound up in thin oak boards taken from Sir Thomas Browne's old house at Norwich; it is an autographed, presentation copy from the publisher, Elliot Stock, to the editor, Dr. W. A. Greenhill; inserted in the book are letters from publisher, printer, binder and various scholars (all relating to publication of the facsimile), two pamphlets on *Religio Medici* by Dr. Greenhill, several pages of notes and corrections, and, best of all, a long letter from Richard Garnett, on British Museum stationery, thanking the editor for his work — a compact bundle of association items done up with this once loved little book, all for a mere shilling! I think I prize it nearly as much as I do the nine volumes of *Tristram Shandy* that I once bought in Oxford for the same price.

Speaking of Richard Garnett reminds me of the day I found, in a small California town, a first edition of William Sharp's *Life of Shelley*. I was not greatly interested until I saw that it was autographed by Sharp in presentation to Garnett, and that, in addition, there was a tipped-in letter in Garnett's autograph, addressed to John Lane, referring to *The*

Twilight of the Gods and mentioning its warm commendation by Professor Furness, to whom that beautiful book was dedicated. This letter now enriches a first edition of *The Twilight*, and thus I have become possessed of two association items for the price of one.

In the shops one may enjoy what one might never care to collect. One will wish to carry away the letters and manuscripts of one's favorite authors : and, though one may not care to own them, one may derive a guilty sort of satisfaction in peeping at the diaries and journals of the merest wastrel who in another age and for his own private satisfaction set down the daily record of his affairs. I remember finding, among the odds and ends on the bargain table of an old shop, six little black morocco diaries done in the late Seventies. I did not want them, but, once begun, I couldn't leave off reading the neatly penned lines. Here was a human heart stripped and naked : an indecent spectacle to those who hold strictly to the conventions of the spirit, but a delight to the vulgar-curious. Tom-the-Peeper is a nasty fellow ; but, I argued for my conscience, this was a case of another sort. The author, dead for a score of years, could not be hurt by my interest in his concerns. And why, pray, does a man commit to a bound book what he does not wish, at some time, to be read ?

"Just a second, please," said the ghost of my noblest ancestor, "have you no modicum of superstition left?"

"Why, I am a Virginian," I replied, "and am accustomed, in moments of extreme inebriety, to call myself a gentleman, therefore, by all the rules of gentleman's logic, I should be a bit superstitious."

"Then," said the ghost with a hint of sternness, "behold this legend on the fly-leaf." His bony hand trembled with indignation whilst I read : "Whosoever steals in upon the privacy of another's heart is a thief and a robber."

But I dismissed at once that unwelcome spectre (an improper sort for old bookshops), and sent him a-streaming back to the valleys of Virginia. For, I reasoned, this was investigation, research, all done in the interest of scholarship. Had the Earl of Carnarvon and Howard Carter been as full of scruples as that whispy old chap, the splendors of Tut-ankh-amen would still be hid to human eyes.

So it came about that I read on and on concerning the love of a young man for his Sophia, and of her unfaithfulness ; and of how, to solace himself, he too had followed in the ways of unfaith and paid his homage to a multitude. Then the breach had been healed, and there were evidences to show the growth of a great passion, of tenderness, of sentimentality. Pasted in were stubs of theatre tickets once touched by Sophia ; a lock of her hair, a fragment of ribbon, a button, a strip of canvas, sacred by its having been pressed in a book that, on a time, had belonged to her. On the last page of that volume, written in red, was the story of her elopement with the false friend. Then there were poems — rhymes, one should call them — written to Sophia, published in the *Argonaut*, and preserved here by their author. Sometimes the verses were signed with a name she gave him —, more often with his reversed initials : always they were intended prayers to his divinity. Pain cried aloud from the tear-stained pages, but to cold, modern eyes the pain is translated into irony. I fear me that the very vocabulary of love in those other days is more than alien to an age of disillusion. The verses will but provoke an unsympathetic snicker :

"Sailed I to Ind for gems or for gold ?
  Spread I my sails amid Fortune's fleet ?
Nay ! with a heart and a hand, too bold,
  I steered for the haven your breast holds, Sweet."

And in the prose, where the modern lad, rent by passion, makes the flat declaration that his girl is "a swell kid," our diarist affirms that "Her most transient smile is holier to me than the blush of dawn to the pale eyes of weary night."

But after the scales had fallen from his eyes, after the "dream-woman" had sailed over western seas with a new lord, the discarded lover began a life that might, in a minor way, be compared to the amorous career of the Chevalier de Seingalt. Pearl and Effie, Kate and Lillian, Anne and Agnes follow each other in swift succession, each leaving behind a lock of hair — mute treasures of faded passion. One was remembered by a glove of fine silk lace ; another by a bit of silver chain ; all these reminders of sentiment neatly sewn to the pages of the diary.

Here, then, was the inmost history of a man who, by his own accounts (supported by a carefully drawn family tree, ornamented by colored heraldric devices), could trace his lineage back to the period of Edward the Confessor ; a one-time student at an Ohio College ; a western labor leader, traveller, writer of fugitive verse : a man saturate with sentimentalism. These are the mere facts, the obvious signs that may be read by a coldly curious reader. But what of the real romance of which we gain but a transitory glimpse ? What of the story which he, poor devil, could not commit to paper ? A poor, silly tale of mawkish love it becomes as, in nightly solitudes, he stammers and sobs over the record : but one feels that

behind the broken narrative was a man who had been
vouchsafed, for an instant, a glimpse of the Immortals. Or, if you will not grant him so much,
know : "Where sorrow is, there is holy ground."

Thus one may waste time over trifles, and not be
much the worse for the wasting, though I mark well
that some book-sellers will cast anxious glances at
those who linger overlong with no intent to purchase.
I maintain, however, that my time has been well
wasted in these trash barrels. Indeed I may point out
that actual discoveries have been made in these unlikely places. In just such a place, in a pile of battered, torn, and disfigured books, I happened to pick
up a common edition of Burton's *Anatomy of Melancholy*, dated 1887. Its binding was in sad need of
repair and its pages were soiled with notes in red ink,
black ink and blue pencil. It was worthless. But
was it? I observed presently that it had belonged to
Professor James A. H. Murray, first editor of the
Oxford Dictionary, also that it had belonged to George
Parker of the Bodleian Library. Then it was that
the notes grew interesting. It seems that Mr. Parker
set out to mark the additions Burton had made to the
original edition of his *Anatomy*, and this he did quite
thoroughly for perhaps forty pages, and then, finding
perhaps the task too great, he had left off. But what
excited me at the time was a note concerning Burton's
life : "Burton was one of the Clerks of the Market
of Oxford, 10 Oct. 1615 & 10 Oct. 1616, his
partner being Everard Chambers." That fact was
unknown to all of Robert Burton's biographers, and,
indeed, had never appeared in print anywhere ! Need
I say that the book was quickly transferred from the
bargain table to my own study ? A letter to an Eng-

lish scholar resulted in verification of the Parker note, and a new page was added to the life of the great Oxford scholar. I never neglect the scrap-heaps.

I shall add but two more incidents to this slight chapter of vain boasting. One concerns the stack of cheap novels usually to be found on the pavement just outside the second-hand shops. One seldom pauses there, having grown used to seeing *Little Shepherds of Kingdom Come*, and the like : yet even there an eager curiosity is sometimes well repaid. One day in passing my eye was struck by a book called *Nancy Noon*, by Benjamin Swift. A little while before I had been reading Laurence Housman's *Echo de Paris*, wherein Oscar Wilde, speaking of Swift (the pen name of William R. Patterson), says, "His style has a gleam of frozen fire. He writes like a sea-pirate driven by contrary winds to a vain search for tropical forests at the North Pole."

Great writers are seldom trustworthy critics, but in the hope of learning the secret of Wilde's admiration for the Scotch novelist I began to turn the pages of *Nancy Noon*. It seemed but an ordinary novel of the period (1896), and I was about to replace it when I noticed a post card between its pages ; a curious little card addressed to "Miss Middleton, 45 Park Road, Haverstock Hill, N. W." The cancelled stamp, bearing the likeness of the youthful Victoria, is dated February 25, '95. I turned it over and, manners or not, read :

15 Clifford's Inn, E. C.
Feb. 25, 1895

Dear Miss Middleton :

Miss Thomas wishes me to send you a Trapanese origin of the Odyssey for a friend — There are one or two very

15. Clifford's Inn. E.C. Feb. 25. 1895

Dear Miss Middleton Miss Thomas writes me to send you a Translation Origin of the Odyssey for a friend. There are one or two not very serious mistakes in the preface but the most important ones are at ff.

9. & 10. The notion Why does Ithaca the river is Jime invention "She" is all wrong. The explanation has been discovered by a Trapanese student & is very pretty & convincing

The cave referred to at p. 16 is also all wrong. My friends took me to the wrong cave. The real South Ithaca corresponds with the 9- is about 80 yards to the South. It corresponds with the 9- in its minutest details — 2 entrances & all — from Od. xiii. 346 on — it is clear that there were two caves near one another in the writer's mind. Believe me yr. very truly S. Butler

Samuel Butler's note on *The Odyssey*

POST CARD

THE ADDRESS ONLY TO BE WRITTEN ON THIS SID

Miss Middleton

45 Park Road

Haverstock Hill

N.W

serious mistakes in the preface, but the most important errors are on pp. 9 & 10 — "The entry of Ulysses into the river is pure invention" &c., is all wrong — The explanation has been discovered by a Trapanese student & is very pretty & convincing.

The Cave referred to on p. 10 is also all wrong. My friends took me to the wrong cave — The real Grotto del Torro is about 80 yards to the south — It corresponds with the *Od.* in its minutest details — 2 entrances & all. From *Od.* xiii. 346, &c.— it is clear that there were *two* caves near one another in the writer's mind.

Believe me yrs. very truly,

S. Butler

I no longer cared about the capacities of *Nancy Noon*, nor her past reputation, but I must confess that in asking the price of the book I did not call attention to its enclosure, nor enquire how it happened to be there ; nor did I hesitate to part with the single dollar necessary to its purchase. Perhaps I left the shop a bit hastily thereafter ; but then I was anxious to insert the card in my copy of *The Trapanese Origin of the Odyssey !* For, you see, I happen to be one of those who believe in the Sicilian origin and feminine authorship of the *Odyssey* — long ago converted by Samuel Butler's logic to a theory that was foreshadowed by Eustathius.*

---

* "Eustathius, the earliest commentator upon Homer in post-Christian times, *circ.* A.D. 900-1100, says Homer took much of his poems from a poem written by a woman" (Butler's letter to H. F. Jones, quoted in *Samuel Butler, A Memoir*, by H. F. Jones, London 1919, Vol. II, p. 388). Let the sceptic read Benjamin Farrington's *Samuel Butler and the Odyssey* (London 1929), and an informative chapter in Clara G. Stillman's *Samuel Butler* (New York 1932).

One of the friendliest book shops I know has a way of ordering uncatalogued lots of books from English dealers, then, after marking them for a reasonable advance, setting them out on the tables for quick sale. There are several advantages in this. The booksellers are saved the expense of cataloguing, and owing to this saving here and abroad are able to offer their wares at a low rate. Moreover in the rapid transfer of books from the brown packages to the table there is little opportunity to discover the peculiar merits of the individual volumes. The customers knowing this are eager to be first at the tables, and the collector who knows his own fields is quite apt to find a rarity marked at an exceedingly modest price.

Thus it came about that I secured Cornelius Paine's copy of Thomas Randolph's *Works*. Perhaps I should prepare the ground a bit?

Cornelius Paine was one of the foremost English collectors of the 19th century, and was used to compete with his greater rival, Henry Huth, in gathering together fine works of the 16th and 17th centuries. Both Huth and Paine were assisted in their collecting by that brilliant scholar and essayist, William Carew Hazlitt, who in 1875 published his edition of the complete poetical and dramatic works of Thomas Randolph. Two copies of this excellent work were printed on vellum, one for Mr. Huth and the other for Mr. Paine. The price was twenty pounds.

Now reprints of these English classics are not in high favor amongst modern collectors, so that one is not surprised at finding them marked down to nothing. This particular set, two fat, dumpy octavos, was in soiled boards, with dingy cloth backs and faded labels, entirely concealing the milk white vellum, beautiful printing and exquisite engravings : the unattractive volumes were tossed out with sermons, almanacks, and old novels. But on opening these volumes one might discover the book plates of Paine, his signature on the fly-leaf, three letters and two postcards from Hazlitt to Paine concerning the production of the volumes and their cost, and Hazlitt's original advertisement announcing his work. For one fourth as many dollars as Paine had paid pounds the books were added to my shelves. Next to a first edition of *The Jealous Lovers* or the *Conceited Pedlar* who could wish for a better Randolph ?

I am tempted to tell how in some such manner, I discovered Eugene Field's copy of *Allibone* with his autograph and notes in all three of the volumes ; Walter Pater's *Lowndes* with four autographs and marginalia ; Michael Wodhull's *Biblia Latina* of 1478, with his records on the fly leaf. But already I know wise men will advise a pilgrimage to Anticyra, where the uses of hellebore are fully known.

For practical men and purposeful collectors may scorn these triflings, and contend that for all the time it takes to unearth our treasures we are but meanly rewarded, but I have failed to note that the sum of their satisfactions is greater for the saving of hours. Meantime I have had my pleasures and would not exchange them for a world full of efficiency.

Non refert quam multos sed quam bonos libros
habeas ac legas.

APPENDIX

CHECK-LISTS OF SOME FIRST EDITIONS

NOTE

FOR most of the writers I have mentioned in this book there are published bibliographies or lists giving sufficient information for the collector's needs. I had prepared a check-list of Eden Phillpotts' books for this appendix : but the recent appearance of Mr. Percival Hinton's excellent bibliography has made it superfluous.

For the check-lists here given I make no claim of finality, though I believe they are more extended than any hitherto published. In fact, I hope they are *not* complete, as otherwise some enthusiastic and zealous collector may be robbed of an exalted moment of discovery !

It is difficult to find any satisfactory list of Cardan's first editions, and while the one here given is far from complete, it will serve to introduce the beginner to his most interesting books.

A CHECK-LIST
OF FIRST EDITIONS BY JOHN TREVENA *
(ERNEST G. HENHAM)

(1) *Under the name of Ernest G. Henham*
God, Man and the Devil ; Skeffington, 1897
Menotah ; Skeffington, 1897
Bonanza ; Hutchinson, 1901
Scud ; Burleigh, 1902
The Plowshare and the Sword ; Cassell & Co., 1903
Krum ; Grant Richards, 1904
The Feast of Bacchus ; Brown, Langham & Co., 1907

(2) *Anonymous*
A Pixy in Petticoats ; Alston Rivers, 1906

(3) *Under name of "John Trevena"*
Arminel of the West ; Alston Rivers, 1907
Furze the Cruel ; Alston Rivers, 1907
Heather ; Alston Rivers, 1908 (Copies with the leaf,
    "An Appeal," being a plea for "Brightly" of
    Furze the Cruel, are especially rare)
Granite ; Alston Rivers, 1909
The Dartmoor House that Jack Built ; Alston Rivers,
    1909
Written in the Rain ; Mills & Boon, 1910
Bracken ; Alston Rivers, 1910
The Reign of the Saints ; Alston Rivers, 1911
Wintering Hay ; Constable, 1912
Matrimony ; Boston : The Four Seas Press, 1912
No Place Like Home ; Constable, 1913
Sleeping Waters ; Constable, 1913

* With the one exception noted, all the above were
published in England.

FOR THE LOVE OF BOOKS

Adventures among Wild Flowers ; (?), 1914
Moyle Church Town ; Mills & Boon, 1915
The Captain's Furniture ; Mills & Boon, 1916
    (American title : A Drake By George)
The Vanished Moor ; Mills & Boon, 1923
The Custom of the Manor ; Mills & Boon, 1924
Off the Beaten Track ; Mills & Boon, 1925

A CHECK-LIST
OF FIRST EDITIONS BY J. MILLS WHITHAM *

Fiction

Broom ; Sands, 1912
Starveacre ; Methuen, 1915
Wolfgang ; Methuen, 1917
Fruit of Earth ; Methuen, 1919
The Human Circus ; Collins, 1919
The Heretic ; George Allen & Unwin, 1921
Silas Braunton ; George Allen & Unwin, 1923
The Windlestraw ; George Allen & Unwin, 1924
Sinful Saints ; John Castle, 1925

History

A Biographical History of the French Revolution ;
    Routledge, 1930

Translations

The Wiles of Women (Turkish Tales) ; Routledge,
    1928
The Shoji, by Kikou Yamata ; Routledge, 1928

---

* All English : all octavo. Collectors will be glad to
learn that Mr. Whitham once wrote an excellent book-
collector's yarn, "Mr. Jordel's Crime," which was published in *The Bookman's Journal* for August, 1925.

APPENDIX

A Check-list
of the First Editions of Mary Webb *

Novels

The Golden Arrow ; Constable, 1916
Gone to Earth ; Constable, 1917
The House in Dormer Forest ; Hutchinson, 1920
Seven for a Secret ; Hutchinson, 1922
Precious Bane ; Jonathan Cape, 1924
Armour Wherein He Trusted ; Jonathan Cape, 1929

Essay

The Spring of Joy ; Dent, 1917

Poems

Poems : and The Spring of Joy. (Introduction by
Walter De La Mare.) Jonathan Cape, 1928

Stories

The Best Short Stories of 1923 ; London, Jonathan
Cape, 1924, contains "Blessed are the Meek"
The Ghost Book ; Scribners, 1927, contains "Mr.
Tallent's Ghost"

A Check-list
of the First Editions of Norman Davey †

---

 * An interesting book telling of Mary Webb's country
is "The Shropshire of Mary Webb," by W. Reid Chappell ;
Cecil Palmer (London), 1930.
 † See also the *Granta*, Vol. 23, No. 520, for May, 1910,
which contains a poem by Mr. Davey on page 363 ; other
oddments by this author may be found in *Punch*, since
1910, and *Touring Topics* for July, 1927.

FOR THE LOVE OF BOOKS

Novels

Perhaps — A Tale of Tomorrow ; Methuen, 1914
(Note : This edition was pulped, owing to the fear
that it might interfere with enlistment in Ireland ;
only a few copies escaped destruction.)
The Pilgrim of a Smile ; Chapman & Hall, 1921
Guinea Girl ; Chapman & Hall, 1921
Good Hunting ; Chapman & Hall, 1923
Yesterday ; Chapman & Hall, 1924. (A reprint of
Perhaps, but in reality its first appearance before
the public.)
The Penultimate Adventure ; Elkin Matthews, 1924.
(A suppressed chapter from *The Pilgrim of a
Smile*.)
Babylon and Candlelight ; Chapman & Hall, 1928
Judgment Day ; Constable, 1928

Short Stories

The New Decameron, Third Volume ; Oxford, Basil
Blackwell, 1922, contains "The Lady's Maid's
Tale," pp. 100-116
The Best Stories of 1923 ; Jonathan Cape, 1924, con-
tains "Sinbad of Sunny Lea"

Poems

Poems (with an essay on Taste) ; London, privately
printed, 4to, 1914, a very limited edition of early
poems.
Desiderium MCMXV-MCMXVII ; Heffer & Sons, 1920

Essays, etc.

The Gas Turbine ; Constable, 1914 (Mr. Davey's first
published book)
Studies in Tidal Power ; Constable, 1923

APPENDIX

The Hungry Traveller in France ; Jonathan Cape, 1931

The Granta and its Contributors 1889-1914. Compiled by F. A. Rice, with an introduction by A. A. Milne ; Constable, 1924, contains a poem by, and several references to, Norman Davey.

A CHECK-LIST
OF ERNEST BRAMAH FIRST EDITIONS
[Only the Kai Lung & Kong Ho tales]

The Wallet of Kai Lung ; * Grant Richards, 1900

The Mirror of Kong Ho ; Chapman & Hall, 1905

Kai Lung's Golden Hours ; Grant Richards, 1922

Kai Lung Unrolls His Mat ; Richards Press, 1928

The Moon of Much Gladness ; Cassell, 1932

The Transmutation of Ling ; Grant Richards, 1911 (is but a reprinting, in exalted form, of a fragment from *The Wallet of Kai Lung*) *

(And, since I mentioned it, here is perhaps the rarest of Bramah books ; English Farming and Why I Turned It Up, 8vo, gray flexible cloth, published by The Leadenhall Press, Ltd., 50, Leadenhall St., E. C. Simpkin, Marshall, etc., 1894.)

(The volume of "*Poems,*" London, (?) 1873, I have not seen.)

---

* The first issue of the Wallet of Kai Lung may be distinguished from the second by the lettering on the back strip of the binding, which reads :

The Wallet | of | Kai Lung.

In the second issue "Kai Lung" occupies two lines. The second issue is printed on thinner paper than that of the first.

FOR THE LOVE OF BOOKS

A Check-list
of First Editions by Caradoc Evans*

Stories

My People ; Melrose, 1915
Capel Sion ; Melrose, 1916
My Neighbours ; Melrose, 1920

Play

Taffy ; Melrose, 1923

Novels

Nothing to Pay ; Faber & Faber, 1930
Wasps ; Rich & Cowan, 1933
This Way To Heaven ; Rich & Cowan, 1934

A Check-list
of First Editions by Charles Whibley †

In Cap and Gown, Three Centuries of Cambridge Wit,
    edited, with an introduction by Charles Whibley ;
    London, Kegan Paul, 1889
A Book of Scoundrels ; Heinemann, 1897
The Pageantry of Life ; Heinemann, 1900
William Makepeace Thackeray ; Blackwood, 1903
Literary Portraits ; Constable, 1904
William Pitt ; Blackwood, 1906
American Sketches ; Blackwood, 1908
Studies in Frankness ; Constable, 1910
The Letters of an Englishman (2 vols.), First Series,
    1911 ; Second Series, 1912, both published by Con-
    stable
Essays in Biography ; Constable, 1913
Jonathan Swift ; Cambridge University Press, 1917

———
* All English.
† All the volumes are octavo, and all published in Great
Britain.

292

APPENDIX

Literary Studies ; Macmillan, 1919

Political Portraits ; Macmillan. First Series, 1917 ;
Second Series, 1923

Lord John Manners and His Friends ; Blackwood, 1925

Some Books Edited by Whibley

Rabelais (in the Tudor Translations), London, D. Nutt,
1900, 2 vols., 8vo.

Collected Essays of W. P. Ker, 2 vols. ; Macmillan, 1925

The Spiritual Quixote : or, The Summer's Ramble of Mr.
Geoffrey Wildgoose. A Comic Romance, by Richard
Graves, with an introduction by Charles Whibley ;
Peter Davies, 1926 ; 2 vols.

The Life and Opinions of Tristram Shandy, by Laurence
Sterne, 2 vols., Methuen, 1894

A story, "Twelve O'clock," is included in *The Ghost
Book* ; Scribner's, 1927

A List of
Cardan's Principal Works

De Malo Recentiorum Medicorum Medendi Usu ; Venice,
1536

Practica Arithmetice ; Milan, 1539

De Consolatione ; Venice, 1542
(This was made English in 1573 by Thomas Bedingfield, and was much used by Shakespeare. Its title
was *Cardanus' Comforte*)

De Sapienta ; Nuremberg, 1544

Artis Magnae, sive De Regulis Algebraicis ; Nuremberg,
1545

Libelli duo. Unus, de Supplemento Almanach. Alter, de
Restitutione temporum & motuum coelestium. Nuremberg, 1543

De Subtilitate ; Nuremberg, 1550

De Varietate ; Basle, 1557

Genituarum Exemplar ; Basle, 1554

FOR THE LOVE OF BOOKS

De Libris Propriis ; Lyons, 1557
Metopscopia ; Paris, 1558
Medicinae Contradictiones ; Venice, 1545
Dialectica, Hyperchen, de Aqua ; Basle, 1556
De Vita Propria ; Paris, 1643. (This was translated into
    English by Miss Jean Stoner ; New York, 1930)
Commentaria in Ptolemai de Astrorum Judiciis ; Basle,
    1554
Ars Curandi Parva ; Basle, 1566
Somniorum Synesiorum ; Basle, 1562
De Utilitate ex Adversis Capienda ; Basle, 1561
Opera Omnia ; ten vols., fol., Lyons, 1663

See also for biographical information : The Life of
    Girolamo Cardano of Milan, by Henry Morley ; 2
    vols., London, 1854 ; and W. G. Waters' Jerome
    Cardan ; London, 1898.

SOME MACHEN ITEMS
NOT INCLUDED IN MR. HENRY DANIELSON'S
Bibliography

Strange Roads ; The Classic Press, 1923 ; Large paper ed.,
    1924
Things Near and Far ; Secker, 1923
The Shining Pyramid ; Covici-McGee (Chicago), 1923.
    Edited by Vincent Starrett.
The Grande Trouvaille ;* The First Edition Bookshop
    (London), 1923. 4to, 8pp. paper covers, illustrated ;
    privately printed and limited to 250 copies
The London Adventure ; Secker, 1924
Dog and Duck ; Cape, 1924
The Glorious Mystery ; Covici-McGee (Chicago), 1924.
    Edited by Vincent Starrett.
Ornaments in Jade ; Knopf (U. S. A.), 1924

* "The Grande Trouvaille" also appeared in "Catalogue
No. 3" of the First Edition Bookshop, March, 1923.

APPENDIX

Precious Balms ; Spurr & Swift, 1924

In Defense, Alfred A. Knopf-Arthur Machen vs. Covici-McGee Co.,— Vincent Starrett. (Contains excerpts from letters by Machen), Covici-McGee, 1924, 4pp., 8vo.

The Canning Wonder ; Chatto & Windus, 1925

The Shining Pyramid ; Secker, 1925 (contains matter not in Am. edition)

Notes and Queries ; Spurr & Swift, 1926

Dreads and Drolls ; Secker, 1926

Tom o' Bedlam and His Song ; The Apellicon Press (U. S. A.), 1930

A Few Letters ; The Rowfant Club (Cleveland, U. S. A.), 1932,— a collection of Machen's letters on literature. Sm. 8vo, 54pp.

The Green Round ; Benn, 1933

Remarks Upon Hermodactylus. By Lady Hester Stanhope. Translated from the French by Arthur Machen, 1933. Privately printed by W. Graves, London.

BOOKS CONTAINING
INTRODUCTIONS OR CHAPTERS BY ARTHUR MACHEN

Among My Books. Papers on Literary Subjects — with a Preface by H. D. Traill ; Elliot Stock (London), 1898, 8vo. Contains Machen's essay on "Unconscious Magic."

The Ghost Ship and Other Stories, by Richard Middleton, with an introduction by Arthur Machen ; T. Fisher Unwin, 1912

Cenotaph, edited by Thomas Moult ; Jonathan Cape, 1923. Contains Machen's "Vision in the Abbey."

Et Cetera, a Collector's Scrap-book, edited by Vincent Starrett ; Covici, 1924 ; contains "English and Irish," and "My Murderer," by Machen.

The Pageant of English Landscape, by George A. B. DeWar ; London, The Classic Press, 1924. Foreword by Machen.

One Hundred Merrie and Delightsome Stories (a translation into English of Les Cent Nouvelles Nouvelles,
by Robert B. Douglas), 2 vols., privately printed ;
Carbonnek, 1924 (New York). Foreword by
Machen.

Afterglow. Pastels of Greek Egypt, by Mitchell S. Buck ;
New York, Nicholas L. Brown, 1924.

The Halt in the Garden, by Robert Hillyer ; Elkin
Mathews, 1925. Introduction by Machen.

The Dragon of the Alchemists, by Frederick Carter ; Elkin
Mathews, 1926. Foreword by Machen.

The Ghost Book ; Scribner's, 1927. A collection of tales
containing Machen's "Munitions of War."

Great Names : an Anthology, edited by W. J. Turner.
Dial Press (N. Y.), 1926.

The Physiology of Taste, or Meditations on Transcendental
Gastronomy, by Brillat-Savarin, with an Introduction
by Arthur Machen ; Peter Davies (London), 1925.

A Conrad Memorial Library. The Collection of George
T. Keating ; Doubleday, Doran (New York), 1929.
Contains Machen's review of "Victory."

Our Father San Daniel, by Gabriel Miro (English translation) ; Ernest Benn, 1930.

Above the River, by John Gawsworth ; London, the
Ulysses Bookshop, 1931. Preface by Machen.

Casanova Loved Her, by Bruno Brunelli, with Preface by
Arthur Machen ; Peter Davies (London), 1929.

FUGITIVE ITEMS, MAGAZINES, PAMPHLETS, ETC.

Babes in the Wood, by J. Hastings Turner & Lauri Wylie.
Their pathetic story told for children. A theatre program for a children's pantomime, which began December 21, 1922, at the New Oxford Theatre
(London); the story here written by Arthur Machen.
4to, 8pp.

Invitation to an Exhibition of the works of Arthur Machen,
December 10, 1923, by Harry F. Marks, 187 Broad-

way (New York) ; 4pp., 8vo. Contains facsimile of
Machen letter written for this occasion.

Cadby Hall (An advertisement written for the J. Lyons
& Co. Ltd., concerning their confections.) 8vo,
16pp., with blue and gold paper covers.

Catalogue No. 6, 1923, of The First Edition Bookshop
(London), contains the first appearance of Machen's
article "The Collector's Craft," afterward reprinted
in the (U. S.) Publishers' Weekly.

Chapman's Magazine (Christmas Number, 1895), Vol.
II, No. 8, contains "The Red Hand"—pp. 390-418.
On the cover of the magazine this tale is listed as
"The Telling of a Mystery."

Arthur Machen's London Residences, 1880-1893. A series
of photographs, mounted, with appropriate comments
from Machen's books. The Ulysses Bookshop, London, 1930.

Arthur Machen's Residences. A second series—1863-
1930. Ulysses Bookshop, 1930. Uniform with
above, both sets limited in number to twenty-five.

* The Publishers' Weekly for Feb. 16, 1924, contains
"The Only Way," by Arthur Machen. (U. S. publication.)

Book Notes for April-May, 1928, contains a Machen
article, "Concerning Cocktails." (U. S. publication.)

The Whirlwind, Volume II (London), 1890, contains "A
Wonderful Woman," "The Great God Pan," "The
Lost Club," and "An Underground Adventure," by
Mr. Machen.

The Academy, Vols. 72, 73, 74, & 75 (London, 1906,
&c.), contained numerous articles and essays by Mr.
Machen.

Walford's Antiquarian Magazine, 1884-1887, inclusive,
contained many small Machen contributions, he being

---

* The Flying Horse for March, 1924 (No. 3) contains
"The Only Way," by Mr. Machen.

at that time with Redway who published the maga-zine.

T. P.'s Weekly (London, 1902-1910), Vols. I to XVI, contains many articles by Machen.

The Gypsy, Vol. I, Nos. 1 and 2 (London, 1915), con-tains two chapters of "The Secret Glory."

Horlick's Magazine, Vols. I & II, contains articles by Machen : "A Fragment of Life" appeared in its pages in 1904 (London).

The Neolith for August, 1918, contains "The Rose Garden"— its first appearance, London, 1918.

Lyons Mail, Vols. V, VI & VII (London), contains articles by Machen, the chapters afterward published in "Dog and Duck."

The Reviewer (Richmond, Va.) for January, 1923, con-tained "The Treasure of the Humble" ; and in July, 1924, printed "The Thousand and One Nights."

Now and Then, No. 27, Spring of 1928 (London, Jonathan Cape), contained "A Note on F. J. Huddle-ston," by Machen.

The Wave, Vol. I, Nos. 1 & 5 (Chicago, 1922), contained "The Art of Dickens," and "The Marriage of Panurge," by Arthur Machen.

MISCELLANEOUS MACHENIANA

(a) *Relating to the controversy over The Bowman*

On the Side of the Angels, a Reply to The Bowman, by Harold Begbie ; Hodder & Stoughton, 1916.

Angels, Saints and Bowmen of Mons, by I. E. Taylor ; The Theosophical Publishing Society, 1916, a reply to both Machen and Begbie.

The Visions of Mons and Ypres, their Meaning and Purpose, by the Author of "The Great Pyramid," etc., London, Robert Banks & Son. 8vo, pink wrapper (n.d.).

APPENDIX

(b) *General*

Arthur Machen a Novelist of Ecstasy and Sin, by
Vincent Starrett ; with two uncollected poems
by Arthur Machen. Chicago, Walter M. Hill,
1918. (This essay was reprinted in "Buried
Cæsars" ; Covici-McGee, 1923.

Arthur Machen a Bibliographical Note, by Nathan Van
Patten ; privately printed ; Kingston, Canada, 1926.

An Unacknowledged work of Arthur Machen ? by Nathan
Van Patten ; reprinted from the papers of the
Bibliographical Society of America, Chicago, 1928.

The Rose Garden, by Arthur Machen. Fifty copies privately printed for Nathan Van Patten, 1932 (Stan-
ford University ?). This item is reprinted from
"Ornaments in Jade."

The Hesperian (Summer issue for 1930, San Francisco)
contains an article on "James Branch Cabell and
Arthur Machen, Certain Analogies between their
Early Works," by Nathan Van Patten.

On Strange Altars, by Paul Jordan Smith ; Albert & Charles
Boni, 1924, contains an essay on Arthur Machen.

INDEX

INDEX

INDEX

305